Wilhelm Landau

**Travels in Asia, Australia and America**

Wilhelm Landau

**Travels in Asia, Australia and America**

ISBN/EAN: 9783337320706

Hergestellt in Europa, USA, Kanada, Australien, Japan

Cover: Foto ©Andreas Hilbeck / pixelio.de

Weitere Bücher finden Sie auf **www.hansebooks.com**

# TRAVELS

— IN —

# Asia, Australia and America,

COMPRISING THE PERIOD BETWEEN 1879 AND 1887.

BY

## BARON WILHELM VON LANDAU,

(Saxe-Coburg-Gotha,)

*Dr. phil. F. L. S., corresponding member of the American Geographical Society, etc., etc., etc.*

PART I.

NEW YORK: GEORGE LANDAU,
1888.

Entered According to Act of Congress, in the Year 1888, by

BARON WILHELM VON LANDAU,

In the Office of the Librarian of Congress, at Washington, D. C.

TO THE HONORABLE

# CHARLES P. DALY, L. L. D.,

President of the American Geographical Society and Ex-Chief Justice of the Court of Common Pleas, of the City of New York;

Honorary member of the Imperial Geographical Society of Russia, of the Geographical Societies of Berlin and Turin, and corresponding member of the Royal Geographical Society of London;

Honorary member of the Metropolitan Museum of Art, Medico-Legal Society, and Mercantile Library Association of New York,

**WITH HIGH ESTEEM AND GRATITUDE.**

*THE AUTHOR.*

# PREFACE.

*THE leading idea which has governed the preparation of this little work has been to precisely relate the personal experiences of the author in different parts of our planet. The standpoint which he takes is partially that of a tourist, at the same time offering all the statistical and geographical data he possibly could obtain, and he wishes to be distinctly understood that in making these extensive, long lasting travels, he **was** not led by any other motive than the mere love for science, nature and art.*

*Though, among explorers, only one of the "Dii minores," I found sufficient reward in the honorable mention of my expeditions and the scientific appreciations in the reports of the "Gesellschaft für Erdkunde" (Society for the Enrichment of the Knowledge of the Earth), the Ethnologic Periodical and the lectures of Professor Doctor Virchow, of Berlin.*

*Many of the tropical and sub=tropical plants, etc., with which I had supplied some countries in Europe and Africa for acclimatization, thrive well according to statements received, and promise to become a **source** of revenue.*

*This also, adds to the pride I feel in passing revue over a period of eight years' travelling, devoted exclusively to science.*

*Owing ~~to~~ the success of my explorations, especially in the thinly populated wild islands in Oceania, to the kind and generous assistance of the Governors, Regents, Residents, the Roman Catholic Curas and the Commandants of the Guardia Civil, I herewith express my heartfelt thanks to each and all of them.*

*THE AUTHOR.*

IT was in Autumn of 1879 when I left dear, old Berlin, to realize the dream of my youth: to visit the "mythic cradle of the human race," the distant India.

Armed with everything necessary for such a trip, a good constitution and a certain degree of self-denial, as well as with my Doctor of Philosophy in my pocket, I looked cheeringly into the future.

Munich, the Brenner, Verona and Bologna were passed and Brindisi reached, when passage was taken for Corfu on board a steamer. As I had stayed before in Corfu, I hastened my departure from the latter place to Alexandria and by rail through the Delta to Cairo. I did not remain there any length of time and after visiting Doctor Schweinfurth, whose acquaintance I had made on former travels and at whose residence I was introduced to some members of the Nordenskjoeld Expedition, I sailed for Suez. My stay in Egypt, as mentioned before, was a very short one on this occasion and for this reason and former descriptions of the country, published by me, I omit to say anything about it.

I boarded the steamer "Jemna" of the French Messagerie national line bound for India and after passing Pondichery and Madras I reached Calcutta through the Hoogly, an arm of the Ganges.

Calcutta, the capital of British-India, with 870,000 inhabitants, has but few remarkable curiosities. The houses of the Europeans and of the wealthy Natives, the Baboos, are spacious and elegantly furnished. Poonkhas, or ventilators, suspend from the ceilings and the numerous windows of the pretty high houses have awnings. Most everybody here has his own servant. The mode and way of living here is very luxurious. The botanical garden, situated on the other side of the river Hoogly, contains a great many of ornamental flowers, among which the beautiful specimens of the Burmese Amherstia nobilis and Bougainvillia spectabilis are the most prominent. Doctor King, the director of the botanical garden, to whom I am under great obligations, enabled me to send a large collection of plants, flowers, seeds etc. to the botanical garden of Berlin.

A peculiar spectacle surprises the stranger in Calcutta, half an hour before and half an hour after sunset, on the so-called Esplanade, a tract of land, four miles in length and one mile in width, situated on the banks of the Hoogly, when the Parsee, the Hindoo, the Mahometan and the European with their original vehicles, their richly liveried coachmen and servants make their appearances, thus outrivaling the Roman or Parisian Corsos.

An excursion from Calcutta on the North Bengal Railroad, over the Ganges, to Darjeeling, thirty miles in the interior of the Himalayas brought me to the highest Tea-plantation in the world, 7,000 feet above the level of the sea. From the top of a mountain in that region, the highest mountain of the Globe "Mount Everest" is visible. On my return to Calcutta, over a different road, I passed a Cinchona plantation, 5,000 feet high, and started for the West, by way of Patna, to Benares.

Benares, the Athens of India and the sacred city of the Hindoos, is famous for the great mosque "Aurung zebe," so called after the emperor, who had this symbol of Islamitic faith erected on the ruins of the Hindoo temples.

The astronomic observatory in Benares was built in 1600 by Mânasimha. Among the many temples of the Hindoo, those in which the "Ape" receives godly homage are the most numerous. Hundreds of these little "Deities" are found in the groves and orchards and are fed by their "Worshippers" with all kind of delicacies.

Benares has about 50,000 Idols, exhibited for public worshipping in niches, cases etc. The temples where the bulls are adored, swarm with filth, especially the niches in which other lifeless Gods are enshrined. Their faces and bodies are literally dripping from oily substances,—remnants of offerings—, thus creating an intolerable odor. From the ceilings, diminutive bells dangle down and are frequently rung, to remind the negligent "Deities" of their obligations.

There are many antiquities in Benares.

The Ghauts, a prolongation of the stony steps, descending from the rocks, form a platform and are constantly thronged with people, flocking down to the river to purify themselves with its holy water or to perform some other work. On the extreme end are beautiful Stone-Kiosks, also harbors of some abominable "Deities."

On the 4th of June 1857 a great many Europeans were murdered in this city by the rebellious natives.

From Benares I traveled to Lucknow—the old capital of the former kingdom Oudh—with famous forests in the neighborhood.

Several edifices, built by a Frenchman, create sensation by their peculiar style.

In the environs of Lucknow is Cawnpore, where, on the very day on which the Mogul Empire was proclaimed, viz.: the 12th of February 1857, the horrible massacre of Europeans by Nana-Sahib and his Sepoys was perpetrated. A second slaughter, not less brutal than the first, took place on the 16th of July of the same year. On the following day the distressed received succour from General Havelock. After a brief stay in Cawnpore, I started for Saharampore, from where another collection of seeds, etc., was dispatched to Europe. Here also, the Director of the botanical garden—the latter properly a place for the cultivation of domestic plants—Doctor Dutton, favored me with his kindness. The Siwalik hills, where tertiary fossiles are excavated, were duly explored by me.

Between these geologically famous hills and the real Highmountains in Dehra-Dhoon, the culture of silk-worms is carried on and tea-plantations found.

From the Sanitarium Massory, where I received the membership of the Himalaya Club, the Snowmountains present a magnificent view. Landowr, also a sanitarium for soldiers, enjoys the neighborhood of Ale-breweries. The way leads now to Agra, one of the former residences of the Mogul Emperors, about hundred miles distant from Delhi. In Agra is the most splendid mausoleum in the world, the celebrated "Taj-Mahal." It is impossible to give a true description of the Taj-Mahal with its harmonious proportions, its Mosaic work, the immaculate snow-white marble etc. According to accounts in Agra, Taj-Mahal was founded in 1631 under the reign of the Mogul Emperor Shah-Jehan and devoted to the memory of his spouse Moontaj-i-Mahal. Tavernier relates that 20,000 people had worked for twenty successive years on the completion of this wonderful mausoleum.

The Moti-Musjed or Pearl-mosque deserves to be mentioned as also the Jumna-mosque. The latter, though not so nice as the Pearl-mosque, towers above all other Mosques in Agra, its site being the loftiest.

The sepulchral monuments of Elmadaod-Doulah and Akbar are magnificent relics of oriental architecture.

In the vicinity of Agra is the native state Sindhee

with an English cantonment. Splendid temples and ruins of such, of an extinct Hindoo religion, the so-called Jaynes, are abundant. The soil contains plenty of iron-ore.

Among all the attractions in India, the architectonic monuments of the past, cause the travellers admiration and astonishment, but above all, the relics of the glory and power of the Mogul Emperors. It was in Delhi—of historic fame—where I had occasion to admire the well preserved remains of architectonic monuments of the great Mogul Emperors.

On the 11th of May, 1857, during an insurrection of the Natives, a terrible massacre of Europeans took place in Delhi. The English attacked the insurgents on the 14th of September 1857, and the city was taken by the former on the 20th of the same month. The day following, the last of the Mogul Sovereigns, Surazoo-deen, was captured and several of his grandchildren and princes executed.

Of all the curiosities in Delhi, the Dewani-Khass or Presence chamber (Audience hall) excites the greatest attention of the visitor. This edifice too, like the incomparable Taj-Mahal, owes its origin to the above mentioned emperor Shah-Jehan.

The imperial palace, turned into ruins by the English, was considered the finest residence of any "Despot" in the East.

The Dewani-Khass is an arched pavilion, rests on low, solid pillars and measures 150 feet in length, and

50 feet in width. The material is of the finest white marble. The sculpture, engraving and ornamenting of the pillars and walls is almost inimitable. Flowers, blossoms, leaves, fruits and Arabesques in Mosaic, composed of precious gems, appear to the visitor as if alive or painted on canvas. In the Arabic-written characters, on different places of the hall, resembling Arabesques, citations from the Koran are found, among others, the lines, glorified by Moore in "Lalla Rookh":

"If in reality, there is an Elysium on earth,
It is this, it is this."

Below the central arch of the pavilion is a low marble tribune, on which stood the famous Peacock throne. Bernier, who has seen the throne, gives the following description of it: "The throne consisted of two massive golden peacocks, whose plumages were composed of the most precious stones. The seat was inlaid with diamonds and supported by six solid golden legs, also sumptiously covered with diamonds and rubies. Six wide, massive silver steps, likewise containing different jewels, led to the throne, the cost of which, according to the above named traveller, was from 20 to 30 Millions of Pounds Sterling."

The throne was stolen by the Persian conqueror Nadir-Shah, and the precious diamond "Koh-i-noor," worn by the Mogul Emperor, wandered to England, where it now ranks highest among the crown jewels of Queen Victoria.

Of great attraction also is the Private Imperial

Mosque within the fortified palace, built of white marble. The Jumna Mosque, situated in a different part of the city, is one of the finest of its kind and from the Minarets the celebrated lonely "Kutub Minar" column, undoubtedly the loftiest structure in the world, is visible. The environs of Delhi, to the extent of 15 miles along the banks of the Jumna, are literally covered with fragments of tombstones, walls, mosques, palaces and astronomical observatories.

These are remains of the Delhi of the past, for the first Delhi was already built 2,000 years ago.

Here, as in some other parts of India, the boil-disease (covering the whole body with protuberances) appears during the hot season and gets many victims.

From here I started for Simla, by way of Umballa, a very tedious and troublesome voyage. One is dragged with difficulty in the clumsy vehicle, the so-called "Garre," over the plains and through unbridged rivers. The construction of these Garres is such, that they have to serve as sleeping compartments, since travelling in the night time becomes here a necessity, shelters nowhere to be found. Naturally enough, there is but little comfort in them.

Here it was, where the three brothers, Herman, Adolf and Robert Schlagintweit met in the month of May 1856, to complete their equipment for the intended journey to Cashmere. They arrived in Bombay towards the end of 1854, and first crossed the "Deccan" to Madras over different roads. They separated in Madras in the following spring. Adolf and Robert travelled to the remote Northwest of India and spent their time with examinations of the passes, glaciers, mountains, etc. They advanced as far as Ladak and attempted to climb to the summit of the Ibi-Gamin, one of the steepest peaks. Though the attempt was fruitless, they nevertheless reached the extraordinary height of 22,000 feet, a height which, up to that period of time had not been reached by any mortal man.

During that time Herman made extensive travels in Sikkim and Assam, and through the whole region between Brahmapootra and Burmah, in the tropic low-lands as well as in the unexplored mountainous district.

After the already related meeting of the brothers in Simla, they visited Iscardo, made repeated excursions in the wild region between the Upper-Indus and the table-land of Pamir, and afterwards explored the southeasterly continuation of the great Karakoram chain of mountains in Little-Tibet, thereby fixing the altitude of the Dapsang to 28,278 feet.

They were the first Europeans who, after passing the Karakoram over a pass, 19,000 feet above the level of the sea, had seen and crossed the Kün-lün. Unexpected circumstances forced the brothers to return to India, and Herman and Robert embarked for Europe in the Spring of 1857, whilst Adolf was determined to profit from their mutual discoveries, and to explore Central Asia as far as to the Russian possessions north of Thian-Shan. Rumors of the progress of the Tartaric rebellion against the Chinese supremacy, had by this time reached Little Tibet, and the task at which Adolf aimed seemed practicable to him. After crossing the Kün-lün he marched towards Yarkand, but was sent back and proceeded to Kashgar, presenting himself to Wallé-Khan, the leader of the Insurgents, who at that time was besieging the Chinese forts. All that the world got to know about the fate of this indefatigable traveller, was, that he was murdered by the order of Wallé-Khan.

The great Sanitarium in this place is about 8000 feet above the sea.

The Viceroy of India, as well as the Commander-in-chief, and the Lieutenant-Governor of the Punjab reside here during a period of eight months in every year. The seat of the government (wandering with the Viceroy) is also here during the summer.

My stay in Simla was a pretty long one, enjoying the acquaintance of the Earl of Lytton, and of his successor, the Marquis of Ripon. I made frequent excursions to Tibet as far as to the Chinese borders, but was not permitted to step over the boundaries. On that journey, at the Mission Station Kothgur, I met a missionary from Berlin, a Mr. Rebsch. Before this last place is reached, Narkanda has to be passed, where a splendid view of the snowmountains presents itself.

Doctor Lucius, the present Minister of Agriculture in Berlin, was here some time before my arrival.

The road leads now right through the snow-mountains with their gorgeous valleys and luxuriant pine- and cedar-forests up to the lofty boundaries of vegetation. In the former grows the eatable pine. The alpine vegetation is not so abundant as in the Swiss alps, but the cultivation of the vine is very productive on account of the scarcety of rain.

Back of Kothgur, the Sutlej, an important river with canyonlike banks and peculiar windings, discharging into the Indus, was reached.. We started now from Murree over the mountains for Cashmere.

The voyage lasted full fourteen days. In daytime travelling was seldom interrupted and the nights were passed under shelter.

The river Jhelum, in the neighborhood of the capital, Shrenaga, describes the most peculiar windings imaginable, which latter are imitated in the patterns of the Cashmere Shawls.

Our way up hill, in tents, brought us to Sonamag, which is very high situated. After we had left the last named place, a christian church was consumed by fire and we were charged with the deed, though Mahometans had caused it.

The established church in Cashmere is "Mahometanism," that of the court "Hindoo."

The principal passage to Central Asia and Turkestan leads over Sonamag. This same course was taken by Schlagintweit and the English Embassy.

There is a large stock of game on the table-land of Cashmere, and hunting is very frequent. The interior of Cashmere is only during the summer inhabited, at which time the Maharajah and his court reside here. During the winter the court resides in Sommoo.

On my return to India over the old disused highway, laid out by the Mogul Emperors, I found now and then ruins of seraglios and caravanseries, which afforded night-shelters. This road is in a very bad condition and therefore not so much in use as the Murree road.

The manufacturing of shawls, in former times carried on on a large scale, is now, since they are out of fashion, almost extinct, and only Shrenaga produces some. Oxen are the beasts of burden in Cashmere, and horses and donkeys are used for riding. The killing of cattle and fishes is strictly prohibited, because they are worshipped.

A short distance from Shrenaga, some large lakes, palaces in ruins, formerly summer seats of the Mogul sovereigns, and gardens with beautiful cascades, are to be found. The vegetation here, with Italian and other poplar trees, bordering the lakes and adorning the streets, is almost northerly and puts one in mind of home, especially when arrived from India.

Cotton and Indian corn, the former with yellow blossoms and sesam, from which the sesam oil is obtained, are raised to a considerable extent. During my sojourn there, a Belgian pressman was summoned to Cashmere to introduce the cultivation of fruits, vine and other plants, and for the construction of press-houses. Some species imported from France and Germany throve—as I was informed afterwards —very well.

To reach Cashmere, it was necessary to obtain special permission from the Government of the Punjab in Lahore. The reason for this precaution was the insufficiency of provisions after the rage of a famine in that region. We found many skeletons of cattle, killed by starvation, on the road from Murree to Cashmere.

This journey was performed in the middle of summer, the so-called rainy season, which differs from the rainy season of the southern or eastern part of the Himalaya. The rain in these regions, with but short interruptions, lasts throughout the season. Special permission for the use of the roads from and to Cashmere is also required, as there are only a few designated by the Government. Foreigners are submitted to a strict control on the part of the English resident.

My sojourn extended to three months, and I made frequently excursions to the Valley of Cashmere, where I had splendid views of the snow mountains and to the Jhelum river.

The want of tents, or other shelters, necessitates many families to live on boats, and the river is crowded with them. Hunters, coming from India, either for pleasure or for the recuperation of an undermined health, are often met with. Hotels are entirely unknown here and one has to content himself with the tent or house he is put into by the Maharajah.

The morals and customs of the Mahometans are looser than those of the Arabians, the women for instance do not veil themselves so close. The public worship and instruction of the Hindoo, on the contrary, inasmuch as a stranger has a chance to cast a look into, is strictly regulated and profoundly moral.

Returning over the same road, I proceeded to the Punjab with its capital Lahore, which, though worth seeing, can not be compared with either Agra or Delhi.

During my brief stay in Lahore I had the honor to form the acquaintance of Professor Doctor Leitner, the celebrated Orientalist, to whom science is greatly indebted for the interpretation and explanation of several old Indian idioms. On his first voyage from India to Cashmere, Professor Leitner had to endure a series of hardships and privations, whilst I enjoyed the advantages of the present improved conditions. It was Professor Leitner, if I remember well, who proposed the establishing of a High-Shool in Lahore, now in an excellent state of progress.

On reaching the Punjab, we enter the sphere of a nation which occupies a great part of northwestern India, and who are neither Mahometans nor Hindoo, though inclining to the former, the "Sikhs," a beautiful race of men. From their midst soldiers and policemen are selected. They possess magnificent temples. In the vicinity of Umritsar, with a luxuriantly outfitted temple, especially in Loodhiana, the manufacturing of imitations of genuine Cashmere shawls is one of the important features.

The Punjab in the neighborhood of Lahore, is rich in rivers, and in Summer, shows one of the highest temperatures in the world. In the other parts of India where there is frequent rain ~~before~~ summer comes, the temperature is milder, but in the Punjab and the westerly, desert-like region on which the former is bordering, and where there is but little rain, the temperature rises from 120 to 130 degrees.

This country is frequently visited by whirling clouds of dust. At the approach of them, the inhabitants retire to their huts, which are covered with Koosh-koosh grass, thus reducing the temperature within, but when the wind abates and the heat becomes unbearable, the Thermantidod has to be put up. Many other arrangements such as Poonkhas or fans and ventilators pulled by Kulies, etc., are in use.

Every four or five years the Viceroy of India arranges the famous "Durbar," a festival of enormous brilliancy, and to which the Maharajahs of the corresponding districts are invited. On that occasion they display an extraordinary splendor. The suite of attendants with their richly ornamented liveries, the elephants and camels with covers trimmed with jewelry and thousand other attractions captivate the senses. The Maharajah of Cashmere who was present, displayed a fabulous pomp and I must confess that I rarely ever had such a delight of the eyes. From Lahore I traveled by way of Umballa, Saharampore with but a short stay in Delhi, to Agra from where I turned aside to the confederate Rajpootana state. The English Resident (native government) whose hospitality I enjoyed, had the kindness to place an elephant and domestics at my disposal for the trip to Ambher, the former capital.

The gardens and palaces of this place are worth seeing. Tigers used to invade the city because the Hindoo never shoots them unless he is in immediate danger. They are now decimated by Europeans and others who frequently arrange hunting parties.

In this part of India I received a communication from Doctor Schweinfurth, at that time in Egypt, to send him plants, seeds, etc., for transplantation in Africa where they thrive well, especially the Bamboo, Doctor Dutton and others in Saharampore acommodated me kindly with the required plants, etc., thus enabling me to accomplish the wish of my worthy friend, whose intention it was, to experiment with them on the farm of Professor Doctor Soyaux on the Gaboon.

West of Jaypore is a salt lake and a very productive salt mine. The palaces in Jaypore are noteworthy as are also the dyeries in which homespun materials, mostly cotton-goods, are dyed.

On the road to Ajmer numberless monkeys (Baboons) rove about and are very bold because they are worshipped by the natives.

Not far from here are temples of Brahma, whilst only such of Shiva and other By-Gods are found in other parts. The Hindoo faith was originally "Monotheism" and is still considered as such by the better class of its followers. Brahma was an invisible and allmighty God, the creator of heaven and earth and like the deity of the Buddhists too great to be conceived by mortals. The three descendants of Brahma are more personifications of his attributes than separate personalities. These three, the "Trimurti" or the Hindoo-Trinity are: Brahma, the creator, Vishnu, the preserver, and Shiva, the destroyer. Among the emblems of the latter is a child, thus signifying that "life" is constantly deriving from the "dead."

Out of the three, a multitude of inferior Gods sprung up and with their descendants number thirty millions of which only three millions are bad. From this proportion the kindness of the ruling deity is perceptible. The original faith is much degenerated at present and dark superstition substituted.

In the lakes of Rajpootana both sexes of the natives enjoy frequent bathing.

Travelling in the western part of the states is very troublesome and can only be performed on camels-back. A habitation here, forms—so to say—an oasis, the distance from each other being so great.

Ajmer is pretty mountainous and there is great abundance of wild fruits.

On my return I had again to put up at Agra,

from where I visited the fortified place of Allahabad, the seat of the British government. In this place I enjoyed the most generous hospitality of the English representative, Lieutenant-Governor Sir Henry Cooper.

The drainage in Allahabad is one of the grandest in India and I was greatly disappointed that I could not inspect the same on account of the cholera raging there at that time.

Cholera in the eastern parts of India, appears during the hot season; the absence of the extremely moist atmosphere at that time favors the disease. In the west it appears in the course of the rainy season, because both, the soil and air contain too little moisture to promote bacillar or parasitical activity. The climate of India, in general, is unhealthy for Europeans. The rainy season is followed by the cold and lasts during the months of October, November, December, January and February. The degrees of cold are not high; the normal temperature in the coldest month of the year, the month of January, is in Calcutta 67°, in Madras 77°, and in Bombay 78°. The hot season begins towards the end of February and lasts till rain commences in the month of June. The different seasons in India deviate greatly—India extending over a latitude of over 2000 miles. On the west coast for instance, the rainfall is stronger, in the north is the cold severer, and in the south heat reigns almost throughout the year.

After a brief stay in Allahabad, I boarded a train

of the Great Peninsular Railroad for Central India and proceeded next to Jabalpore, in whose vicinity are diamond mines, belonging to a Rajah, and to which access is gained under great difficulties.

Jabalpore is situated on the famous Nurbuddha river, on whose banks grows the sacred tree of the Buddhists, the Pippal tree, Ficus religiosa. The adoration of this tree bases upon the ground that, under it, life was imparted to Vishnu and that Buddha has rested under its shade. Many other beautiful trees adorn the banks of the river, as for example the Banyan-Pagode, or Indian Fig tree, Ficus indica. Geologically, this territory is marvellously beautious with its formation of marble. The tropic vegetation develops the greatest luxuriancy, and the cultivation of cotton is carried on on a very large scale up to the coast (especially in Guzerattee) and almost as far as Bombay. There are a great many tigers around here.

After a two days' travel through beautiful forests of cocoanut trees, with extraordinary specimens of the cocos nucifera, I reached the "Elora" cave. In the interior of the cave, situated in the high-land of Deccan, are Buddhistic and Hindoo temples.

From Elora back, along the coast, over islands, the train of the Great Peninsular Railroad carried me to Salsette. The climate on the coast is very unhealthy and all kinds of fevers, especially Malaria, rage all the year.

Between the continent and Bombay, on a formation of basalt, is the Island of "Elephanta," which place—as I had already reached Bombay—I visited later.

The city of Bombay is divided in two parts; in the fort, situated within the old Portuguese fortifications, about one mile in length, ending on the beach of the bay, surrounded by moats, the stagnated water of which produces fever; and in the new city quarter, north of the Esplanade. Bombay is a very rich city, the wealth mostly to be found among the Parsees.

It might not be superfluous to say a few words about the followers of "Zoroaster," whose doctrine—as is known—teaches the existence of a God and an evil principle, both together ruling the Universe. They settled on the Malabar coast about 800 years ago, when expelled from Persia. The sun, as the representative of God, fire and the sea are worshipped by them. Immediately after sunrise they perform their prayers. In their temples, Idols are not to be found, but the sacred fire is kept burning all the time. They neither burn nor bury their dead, but expose them to the air on the top of a hill, where they decompose or are devoured by beasts of prey. They marry their children at the tender age of 4 or 5 years, bring them up together and unite them when of maturity.

Bombay possesses many Parsee temples. The "Tower of Silence" is inaccessible to other believers, the sight of which dare only be seen from a distance, but models of it are everywhere procured. The Meteorological Observatory is under the direction of

Doctor Chambers. The museum in the Victoria Garden and the hospital for sick animals deserve to be mentioned. Public conveyances consist of cabs, buggies and palanquins, carried by four carriers. Most everybody here has his own servant. Bombay is the second important commercial city in India after Calcutta.

A short distance from Bombay, in the suburb Mazagaun, are many serpents in the adjoining djungles. Here resides the Jewish Sassoon family, eminently rich. The accumulation of their wealth derives from trading in opium with China.

The residence of the governor,—who was kind enough to furnish me with recommendations to the government of Hyderabad—is near Bycola. Of all the Indian cities Bombay resembles most a European town. Objects manufactured of sandal, rose and other fragrant wood are offered for sale on every way and passage in the city.

The route from Bombay to the island of Elephanta, seven miles in distance, is performed on a small boat, Mazagaun has to be passed. The bay is admirably beautiful. The small islands with their magnificent vegetation and charming hills on one side and the peaks of the Malabar Ghauts on the other side afford an unusual sight. Malabarhill, the favored place of the Europeans with their pretty bungalows, makes an excellent impression upon the traveller on passing it.

Elephanta is one mile in length and has a

luxuriant growth of palm trees and tamarinds. The form and situation of Elephanta are of a charming beauty; the highest point is divided in two peaks, one higher than the other. A short ascent leads the traveller to the front of the temple between the two peaks where a splendid view of Bombay and Salsette presents itself. The beauty of the vegetation in the foreground is beyond description. The interior of the temple, entered upon very suddenly—doors not existing—shows a spacious chamber on each side of it. The roof is supported by pillars hewn out of the rock, beautifully sculptured. A single glance of the visitor meets with the triple bust of the "Trimurti," the Hindoo trinity, cut in stone and measuring twelve feet in height.

Returning to the city, I visited the botanical garden with its palm trees and the abundance of tropical and other bright-colored flowers, etc., amongst which the Persian roses are of an unusual brilliancy.

An excursion to the Ghauts, with their picturesque outlines, and the sanitarium in the midst of extremely beautiful basalt formations, with extensive sandal wood forests at the basis, is worth while undertaking.

Farther on in the mountains is Mahableshwar, where—at times—the rainfall reaches the abnormal height of 250 inches. Arrived in Karli, by way of Khandalla, the caves with Buddhistic temples in the interior were examined.

East of Khandalla is the unsurpassable breach

of the above mentioned Ghauts, the train passes right through to Poonah.

In Poonah resides a German Savant, a celebrated interpreter of the Sanscrit, whose name—I am sorry to say—I have forgotten. On my return to Bombay, I started for the south on board an English steamer, and leaving Goa, the Portuguese colony sideways, I landed at Baypore-Calicut, 12 to 13 degrees north of the Equator, consequently a very hot place with an extremely moist and tropical climate.

All Indian palm trees are here represented.

The inhabitants, because not intermixed with negro blood, present a brighter and purer complexion and one is inclined to call them pretty.

A day's journey from Baypore-Calicut, and not distant from Cochin, exists a peculiar race of white and colored Jews.

The next voyage was to the East per Madras railroad, and to the foot of the Neilgherre chain of mountains, with the highest point 8,500 feet above the sea. The climate is very mild and coffee and tea grow abundantly. The cinchona plantation in Neddiwattam belongs to the government. The sanitarium Oatakamund has a charming site.

In company of the director of the botanical garden I rode to "Dodabetta," the highest point of the Neilgherre, with an imposing view toward the surrounding country and the southerly chain of mountains. In the hotels of this mountainous country, the departments of the sexes are strictly seperate.

The governor of Madras, and the aristocracy reside here during the summer. Though it was winter when I was there, the weather was nevertheless very mild. To the north is the native state of Mysore with important coffee plantations and gold mines.

From Bangalor, in the distant east of this State with an English cantonment, I proceeded to Madras on the south-eastern coast by rail, and arrived there in the month of January. The heat was almost unbearable and sleep could only be procured under the Poonkha or fan, and even then I was terribly tortured by mosquitos and sand-flies. The rainy season lasts from the end of October to the beginning of January. I was furnished with a very warm recommendation by the late Mr. Bruhns, director of the astronomical observatory in Leipzig, Germany, to Professor Pogson, on whose Astronomic-Meteorological Observatory the scientific observations are published by the Professor's daughter. A famous Israelitish Philologist, Mr. Oppert, is Professor on the Madras College.

The garden of acclimatization interests on account of the various plants, and the government forts are worth an inspection. Towards the end of January, I embarked for Point de Galle on a steamer of the British India Steamship Company.

This place was formerly an important seaport until Colombo has gained the advantage over it.

On a trip to a lake in the vicinity of Point de Galle I saw the Totapella, a mountain second in height of all the mountains in Ceylon and after a short stay in Point de Galle, I travelled to Colombo the capital of Ceylon. Properly, the Djungle region begins here and ends where the country rises terrace-like, thus developing the tropic vegetation (especially on the west coast) to the utmost. Coffee, transplanted from Africa, blossoming and fruit-bearing at one and the same time, is but little aromatic. There is not much activity in the capital of Ceylon. Cinnamon grows almost everywhere and in the Cinnamon garden—a place of a Djunglelike description—extraordinary specimens of cinnamon bushes can be seen. The cloudless sky with a burning hot sun and the blinding white sand contribute greatly to render the stay in Colombo disagreeable. The natives or Singaleses in their provoking white garments do not increase the attraction of the place.

After a short voyage from Colombo, Kandi is reached, a famous place of pilgrimage with clean, tidy houses and some commerce, part of which is in the hands of a few German firms.

In a temple, in this place, the sacred tooth of Buddha is preserved, thus forming the attractive power of the pilgrims. To the German residents in Colombo I am greatly obliged for the many favors shown to me. In Paradenya, a suburb of Kandi, I was introduced to Doctor Tryman, the director of the botanical garden and author of a work about the cultivation of trees from which Caouchouc is obtained. The botanical garden contains exceedingly fine specimens of the Giant-Bamboo and Talipat palm-tree of an abnormal height, also Caouchouc supplying fig-trees, Ficus Indica and Ficus Tocicaria.

The richly ornamented leaves of the Talipatpalm, Corypha umbraculifera, growing to a height of over a hundred feet, are spread—like a parasol—over the heads of distinguished Singaleses by their servants.

Above Kandi are many cinchona and coffee plantations belonging to private people. The coffee crop did not yield, when I was there, on account of the appearance of the devastating Hemileia vestatrix.

To the sanitarium "Nuwarra-Ellia," a distance of 47 miles through the Ramboddé pass, about 13 miles in extention, an altitude of 6,000 feet has to be climbed, and after a descent of about two hours, the road, leading to the sanitarium, is reached. Surrounded by mountains, Nuwarra-Ellia extends very romantically, valley-like, to a length of two and a width of one mile.

In the neighborhood of Nuwarra-Ellia resided Sir Samuel Baker, the celebrated traveller and explorer of the Nile, whose acquaintance I had made the year before at a reception, given by the Viceroy of India, in Simla. Sir Baker was a great sportsman, and often had occasion to use his couteau-de-chasse in encounters with beasts of prey infesting this region. Leopards, wild Elephants and Woodstags, etc., etc., are in abundance in these woody mountains.

After scaling the summit of the highest mountain in Ceylon, the "Petrotallagalla," 8,300 feet, I returned to the plains.

The other high mountains in Ceylon are: the "Totapella," 8,000, the "Kirigallapotta," 7,900, and the "Adams Peak," 7,700 feet high.

In the plains of Nuwarra-Ellia as well as in the plains of Moon stone, Kondopallé, Elk, Totapella, Horton, Bopatalava and Augura, (all these together comprising a district of about 30 miles) remains of mines for the produce of precious stones are found. There can be no doubt, that the produce of jewels in former times has been a very lucrative one, for even now, small rubies, sapphires, emeralds, turmalines and chrysoberyls are found in the so-called Ruby-valley, below the surface in a stratum of gravel.

The animal kingdom in Ceylon—as already mentioned—is well represented, from the small house lizard to the iguanon, about four feet long, and the elephant. A peculiar species of lizards, nowhere else to be found, habitates Ceylon. Small in size and thorn-backed, with a long horn protruding from the upper portion of the mouth, it resembles the antediluvian monstre, the "Iguanodon."

After my return to Colombo I made frequent excursions, either on horseback or in some vehicle, to Point-de-Galle through the splendid cocoa tree forests.

I was now on the point of visiting another part of the globe, "Australia," and must confess, the very thought of leaving India, especially Ceylon, the "Paradise of the East," fell heavy upon me. To get an idea of the vastness of this wonderful country, one must consider, that 23 distinct languages are spoken in India, the written characters of all these languages differing from each other as much as Roman does from German. The languages spoken are : 1) The Urdu, (the proper Hindostan language) the "French" of India, the language of the Mahometans and of the trading people, mostly spoken in Rohilcund, Doab and Oudh. 2) The Hindoo, in Rajpootana, Oudh, Rohilcund, Malva, Bundlecund and by the agricultural Hindoos. 3) The Bengal, in Bengal and the East. 4) Pushtoo, in Peshawar and in the far West. 5) Sindhee, in Sinde and the Cis-Sutlej states. 6) Punjab, in the great Indus Valley. 7) Nepaulish, in Nepaul. 8) Cashmerish, in Cashmere. 9) Guzerattee, by the Parsees and in Guzeratte. 10) Assamish, in Assam. 11) Burmese, in Burmah and Pegu. 12) Cutchee, in Cutch. 13) Bhootish, in Bootan. 14) The Kaeren, in Burmah and Pegu. 15) Singhalese, in Ceylon. 16) The Malay, in Travencore and Cochin. 17) The Tamul, from Madras to Cape Comorin. 18) Canarese, in Coorg and Mysore. 19) Teloogoish, in Hyderabad and along the eastern coast. 20) The Cole and Gond, in Berar. 21) Khassiyaish, in the northeast. 22) Ooryaish, in Orissa. 23) Mahrattan, in Bombay, Nagpore and Gwalior.

In addition to these 23 languages, the better classes converse in the English, Pali, Sanscrit, Persian and Arabian languages and what is said about differences of opinions: "Quot homines, tot sententiae" can be said about the languages in India

The Hindoos, undoubtedly the proudest nation on earth, consider their country to be the primitive source of all that is good and nice and from where the rest of the world receives the blessings. The Indian Empire is divided into British territory and fendatory States, acknowledging sovereignity of Great Britain. British-India is the richest and most populous dependency of the English crown. Area, 1,383,504 square miles. Population, 253,906,449.

The Government is entrusted to the Secretary of State for India. He is aided by a council of 15 members. The executive authority is vested in the Governor-General, appointed by the British crown and a council of 7 members. The salary of the Governor-General amounts to 25,000 pounds sterling per year.

The population is dense. The density varies from 441 per square mile to 43, average for all India being 184. Agriculture is backward. The means of transportation poor, but improving. Eight famines have visited India and decimated the population of various provinces.

The soil is productive, rice, corn, millet, barley and wheat are growing; cotton, indigo, opium and sugar-cane are largely exported. Education is improving. The European and Native army numbers 190,476 men. The Native States have an army of 349,835 men.

The island Ceylon, situated in the Indian Ocean, south-east of India, has an area of 25,364 square miles, is 260 miles in length and has an average breadth of 100 miles. The climate is much more pleasant than that of southern India. The government is administered by a Governor with an Executive Council and a Legislative Council. Minerals abound and precious stones are often found. The pearl-fisheries of the western coast are famous. Bread fruit, cinnamon, pepper, rice, cotton and tobacco are among the chief products of the soil; and coffee, tea, cinchona bark, cocoanut-oil among the export. The population is estimated at 2,700,000. There are only about 4,000 Europeans in Ceylon. I remained in Point de Galle, waiting for a steamer of the Oriental and Peninsular Line, and procuring passage for Australia, I bade "India" good-bye.—

The sea voyage from Point de Galle to South Australia—passing Cape Lewis—lasted sixteen days, the first landing-place being Albany, situated on the south coast. The voyage was a very quiet one till we reached Albany, then we had violent storms for the rest of the voyage. Here resides a brother of the well-known explorer of South America, Mr. Schomburgk.

Adelaide, the capital of South Australia, with 38,000 inhabitants, of which a great many are Germans, is quite a lively place.

After a brief stay in Adelaide, I proceeded to Melbourne, the capital of Victoria, with 290,000 inhabitants. It is difficult to reach the port of the city on account of the heads,—so-called capes—dividing the outer from the inner harbor. Melbourne indulges in the protection of the Tariff in opposition to the colonies who are free traders.

My sojourn in Melbourne during the International Exposition and extending to four months, was a very pleasant one. I formed many valuable acquaintances and through the kindness of my worthy and learned friend, the famous botanist and author of works, on the "Flora" of Australia, Baron von Müller, formerly director of the botonical garden, now Governments' botanist, I was enabled to send a rich collection of seeds, fruits, cones etc., to the late Professor Eichler, director of the botanical garden and museum in Berlin. To Baron von Müller and the director of the museum of Physical Sciences and the director of the botanical garden I am under deep obligations for the honor conferred upon me,—in proposing and electing me a Fellow of the universally renowned "Linaeus Society."

The astronomical observatory with colossal telescopes—director, Mr. Ellery—is a very fine institution. The botanical garden near the river Yara-Yara, which latter almost touches the city is romantically situated and was completely transformed since Doctor Gilford is the director.

The goldmint is very important. Of the secretary of the Minister in Victoria I received valuable scientific records and statistics. On one of my excursions to the interior and to the gold regions, I visited Balarat with Alluvial mines, almost extinguished, whilst the Quartzgold mines are in a blooming condition.

Sandhurst, formerly called Bendigo, as well as the whole gold region do not produce so much now as in bygone times.

North of Balarat I visited the famous Sheep-breeding establishment of Sir Samuel Wilson and went from there on the Northern boundary to the Murray river and the Riverina district on the other side. This region is notorious for its fertility and belongs to New South Wales with the capital Sidney. The climate is mild, because northerly.

On another trip to the Australian Alps, northwest of Melbourne, I ascended Mount "Kosciusko," the highest point, 7000 feet above the level of the sea. In Fernshaw, in the Australian Alps, the giant trees of the Eucalyptus amygdala gigantea reach the extraordinary height of over 400 feet.

In the course of the winter I was introduced to Professor von Haast, the famous geologist who resided in Christchurch, New Zealand, and to Sir Henry Parks, the most important statesman in Australia, whilst Graham Berry, the defender of the trade protective policy, is a deciding authority in all colonial affairs.

I applied to Sir Henry Parks to effectuate a resolution of the Parliament to grant the necessary means for the discovery of the remains of the scientific traveller Leichhardt, and to my great gratification I have met with success.

East of Melbourne is the Gipsland, famous for its mild and moist climate.

I now set out for Sidney on the incompleted railroad, crossing the river Murray. In Albury—North South Wales—on the other side of the Murray river, important cultivation of vine is carried on, mostly by Germans.

On the road from Albury to Sidney I halted at Wagga-Wagga, memorable through the Tichborne trial. The construction of railroads is after the European system.

The capital Sidney with about 220,000 inhabitants is beautifully situated on the Sidney-bay, the latter making deep indentations, thus producing an amphitheatrical view of the city.

The botanical garden is not as large as that of Melbourne, but is much nicer situated and noteworthy for its Araucaries. There is also a museum and an observatory here.

I had the pleasure to make the acquaintance of Lord Loftus, formerly English embassador to Prussia and now governor of New South Wales and of the German Consul General for Australia and the Fejee-Islands, Doctor Krauel.

An invitation of Mr. Godefroy, residing in the Fejees', to visit him had to be respectfully declined on account of an indisposition.

Doctor Bennett, the Ornithologist, who possesses

a considerably large library, was also one of my newly acquired and valuable connections.

The kindness of Doctor Moore, the above mentioned director of the botanical garden in Sidney, who deputed his assistant, Doctor Weber, a German, to accompany me to the Illawara district in New South Wales, will never be forgotten. Here I had a good opportunity to study the "Flora" of Australia, especially the Palms. The coal region extends all along the eastern coast of New South Wales.

The export of coals from New-Castle, north of Sidney, (which I visited) to China and Japan is very large. On the other side of Sidney harbor is a tower, erected by a philanthropic German, which affords a lovely prospect of the city and the surroundings.

West of Sidney, in Paramatta, are beautiful orange groves and cottages. A branch line of the railroad carried me to the Blue Mountains, a brilliant, resplendent sandstone-formation. The highest summits of this mountain chain, not exceeding 3,000 feet, consists of basalt, and with the slope, Bathurst, a coal and iron mining district is reached.

I returned to Sidney, intending to go to New Zealand but was prevented from doing so on account of the detention at quarantine in Aukland—the nearest landing-place—where every passenger coming from Sidney had to remain a period of time, Variola at that time raging in Sidney.

A sea voyage of two days brought me to Brisbane, the capital of Queensland, with 36,000 inhabitants, situated on a river having the same name. Brisbane is the seat of the colonial Parliament. The botanical garden is of secondary importance. Doctor Bailey, the director of the museum in Brisbane, is the author of several scientific works.

The cultivation of the sugar-cane commences in the environs of Brisbane, 28 to 29° southern latitude and still far northerly—as in all Australian colonies— isolated gold fields are to be found.

On the high plain, west of Brisbane, lies the city Toowoomba, 1500 feet high. Warwick, in the midst of extensive pastures, has famous cattle and sheep breedings on the farms.

In Stanthorp—on a granite formation—tin is obtained from the rivers and the cultivation of fruits largely pursued.

I travelled back to Brisbane and found it very warm there, it was already in August, and sailed along the east coast and the coral reefs, 1,100 miles in length, where several stoppages were made. Steering northward now, the course of the coast changes after a few days westerly, and leads to Thursday Island with important pearlfisheries, and from where —the weather permitting—the coast of New Guinea is clearly visible, and along the Gulf of Carpentaria and several islands of the Sunda sea, as for instance Timor, Sumbava and Bali, well-known from former visitations of earthquakes.

Leaving Bali, the east coast of Java appeared in sight and we were most disagreeably surprised to see the yellow flag hoisted—a warning that the Cholera was raging in Java. Batavia, the capital of Java, has about 99,000 inhabitants. The European quarter is at Weltenvreden, a suburb of Batavia. Here is the winterpalace of the Governor-General.

The zoological garden contains beautiful specimen of Ourang-Outangs. The many military and civil clubs heighten the attraction of the place. The commerce in staplegoods and the trade in coffee and sugar is important. 80 miles from here, at the basis of the mountains is Buytenzorg.

The Governor-General s' Jaacobs had the goodness to furnish me with recommendations to the residents in the country and to his friend, Mr. Holle, the owner of large tea plantations in the interior.

Buytenzorg, in my opinion, has the most important botanical garden in the world. It is almost impossible to give a description of the variety of plants, etc., which delight the eyes of the visitor of this lovely spot. Nepenthes of an unusual brilliancy grow here abundantly. Here also, as somewhere else, the director of the botanical garden, Doctor Treub, favored me with his kindness, so much so, that the botanical garden in Berlin again received a valuable sending of fruits, plants, seeds, roots, etc., etc.

In the hospital for Berri-berri patients—this malady appearing in some tropical climates—beginning with Oedema of the lower extremities and generally ending fatally—I found a great number of persons afflicted with this dreadful disease—some of them in a dying condition.

The agricultural institute is very important.

The summer palace of the Governor-General is also here.

Domestic weapons are offered for sale everywhere in this palace.

To reach Sindanglaya, 3,800 feet above the sea, vehicles, drawn by ponies, had to be hired. The road is in a very good condition, and leads through a magnificent Flora. Every five miles the caravan passes through a so-called Tal (an old post station), and rests for a while. The latter part of this journey is performed over a mountain pass of the Ghedde mountains.

The valley of Sindanglaya is pretty well settled and cultivated, the climate of which is very healthy, and affords protection against all kinds of fevers.

The cultivation of rice — like almost everywhere in Java — is carried on in a large style, drainage universally.

My next aim was Wandong, the capital of Preanger, 2,500 feet above the level of the sea.

Wandong is the seat of the Resident and the Regent, and is surrounded by mountains. The Regents in Java are former land proprietors and Mahometan princes. Their duties consist in settling disputes amongst the Natives (Mahometans) and in procuring shelter for travellers.

The morals of the Natives in this country are

not as strict as those of their co-religionists in India or elsewhere. They indulge in wine and entertain an almost amicable relationship with Europeans.

The Resident van Vloeten, to whose family I had already been introduced in Batavia, received me most cordially, and I shall never forget his kindness.

A visit to the cinchona plantation, 5,000 feet above the sea, on a volcanic formation, was worth the troublesome travel.

The bark of the Calisaya Ledgeriana, here cultivated, yields from 10 to 12 per cent. quinine, whilst from the Indian scarcely 3 per cent. is obtained.

Messrs. Junghuhn and Haszkarl, two well-known savants, authors of many valuable works on natural sciences, deserve the credit to have added greatly to the introduction, respectively the cultivation of quinine on the Island.

The mountain Flora of Java has been minutely described by Mr. Junghuhn, whose monument is found at the base of the mountain on which the above mentioned plantation is situated.

A rich tropic vegetation surrounds the traveller until Lembong is reached, when a horse has to be mounted in order to ascend to the cinchona plantation.

The lower part of the mountain is planted with tobacco.

My reception on the plantation by the Natives will never be forgotten by me. They did all in their power to make my stay there agreeable — dancing, singing and performing all sorts of native juggleries, going on all the time.

Returning to Sindanglaya I made preparations for the intended visit to the Volcano Gheddé, 10,000 feet above the sea.

I found a companion in the person of the Dutch Colonel Smith, and at about nine o'clock in the evening we started on horseback, with our guard and torchlight bearers in the front and rear.

The way leads through dense forests and an immensely rich tropical vegetation.

Here also, as on the ascent of the Kawa Opus crater, the cavalcade rests at the different stations, and at the break of day the open plane, underneath which is the little hut where travellers make a long siesta, is reached.

It is superfluous to describe this volcano, as it resembles in every respect the Kawa-Opus and Kawa-Ratu, the same desert-like surroundings, total absence of any vegetation, or dwarf bushes here and there, contrasting with the lovely verdure of the lower parts of the mountain. The approach of the rainy season was to be expected soon — it being November; the heat was almost unbearable, not less than 100º in the shade, and I was, therefore, anxious to leave the Island and take passage in Batavia for Singapore.

A peculiarity on the Island of Java is the law which prohibits the hoisting of any other flag than the Netherland.

In the eastern part of the Island the Japanese language is spoken ; in the west the Sundanese, and on the coast Malayan, whilst French and Dutch are in general use, especially by commercial people.

Agriculture, formerly feudalistic, is progressing favorably now, and has been ever since that system was abandoned, and the population is becoming somewhat prosperous.

The most important colony of the Netherland Indies is Java, which politically includes the neighboring Island of Madura. The total area, 50,848 square miles. Population, 20,259,000.

Java is governed under what is termed the Culture system, which was established in 1832.

By far the larger part of the commerce of Java is with the Netherlands.

The principal exports are sugar, coffee, rice, indigo and tobacco.

I left Batavia in the first part of the month of November on a Dutch steamer carrying troops for Acheen, one of the two capitals of the Island of Sumatra, and intended to proceed to Singapore.

The voyage was not very pleasant for me.

We had not reached the Island of Rhio, when, to my great horror, Asiatic cholera was raging among the soldiers on board the ship, decimating them and leaving us in constant fear to be also subjected to this terrible scourge.

Notwithstanding the protests of the authorities of Rhio, the landing of all the sick was effected there, and we proceeded on our journey, leaving them at Rhio, situated on the Equator.

I remained for some time in Singapore, whose population consists mostly of Chinese, some of whom are very wealthy.

Singapore is a free port. The climate, though in the dreaded neighborhood of the Sunda Islands and the Indian continent, is tropical and healthy.

The environs of Singapore are almost infested with tigers, and one is assured here that not a single day in the year passes without that at least one Chinese is devoured by the brutes.

There are extensive plantations of tapioka, a Maranthus, in the interior. The cultivation of betel pepper and cocoanut palms is also very important, and from the many odoriferous grasses and weeds essential oils are extracted, especially from the lemon grass.

By the kindness of the English Governor, Sir Frederic Weld, residing here, who gave me a very cordial reception, I was introduced to the Resident of Perak, and was invited by the latter to visit him.

A special invitation of the Maharajah of Johore, whose magnificent palace is situated in the extreme south of the Malayan peninsula, to be his guest, was heartily welcomed. After a three days' stay there, he requested his nephew to accompany me to the Gambir and Pepper plantations, in the interior; and to the Indigo, Yam and Sago plantations in the southwesterly part of the State.

In order to reach these latter, the so-called straits — a waterway — have to be crossed, and for that purpose the Maharajah had a small steamer, used only by himself, in readiness for us.

The great kindness and generosity of the Maharajah enabled me to study the country profoundly.

On this journey I found remnants of an abandoned nutmeg cultivation.

Livery and coachmen in this part of the country recruit themselves from India, whilst the rest of the serving class consists of Malayans.

The language is Malaye, the religion Mahometan or Hindoo.

On an excursion to the Island of Penang, 4° north between Sumatra and the Malayan Peninsula, on which way Malacca has to be passed, I had the honor to be the guest of Lieutenant-Governor Anson.

The city of Penang is romantically situated; the population mostly Chinese.

On board a steamer belonging to the Government, and generously put at my disposal, I proceeded to Perak to visit the Resident, and traveled from there to the tin-mining region, worked by Chinamen.

Many coffee plantations are found in this mountainous country, and to visit the Government's plantation I had to ride on the back of an elephant. The cultivation of Durian, a fruit, tasting like cheese, and which reaches the size of a child's head, is carried on here.

— 49 —

At the request of the German Consul-General, Mr. Bieber, to study the cultivation of sugar cane in the Province of Wellesley and elsewhere, and to procure all possible statistics regarding the same, I started after my return to Penang for Wellesley.

This country is very low, on a level with the sea. I found all plantations, etc., alike. There are a great many canals, serving to drain the country and to ship the cane, sugar, etc. I also went to Siam, the neighboring state of Wellesley, and gathered all profitable knowledge about the sugar cane cultivation and the manufacturing of sugar, and after communicating the same to the Consul, I returned to Singapore.

The Islands of Singapore and Penang, and the territories of Malacca and the Province of Wellesley constitute the Straits Settlements of Great Britain, which, politically, with six provinces in Siam and a number of small Malay states, either tributary to, or in treaty with the above powers, belong to the Asiatic peninsula, Malay, the southernmost point of the Continent.

The area of Malay is about 70,000 square miles, and the estimated population 650,000. Of the interior of this country there is less known than of any other point in Asia. The surface is very uneven, the climate moist and hot, the temperature on the Makran coast and in the Persian Gulf is $110°$ and at times $125°$.

Out of 365 days, 190 are rainy, the rainfall from 100 to 130 inches.

. The straits settlements have an area of 1,445 square miles and 423,384 population.

From Singapore to Hong-Kong the sea voyage lasted eight days and was a very unpleasant one, as we had to suffer from very vehement northeast Monsoons.

Hong-Kong is a colony of Great Britain and was formerly a part of China. It consists of the Islands of Hong-Kong, ceded to Great Britain in 1884 [1841], and the opposite Peninsula of Kow-loon, ceded to England in 1861. The government is administered by a Governor, aided by an Executive Council. There is also a Legislative Council. The total population of Hong-Kong is 160,420, of whom but 7,900 are white persons.

Hong-Kong forms the centre of trade for many different kinds of goods. Its commerce is virtually a part of that of China, and is chiefly carried on with the United States, Germany and Great Britain.

The tea and silk trade of China is largely in the hands of Hong-Kong firms.

The country is but little cultivated and crossed by a sinister mountain range. Most all the vegetables are shipped from Macao to this country.

A very bad fever, called the Hong-Kong fever, a combination of cholera, yellow and typhoid fever, is raging here, but is diminishing now on account of the sanitary precautions.

The principal place is Victoria, situated in the north of the Chinese coast.

South of the city, on a high mountain, are the fortifications, separating the city from the sea.

The commercial part of the city is close to the port, the other, in a terrace-like elevation, extends to the mountain south of Victoria.

There are many Portuguese here intermarrying with the Chinese populace.

At the time of my stay in Hong-Kong, Doctor von Moellendorf, the well-known zoologist, was the representative of the German Empire there.

Here also it was, where I received the honorable commission from Professor Bastian and Doctor Jagor, of Berlin, Prussia, to extend my travels to the little explored Philippines for the purpose of ethnographic studies and the collection of anthropological and ethnological objects, thus to enrich science.

I will show later, how I managed to meet the gratification of these two "Hommes celêbres" and the famous pathologist, Professor Doctor Virchow, in Berlin.

I made frequent excursions on steamers—all of which were well armed, to stand an attack of the pirates—sailing through the bay and along the Pearl river. From the deck of the steamer, when on the river, the most prominent Pagodes of Canton are visible.

On one of these extravaganzas, I visited Canton, and after inspecting the open vaults with their costly sarcophagos and admiring the gorgeously ornamented Pagodes and the pretty Jade works manufactured here, I left Canton, not without having seen the "Public Execution Grounds," and returned to Hong-Kong to make arrangements for the probably long lasting tour to the Philippine Islands.

Having succeeded in procuring some indispensable vademecums for that voyage, I hastened my departure from Hong-Kong, and landed first in Macao, a Portuguese possession on the Chinese boundary.

Macao is a beautifully situated city, the bay one of the finest.

Partially surrounded by verdant hills, with lovely flower gardens and villas in the centres, the city makes a favorable impression on the stranger. Were it not for the almost uninterrupted tolling of the many church and convent bells, which is often deafening, the sojourn in Macao would be very agreeable.

The population is very mixed, and one is surprised to find so many idlers in the streets and squares.

Portuguese, Chinamen and Negroes, are met with at every step; also, Priests, Patres, Fratres and Nuns.

Women, most of whom are of a dark color, dress in the Portuguese style, with the indispensable Manto and the high colored cloth wound around the head.

The gambling dens of Macao are of world-fame.

From here it takes three days for Manila, the capital of Luzon, one of the Philippine Islands.

A small boat with four or six rowers brings the traveller to the city, only to be subjected to great troubles by the custom officers (Duana). Manila has a botanical garden, small, but exceedingly pretty.

Here I had the great honor to form the acquaintance of Captain-General Primo di Rivera, the famous botanist Vidal, the Jesuit, Padre Faura, whose scientific works on the Chinese Tai-Fun are well-known, the German Consul-General Kemperman and the chemist Grupe, all of which were instrumental in my successful explorations.

Padre Faura requested me to visit the district of Dupax, where, especially in the last twelve months, frequent earthquakes occurred. I gratified the wish of that gentleman as will be seen hereafter.

Of the population of Manila, Indians of the Malayan race are in plurality. They are called Indianos. The rest of the inhabitants consists of Negritos, Mestizos and Europeans.

The Mestizos are a beautiful set of men, and most all of them are in good circumstances. The Singleys, cross-breeds of Chinese and Indianos, are also well to do. Population of Manila, 160,000.

Though not a professional Ethnologist — my favorite studies were always Natural Sciences — I accepted the honorable commission of the celebrated German Savants, to explore the north of Luzon, the largest island of the Philippines, with great joy and a pride, impossible to describe.

The science of Ethnography up to that time was a "terra incognita" to me, and yet I was full of hopes to meet with success.

Of all the distant islands and groups lying just off the coast of southeastern Asia, in Malaysia, none had been less explored by scientific travellers than the Philippines; whether from their geographical situation in that remote corner of the world or from the hardships and exposures to which one is subjected in the uncultivated and wild interior, is a mere conjecture.

Of the few visitors of scientific-literary fame, who explored part of the Philippines ethnolgically or for the purpose of natural sciences, the following gentlemen have to be mentioned: Professor Carl Semper in Wuerzburg, von Drasche, Doctor Jagor and Meyer, all Germans.

The explorations which Professor Semper made amongst the Negritos, are undoubtedly the most important. Doctor Jagor's work, in which the learned gentleman describes the Philippines, has been translated by my worthy friend, the botanist Vidal in Manila, into Spanish.

I found a companion for the probable wearysome tour to the north, in the person of the Literary, Mr. Au, a German, and preparing ourselves for this extensive journey, we intended to start from a certain point, in different directions and meet again, but had to abandon this plan on account of the unsafety in this country.

It would fill pages to specify all the articles which we bought for the trip, suffice to say, the apparatus for photographs, cooking utensils, tent, arms and provisions, were a great burden to us.

Before starting from Manila, we visited the Lagunas in the vicinity, the Botocan Cascades and the Volcano Tal.

On the morning of the 20th of March, the little expedition left Manila in the best of humor, and crossed the northeasterly point of the bay to Bulácan and thence through well cultivated land and Quingo, Balinag, San Miguel de Mayum to San Isidro, where we were hospitably received by the Commander of the Guardia Civil, Mr. Scheidnagel, having been recommended by Mr. Vidal.

Mr. Scheidnagel takes a great interest in natural sciences, and is the author of a work on the Philippines and on Benguet in special, which latter he describes in a separate little book.

In the latest German ethnographical works the name of Scheidnagel is honorably mentioned, and his work recommended.

For our scientific purposes, his letters of recommendation to the Governors of the provinces of Nueva Viscaya and Principe, and to his subordinate Chiefs of the Guardia Civil were of incalculable advantage and gave us the right to demand a military escort in case of necessity.

Finding nothing of interest in this and the middle part of Nueva Ecija, we proceeded to the north, passing Calavetuan, Talaveras, San José and Punkan.

We remained several days in Caraglan, in whose neighborhood Rancherias' of a wild tribe, the Ibilaos or Ilongotes, exist.

The Franciscan Monk in Caraglan possessing a great knowledge of the country and the people inhabiting the same, participated in our undertaking, and in company with the sergeant of the Guardia Civil stationed there, conducted us to the distant Rancheria of the Ibilaos, giving his best advises as how to procure ethnographic objects.

Of the many photographs which we had made in this Rancheria of the wild tribe, only one was successfully obtained, the high temperature of the water and its limy contents damaged them considerably.

Thanks to the indefatigable Frater, who also acts as a spiritual functionary, we succeeded in procuring great quantities of ethnographic objects, such as arms, ornaments and articles for domestic use.

All these objects were received by us in exchange for clothes, jewelry, etc. . After leaving Caraglan we crossed, north of the latter, the Carabalho mountains, which divide the two provinces of **Nueva Ecija** and **Nueva Viscaya.**

On both sides of the mountains live the above mentioned Ibilaos or Ilongotes.

From the Carabalho Sur (southern Carabalho) on the east and southeast to Cassiguran and Buler, and in the south, extending to Caraglan, San José, etc., Ibilaos Rancherias are scattered everywhere.

The Carabalho Sur divides the middle of northern Luzon and inclines in the western and eastern part of the island toward the north and south, thus forming large sized central planes in the north and south.

On the other, the northern part of this Cordillere, called Carabalho, and along the many branches, as far as to the eastern part of the mountains in Nueva Viscaya, Ibilaos are also living.

The Cordillere in the east of Viscaya is but little known.

Opposite Bayambong in the East is a mountain 4000 feet above the level of the sea, and considered to be the centre of the earthquakes of late.

We could not get any information about this mountain nor the dense, primitive forests or the inhabitants.

The Ibilaos of other districts only knew that their enemies inhabit that region. They called them Ibalaos or Ilongotes like themselves and would not —under any consideration—accompany us, so much afraid were they of them.

As there are a great many Rancherias, I will only mention a few of them, the names, as given by the Ibilaos. In Carabalho Sur are three, high up in the West, Liroc.

Along the east coast, south of Cassiguran in the adjacent mountains, are Dagan, Ampatan and many unknown small ones. Near Buler (Principe) Patang and Gumiat.

To the south and west of Buler live Balugas, also called Dumagas, belonging to the Negritos which are spread almost over the whole north of Luzon.

The inhabitants of Cassiguran (Contra Costa) are called Ipogaos.

Rancheria Rosale, which we visited, contains from 12 to 15 houses and has tobacco, sugar cane, camote and banana plantations.

In the gardens of the Ibilaos, Camote, (Convolvulus batata) Gave, (Calladium esculentum, or Sagittae folium of Linné) of which only the root and the leaves are eaten, corn, onions, garlick and rice are cultivated.

The rice crop yields but little, drainage not existing.

The Ibilaos of Rosale communicate with the Indians and seemed to be of an obliging and trustworthy character and quite harmless.

According to their own statement, they have a kind of a religion.

Though the sun and the moon are not worshipped by them, they nevertheless consult them as oracles.

The halo of the moon or the sun, the appearance of these bodies when they rise or set, whether stars are visible in their neighborhood, or if nebula exist and how they are formed, all this influences the Ibilao in all his undertakings. Deductions are made from them and their natural superstition is systematically nourished.

Monogamy is the only legal form among the Ibilaos and fornication is punished with the death of both guilty parties, it becoming the duty of the nearest relatives of the incriminated to put them to death.

At a very early stage of life children marry, (the parents stipulating a verbal marriage contract) and unite when at a mature age, then the real wedding takes place.

The dowry consists of a certain number of weapons, domestic utensils and pigs, and is selected, naturally under the influence of her parents, by the bride.

Intermarriages in large families are common, but never does a brother marry his sister.

Newly born infants receive a kind of a baptism, water is spilled on their heads and salt put into the mouths by an old woman.

Baptisations, weddings and funerals are always followed by bacchanalies, the same as with the Indians.

The Ibilaos do not know any divisions of time or seasons except the time of the harvest.

Nuños, their evil spirit, is very much feared by

them, as it is he who sends all the misfortunes, and he is therefore invited to all their festivities.

Of medicinal plants they only know a few herbs and barks of trees and these are only used for external wounds, etc. Their weapons are the campilang, a sheathknife, the lancet, arrow and shield. Earrings, necklaces and bracelets are worn on the upper part of the arm by both sexes and the waistcloths are the usual ornaments of the Ibilaos.

Cowards by nature, they are very treacherous and very much feared for their cruelty and brutality, not only do they persecute their greatest enemies, the Negritos, but are in constant war with their own tribes or even kinsmen.

Armed from head to foot and using the same weapons as their western neighbors of the Central Cordillere, the Igorrotes, they are born warriors.

The industry of the Ibilaos is very limited and is confined to the weaving or rather binding of the fibre of a plant into Parneros, (sieves) and Cribas de bejuce (baskets), also in the collecting of honey and wax. All the mentioned articles are either sold or exchanged in the Christian villages.

Hunting is one of their favorite sports. Their cruelty is without limit and their bloodthirst makes no distinction between friend or foe.

They murder Negritos and Indians of the neighboring villages, where and whenever they get a chance to do so, but not like the Igorrotes for mere bravado. The motives of their killing in most instances is superstition.

The most precious thing a young man tenders to his affianced is a finger, an ear or any other limb of a person murdered by him.

To-day, several tribes unite to execute their fiendish purposes of killing harmless persons, and to morrow, perhaps, we find these same tribes as bitter antagonists, murdering each other for no cause but to satisfy their bloodthirsty passions.

In these bloody expeditions the young sons of the Ibilaos participate, or when of too tender an age, are instructed by their fathers in the art of severing the head from the body of a murdered person.

At the death of a member of a family, the latter, accompanied by friends, leave the Rancheria in a procession and murder whoever comes in sight of them, thus avenging the dead.

This same bloody ceremony is performed by the Ibilaos after harvesting, to offer thanks to the infernal gods.

The density of the mountain-forests and the almost impassable, narrow and uneven roads are the cause that these barbarians can not be persecuted.

Though, as already described, well armed, they also use Puas' (traps) from which—once entrapped— no one can extricate himself.

Rarely are two Ibilaos seen wandering the same way together, for fear that their footprints would be followed and the place of concealment revealed.

According to Professor Blumentritt, the Ibilaos of Carabalho Sur live only towards the North and Northwest, their habitations extending to the Carabalho de Buler.

The same author describes them as of small stature and weak physical strength, that Negritoblood flows through their veins and that they have no agriculture.

Our observations differ greatly from the above, inasmuch as we have already described, that we had seen their cultivation of cereals and fruits, etc. The statement about the Negritoblood can not be applied exclusively to the Ibilaos, since Negritos are spread all over the Philippines and not only over Northern Luzon.

Buzeta and Bravo, two Spanish authors, say that the Ibilaos lead miserable lifes and are deficient of even the smallest luxuries.

We cannot agree with them.

All the Rancherias which we visited were not in such bad conditions as described. The Negritos are much poorer in their ways and modes of living. In Blumentritt's essay, the Ibilaos of the neighborhood of the Contra Costa are called Ilongotes. We differ also in this respect, referring to authentical sources and our own researches.

From Caraglan in a distance of six miles we visited a Rancheria high up in the mountains.

The expedition was accompanied by the parochial clergyman and the sergeant of the Guardia

Civil from Caraglan, both of which shared in the tedious journey in the most amiable way.

We passed the night in a miserable hut, and started early next morning, in order to accomplish our intended negotiations with the Ibilaos.

Very little money was required — as the Ibilaos preferred the exchange of the articles desired by us for the goods we had in store — and a nice collection of ethnographical objects was procured.

In this Rancheria we found beautiful, classical figures, of imposing physical strength; some others resembled Chinese and Japanese, which circumstance leads to the supposition that they had intermixed with the latter when their habitations were on the west coast.

We returned on the next day to Caraglan fatigued from the mountain trip, and started shortly afterwards for Aretao, north-northwest of Caraglan. Our march led over the Carabalho, which divides the north of Luzon.

From a mountain pass, about 3,500 feet above the level of the sea, and very steep, we had beautiful views of the mountain forest underneath and the distant Contra Costa (Pacific coast) dawning in the east, the sea not visible.

Our first station was made in **Camerin San Lazar**, on this side of the Pass, at about noon, on account of the inclemency of the weather.

The station, consisting of an old hut, open in many places, afforded a bad shelter.

The rear part of this hut served as a parlor and reception room for my companion and myself, whilst the front part was densely crowded by our servants, the Indians and the military escort on this expedition from Caraglan.

A few miles distant from the hut, or blockhouse, the steep ascent of the Carabalho commences.

This road affords an excellent opportunity for botanists; vegetation abounds and is exceedingly rich.

In the quartz sand we found diminutive gold leaves, and concluded that these mountains must contain gold ore, but could not pay much attention to this discovery, our time not permitting it.

The distance from Caraglan to Aretao, the first pueblo on the other side of the Carabalho, is about 28 miles, and the expedition reached this place in two days. On the first day we made only a short march, the weather was too uncertain, but on the second day, though we had to walk a great deal over the high mountains in consequence of the terrible condition of the road, we succeeded in terminating our tour.

On the other side of the Carabalho is also a shelter for travellers, called San Claro. This building is much smaller than that of Camerin San Lazar, but cleaner.

It was late in the night when we arrived at Aretao.

The place is romantically situated, and was the

more picturesque as it showed the signs of the destruction caused by the last earthquake.

The cloister also was a heap of ruins, and the clergyman lived in a small Indian house.

We could not find any other place, so we put up at the spacious school house of the village.

The day following our arrival, we visited the few Europeans of the place, viz.: the Priest and the Officer of the Gendarmeria. The former is a venerable gentleman and a good scholar.

Here, in Aretao, we found ourselves in the region where the earthquakes of 1881 had caused immense destructions and of which the director of the meteorological observatory in Manila, Padre Faura, had given us some accounts, requesting us at the same time to investigate the accompanying phenomena of these terrestrial revolutions.

According to the statements of the inhabitants, the earthquakes occurred towards the end of the summer of 1881, in Nueva Viscaya.

This region had seldom been visited by earthquakes, and for that reason caused a terrible panic among the peacable populace, more so, as the concussion of the earth was so intense and not in a horizontal direction, like in other parts of the Philippines, but vertically, thus giving vent to the fear of the outburst of a new volcano.

This fear was premature, the concussions ceased at the beginning of the rainy season.

Two and a half leagues from Aretao is Dupax or Dupaz.

Here, inmidst a remarkably beautiful mountainous country we halted, intending to remain several days, plenty of work awaiting us there. In the vicinity of Dupaz are a great number of Rancherias of the Ibilaos, of which four were visited by us.

The cura, or catholic priest, of Dupaz, was a venerable old gentleman, doing his best to give us all possible comfort, and though 65 years old, developed great energy, combined with a vivacious temperament and a strong power of will and action.

Devoting himself to the duties of his high office as Parochial Priest of Nueva Viscaya, he nevertheless studied natural sciences, etc.

The Indians respected the pious, old gentleman reverently, and even the Gobernadorcillo (the mayor of the village) trembled when the stentorian voice of the Cura was heard.

All these good qualities of the Priest were of great value to us. With all our efforts and offers to induce the Indians to accompany us to the Rancherias, we did not succeed until the good, old Priest interfered, and all hesitation, fears and resistances on the part of the Indians were instantaneously banished.

We supplied them with arms, etc., and started for the Rancherias in the mountain forests, south and southwest of Dupaz.

The precaution of arming the Indians is an indispensable necessity, and encounters almost certain, even if well armed. The Ibilaos lay in ambush, and one is never safe until far away from their abodes and arrows.

The first Rancheria visited was in the centre of a dense forest, and the houses not in such bad conditions as described by other travellers. The tribunal or town hall, a small, clean building, served us as lodging.

Like the Indians, they have a captain or chief. This captain made himself very useful to us, acting jointly with our interpreter as a medium between the Ibilaos and us, thus enabling us to add greatly to the Ibilaos dictionary, which I began in Caraglan.

Among the men as well as the women we found beautiful specimens. The women are prettier than the Indians down in the valley.

Beside the inhabited houses we found storehouses for the crop, built in Chinese style. These and some of the types of the Ibilaos with their jewelries, leave no doubt that there must have been an intimate intercourse, commercially and sociably, between them and the Chinese in former times.

Around the Rancherias are gardenlike plantations with tobacco, corn, Gabi, (Caladium esculentum) sugar cane and rice.

The Ibilaos bury their dead not far from their houses, near the banks of rivers.

The tribunal in the Rancheria is beautifully

situated on the summit of a pretty steep hill, the lower part of the latter covered by the few houses.

We photographed some of the Ibilaos, in groups and single, in different positions, also houses and landscapes and were very successful, obtaining quite a number.

Satisfied with the results of our expedition in this part of the island, we left Dupaz for Bombang. From the top of a hill, Bombang, with its little church, beautifully situated, affords an excellent view.

The monastery in this place was destroyed by the earthquake, and we took shelter in the tribunal —temporarily erected—the old tribunal, which was a massive stone building, having also been demolished.

We came to the conclusion that Bombang and the surrounding country was the centre of the earthquakes of last year.

In the last Rancheria of the Ibilaos, not far from Bombang, we found nothing of interest.

Already before Bombang is reached, the settlements of the Igorrotes are entered into.

The inhabitants of the Province of Nueva Viscaya have to be divided in three groups. The largest part of this province, to the east, is inhabited by the Ibilaos or Ilongotes, both names being used by the wild tribes. They are the same as the Ibilaos of the Carabalho and Dupaz. The Ilongotes which we had seen in Carig, are like the former, carried the same weapons, articles, arrows, lances and shield, and had also their front teeth broken out.

The Ibilaos which settled in San Niño, near Bombang, used the same dialect as the Carabalho Ibilaos. With the collected words and phrases we were able to make ourselves understood.

Here we made excavations of skulls and bones of the race described, and I was enabled to send a pretty large collection of such to the famous pathological anatomist, Professor Doctor Virchow in Berlin, for anthropological studies.

The number of Ibilaos can not be given, since the districts along the eastern coast are totally unknown.

They wear the long hair in a switch around the head like the Chinese.

The types of the faces vary, from the genuine, broad face of the Chinaman with the protruding cheekbone to the oval form of the Caucasian race.

They have no idols, but are as superstitious as the Igorrotes and like these latter consult their oracles, viz.: the condition and form of the liver and gall bladder of the sacrificed chickens and swines.

Padre Villaverde, whose guests we were when in Ibung, describes their mode of warfare.

They live in monogamy and the housework as well as the work in the fields is performed by the wives, hunting and fishing by the men.

They build their Rancherias near streams and rivers, on mountain slopes or hidden abysses.

Every Rancheria has an Elder who settles domestic troubles and in time of war is the leader.

It was impossible to get any information about their law-business.

The houses are built of caña (cane) and poles, covered with cogon (grass).

They seem to change their abodes frequently.

The plains in the centre, under Spanish supremacy, respectively in Dupaz and Bombang, are inhabited by Indians, who, in appearance, etc., incline to Ibilaos, being descendants of the latter by intermarrying. The Indians in Aretao, from the same causes, intermarrying with Pangarinan and Agno Igorrotes, resemble Igorrotes, and those in Bayambong and Bagabac, the Gaddan Igorrotes.

The Igorrotes near Bombang immigrated from the mountains of the west, those in the vicinity of Aretao from the Agno.

The Pangarinan and Agno Igorrotes have a great similarity with the Igorrotes of Benguet, the same broad faces with flat noses, and are just as filthy and poor as they.

The Gaddanes immigrated in the past century from the Saltan, and settled all over the plains as far as to the mountains of Quiangan and Silipan.

It can not be stated whether they found free land and settled upon, or other Ibilaos occupying already parts of the country.

The third group consists of the Igorrotes of Quiangan, Silipan and Mayoyaos.

They cut the hair round the head. The houses, especially those of the better situated Principales, are built of wooden boards, with neither chimneys nor windows, and contain one door; they are elevated above the ground, supported by poles, and at nighttime the ladder is drawn in and the door locked.

These are very wild tribes.

The Rancherias in Quiangan, numbering 53, have a population of 13,000, and the 81 in Silipan over 15,000.

Near Diadi, where 19 Rancherias exist, the population, mostly Mayoyaos, numbers 2,376.

The Perugianes, their neighbors to the north, on both sides of the river Magat, up to the Saltan district, though of the same tribe, are their bitterest enemies.

According to what the Spanish captain of the boat related to us, there was a fight between the Perugianes and the Mayoyaos, in which 14 were killed and buried by the military, but were exhumed by the Igorrotes the very same night.

All these wild tribes are independent of the Spaniards, notwithstanding the Spanish missions and the frequent military expeditions. Bordering to the north, in the province of Isabella in the Saltan district, from the river Magat in the northwest to the Partido Itabes and the river Bangag, live Gaddanes.

Blumentritt mentions their neighbors to the left, in the southwest and west as Mayoyaos, and Ifugaos in the south and southeast, in the west the

Itetapanes and on the right side, north and northwest the Dadayags, north the Bayabmanes and Itaves, and Calauas in the northwest.

The name "Ifugao" in the Gaddan dialect, as spoken by the Indians of Nueva Viscaya in the pueblos Bayambong, Solano and Bagabac, collectively, means wild tribes, the same as "Calinga" in the Ibanac and Cagayan is a cognomen for wild and not baptized Igorrotes.

In all my wanderings, I never heard the Dadayags mentioned. The map of Luzon points to the district of Pangul, on the narrow plains of the rio Pangul or Pungal, as their habitation and where they cultivate the land and follow the fishing business.

Though I have never seen them, I am convinced that they are the same as those in the Saltan.

The same author says that Igorrotes live only in the Benguet district, and the Itetapanes up to the Cordillere central, as the neighbors of the Busaco Igorrotes from Lepanto and Bontoc. He describes the Itetapanes as resembling the Gaddanes, and unlike the Igorrotes, darker and smaller in size.

My observations and investigations in regard to the Igorrotes lead me to the supposition, that all the 20 or 22 tribes, so strictly distinguished by Blumentritt, are one and the same race, and that the names of the different districts or localities, and the many dialects—corruptions of one original language—as well as frequent exodus' and immigrations have unmistakably added to this ethnographical error.

In my travels through the provinces of Nueva Viscaya, Isabella and Cagayan, Spaniards and Indians knew nothing of such distinctions, and collectively called all the unbaptized inhabitants of the left side of the rio Cagayan: Igorrotes, Calingas or Ifugaos.

How far the Saltan district extends, is not known. According to Spanish statements, it comprises all the valleys on the banks of the rio Saltan and its tributaries and the northwestern part of the province of Isabella, 9 miles from the Cabezera.

The rio Saltan, crossing Isabella and part of Cagayan parallel to the rio Cagayan, and variably called rio chico, Bangag or Pinacpac, must therefore be the head of the great river.

To my recollection, the river discharging near the Rancheria Pinacpo, taking its course in the north and northwest from the mountains, had been called Saltan. It is not improbable that Gaddanes Rancherias exist south of Pinacpo on the banks of the rio chico, but I know positively, that people from the district of the rio Saltan participated in the festivities in Calapo, up on the rio Malhauec or Maluec, and that they were pointed out to me as relatives of the Calapos and Ripangs.

The types of these Calapos and Ripangs were of the ordinary cut, and though we had seen entirely different physiognomies in Pinacpo, some with finely formed noses, we still classified them as Gaddanes. They wore the same ornaments as the Pinacpo people, had their manners and customs, their houses were built of the same material, caña, and had the same rightangled forms. We found these high-roofed houses also in Balario and Aripa, the women wearing armrings and bracelets like those mentioned above and the men the same garments.

As the district of the Calauas, better Rancheria Calaua, the part high up in the second mountain parallel where the rio Maluec takes its origin, was pointed out to me.

On the map of Cuello, contrary to others, who called it Saltan, the partido Itabes is found. The Itabes proper, where he must be looked for now, is undoubtedly in the region between rio Bangag or chico and the rio Cagayan, commencing on the heights of Solano and ending at Nariping. This is the most famous tobacco district.

Balani and Aripa purvey tobacco to the Government.

The Itabes speaking people were generally called Calingas and styled themselves "Poor Calingas" when in a conversation with us, making comparisons.

All the Rancherias stream-upward of Maluec, are enemies of the Apagaos.

Near Maluec, divided by a mountain range, lies Apagaos on both banks of the rio Apagos, but Negritto tribes are also there as in the Maluec district. The Negrittos of Maluec are genuine Negrittos and communicate with the Igorrotes, who tolerate, but do not estimate them. I never saw Negritto women with Igorrote men, or vice versa.

The Igorrotes used Negritto arrows and arches, the Negrittos, instead of bolos, old worn out Aliguas of the Igorrotes.

In regard to the principal usages of all the Igorrotes from Bombang to Aripa, they all have the same customs and the same Anito cultus, the latter not so much a distinct religion or creed as an observance of a certain pious and devoted regard for the dead.

The ceremonies at funerals, etc., are all alike. They bury their dead underneath their houses and on changing their abodes take them along.

The sacrifices on behalf of the sick, the contracting of marriages and the dissolution of such are exhaustively described by Padre Villaverde from his experiences in Quiangan and Silipan.

The Benguet Igorrotes, too, have the very same observances.

All these little tribes have no state constitutions, no judiciaries and no properly elected chieftains.

In which way or manner they dispose of their troubles, etc., I could not ascertain. To all probabilities, some old normal usages are observed to which they submit and thus settle matters.

Vendetta is almost a standard law with the Igorrotes.

The dead, without avenge, does not find any peace in the grave and causes the family great trouble.

A certain class of these wild tribes, prominent through their wealth, a kind of patricians, are very influential and domineering over the poorer.

They loan to the latter victuals or other things and take usurous percentages.

Not able to pay the interests, which, in a short time exceed the capital, they gradually sink into a sort of slavery and have to work for their oppressors in the fields or in the houses, thereby leading a miserable existence.

The mountain Igorrotes have but little even land on which to sow or plant, and as ploughs are unknown, a piece of wood, pointed on one end, is used for turning the soil and making furrows.

Carabaos (buffaloes), which have to work in the fields, etc., I have only seen in Balan and Aripa, where the tribes were tamer and where the cultivation of tobacco for sale was carried on, elsewhere only the work of man. In Quiangan, where this primitive way of working the fields is used, rice is the principal and most important crop. The narrow or broad terraces, constituting the fields, are built up with grassy soil and stonedams, a very wearysome work.

The smallest space of land is of an enormous value in this part of the island and is inheritable.

This fact, and the solid wooden houses, lead to the belief that the inhabitants never change their habitations.

The climate is cooler than in the promontories, and hence the massive buildings.

In the Saltan, the houses are not so solid, and from the finding of big trees and logs, half charred, it seems to be certain that the country was settled in former times.

There is no industry amongst the Igorrotes, their weapons, domestic utensils and jewelries are exchanged from other Rancherias. From the valley of Sapao, up in Bontoc, most of the bolos are gotten from, and the woven clothes from Balani.

The so-called blacksmith shop in Pinacpo was a very primitive affair, the hammers of which were loaned to another Rancheria.

The art of forging iron is kept a great secret with them.

Ollos are manufactured of clay in the districts where the latter is found.

It was in Pinacpo where the religious festivity, of which I made mention above, took place. The origin of it was as follows: A family lost a child by death over a year ago, and shortly afterwards the pater familias was suffering from a sore leg. This incident leads them to the belief that the dead child endures great hardships in heaven, amongst others, that it is badly, if ever, nourished and therefore plaguing its parents. To pacify the spirits, a continued sacrificing of chicken, pigs and other animals was ordained, and for 21 days this was done under the almost uninterrupted songs of both sexes.

It was just toward the end of this feast when we arrived in Pinacpo, and we had a good opportunity to witness the rites and ceremonies of the Anito observances.

The wine which they drank on this occasion, was made from the juice of sugar cane, and is very intoxicating.

Ropes are manufactured here from ratan and the fibre of the Anabu. Basket making is one of the principal industries of the Igorrotes, and the Tagearabos, or headclothes, also from the fibres of certain plants, are as fine as linen.

They use either old iron or steel bars from the Indians, the forging of iron, etc., is unknown to them, even their wooden shields are bought, and the poorer class, not possessing any, have to lend them from the richer when they intend to go hunting.

The Igorrote never leaves his house without his lance and shield, the constant feud between the Rancherias dictates this precaution.

We did not see any skulls of murdered persons on the houses of the Saltans and Itabes as elsewhere, but so-called victory columns, and when they are erected after some successful encounters, festivities, etc., follow these events.

The Igorrotes do not bury their killed enemies, believing, that if they remain unburied they will annoy and molest their relations.

Heroism is not to be found amongst the Igorrotes; they seldom fight a battle in the open field, but cowardly kill the enemy from some hidden spot.

I found myself in Aringay, in the province of

San Fernando, with but one servant, unable to procure a few more, and considering the voyage to Benguet with this insufficient protection rather unsafe, I intended to return to Manila, to recuperate from the hardships to which I was subjected during a four months stay in this forlorn corner of the Globe.

Satisfied that the results of this expedition, viz: the commission of Professor Bastian, Doctor Jagor and the request of the Jesuit Father Faura would meet with due acknowledgement and appreciation on the part of those gentlemen, I assorted my collection of ethnographical, anthropological, botanical and geological curiosos and parted from my companion, the indefatigable Mr. Au, who had shared in all deprivations so faithfully.

It is but just to state that the success with which my travels in Luzon were crowned, is mostly due to the generosity and kindness of the different catholic Curas, the Commandants of the Guardia Civil, the Gobernadorcillos, and especially to the druggist Grupe in Manila, by whom I was recommended to the above mentioned, and I here express my heartfelt thanks to them.

Without exaggerating, I can say that the four months travel in the Philippines were of a far more wearysome nature than my two years voyages in the Himalayas, Ceylon and Java.

The Philippines belong to the Malaysia, which latter comprises the islands and island groups lying just off the coast of southeastern Asia, and containing the large islands of Luzon, Mindanao, Celebes, Java, Sumatra and Borneo, and is a division of Oceania.

The export from the Philippines chiefly consists of coffee, cordage, hemp, indigo, rice, liquid indigo, sugar and sapan wood, the proceeds of which were 23 millions of dollars in 1882.

The area of both Luzon and Mindanao, whose capital de Sangan has 10,000 inhabitants, contains about 97,000 square miles, the population 5,190,000. Between the Philippines and 100° west longitude, are situated the islands and groups of Polynesia.

Returned to Manila, I forwarded ethnographical and other collected curiosities to Europe, and reported to Father Faura in a special, herein not contained, extract of my observations and experiences in the region of the earthquakes of 1881, and after a brief stay left Manila for Shanghai by way of Hong-Kong on an English steamer of the Peninsula Oriental line.

AFTER my return to Manila, I reported to the European scientists and to several Spanish geographical authors in different parts of the Philippine Islands and took passage for Hong-Kong, respectively Shanghai, on an English steamer.

Arrived in Shanghai, the sad news of the death of my dear, beloved father had reached me, and thus I was prevented to continue my intended journey to Peckin or Peking.

From Hong-Kong to Shanghai, the Formosa Canal has to be crossed and the Island of Formosa passed.

Wanchau, Ningpo and other places on the shores offer nothing noteworthy.

Here is the famous monastery "Sicawei" and a meteorological observatory.

A railroad, built in 1876 for the purpose of communicating the two cities Shanghai and Woosung, a distance of 20 miles, was bought by the Government the year following and closed.

On account of my short stay in China, I made all possible efforts to collect official Statistics and Data regarding this Empire, and was partially successful.

Area: 4,419,150 square miles, with 371,180,000 population, consequently the most populated country in the world.

The state religion, without any outward ceremonies, has only a few symbolic rites on New Year's day, and consists in the study of the doctrines of Confucius and Lao-tse.

The plurality of the people are Buddhists and public education almost universal, but few adults unable to read and write.

It is asserted that China has had newspapers over a thousand years ago.

23 Cities in the Chinese Empire have a population of over 100,000 and 66 with over 50,000 souls.

The chief exports are tea and silk. The coal mines of China rank amongst the greatest in the world, over 3 millions of tons are annually produced; the mines in Kai-ping alone producing 600 tons daily.

It was absolutely impossible for me to get any correct information about the Chinese "Flora," as there are no reliable sources to be found.

Procuring passage on a Japanese steamer of the Mitsi-Pitsi line, commanded by an American captain, we sailed first on the Leviathan of Rivers, the Yang-tse-kiang, whose length is 3,320 miles and the basin of which comprises an area of 950,000 square miles, and afterwards on the China Sea, when we reached Nagasaki, in whose neighborhood is Decima.

From Nagasaki I visited the inland lakes of Japan. The beauty of these lakes with their surrounding sceneries, and the rich vegetation is almost indescribable.

Hiogo, the seaport of Osaka, an important city and the commercial centre of Japan, is situated on a gradually ascending wooded chain of hills, attaining an altitude of 2,000' and has 20,000 inhabitants.

Several fresh water rivers discharge in the Bay of Hiogo.

Of the national beverage of the Japanese, the Sake or ricebeer, there are numerous breweries in this city. This Sake, to comply with the taste of the Japanese must have the following five qualities: bitter, sweet, sour, sharp and astringent, and the odor of fusel-oil.

It contains from 11 to 17 per cent. alcohol. According to analyzations by European chemists, the Sake is detrimental to health, and still, of the whole rice crop in Japan, 9 per cent. are used for manufacturing this national draught.

I was assured here, that the brewing of Sake in Japan, dates back as far as 2600 years, and that Sake brewers from China had arrived in Japan 400 A. C. to introduce the improved chinese Sake breweries.

Certain rules of etiquette regulate the quantities of Sake to be drunk on different occasions and the revenues of both, the Government and the Brewers, are immense. Sake is brewed between the months of November and March, as it requires a low degree of temperature.

The road from Hiogo to Osaka, a distance of 30 miles, leads through valleys, unbridged rivers and mountain ridges, with eggplants, rice, cotton and beans planted on the river shores.

Azaleas grow here abundantly in a wild state.

At a distance of about one mile from Osaka, the palace, formerly inhabited by the Tycoon, is visible;

it is romantically situated on the summit of a hill, crowned with a forest.

Osaka, on the shores of a great river and many canals has an important commerce, several noteworthy temples and a theatre.

Not far from Osaka, I visited the famous temple of Buddha, in which the colossal bronze figure of Buddha exists.

Hiogo was my starting point for the frequent excursions to the interior of Japan, having been furnished with passports from the Government to Kioto or Miako.

On this route Osaka is also reached. On a visit to the Biwa lake—a nice sheet of water—I was surprised to find in its vicinity an extensive monastery of Buddha of which I had known nothing.

Returned to Hiogo, another excursion was made to the Suonada lake, separating the two islands of Kiusin and Sikopf from the larger island of Nipon (the latter, the main-land and the largest of the groups of islands and therefore called Dai-Nipon or Great Nipon).

This so-called Inland lake extends to the bay of Osaka, has a length of about 200 miles and contains numerous rocks and small islands.

Simonoséki, at the head of Suonada lake has 10,000 inhabitants, some commerce, and is surrounded by high hills. In one of the temples of this place, a cartoon, representing a sea battle, two swords and other relics of Taiko-sama, the great soldier and founder of a small dynasty of but a short duration, who lived at about the year 1582, are shown.

Starting for the gold mines in the northwest and afterwards by steamer to Yokohama, I boarded a train for Tokio (formerly known as Yeddo or Jedo), one of the two capitals.

The population of Tokio numbers 823,557.

One of the most important and famous temples in Tokio is the Aoaxa, situated in the busiest portion of the city; it is also called the temple of Quanona.

The god Quanon, with his 36 arms and 100 hands, is very popular and thousands of people are constantly seen to crowd in his neighborhood.

The pilgrimages to Isje, where the 33 chief Quanquon temples exist, are the largest, and those to the Buddhistic temples of Lin and Cami also of large proportions.

The state religion in Japan is Sinto, or Shinto, and it is a remarkable feature that both, the orthodox disciples of Sinto as well as the Buddhists, visit the Quanquon temples.

Of all the temples, however, the temple of Saif in Sicousin, where Teentin died, is the pre-eminent.

In a northerly direction from here, I visited the famous temple of Nikko, in whose neighborhood is a volcanic chain of mountains where frequent eruptions take place.

An excursion to the Hakone mountains, the most beautiful in Japan, and where the extinct volcano "Fussiyama," a sombre, ragged peak, impresses one most unfavorably, is well repaying the trouble.

To-Kaido, the main road, leads from E. to W.,

from Tokio, one of the capitals, to Kioto the other.

It is surprising to find an almost tropical vegetation in Japan, considering the northern latitude of this country, almost everywhere Palmtrees, Bamboo, Cryptomeria Japonica, Glycinæ cinensis or Wistaria, Thujopsis dolabrata, Retinispora, the family of the Rosaceas and Coniferes to be found.

The cultivation of dwarf-trees and plants, especially of the Padocarpus, is carried on in a grand and unsurpassed style and the export of Coniferes is very important.

The shooting or killing of birds within a circuit of 10 Ri, or 30 English miles from the residence of the Mikado, is strictly prohibited.

Japan, or Zipangu, the sunrise kingdom, is an empire composed of islands lying east of Asia, and is supposed to have been founded 660 A. C. Area, 148,456 square miles. Population, 36,700,118. The population is divided into classes, as follows: Imperial family, 39; Kwazokii, or nobles, 3,204; Shizoku, or knights, 1,931,825; common people, 34,765,051.

The government is an absolute monarchy. The title of the sovereign is Supreme Lord, or Emperor (Mikado). Agriculture is followed to a great extent. The chief agricultural products are rice, wheat and beans. The principal manufactures are silk and cotton goods, Japanned ware, porcelain and bronze. The value of the exports, 1883, was $35,609,000; of imports, $28,548,000.

A law went into effect in 1874, by which the government gives nine bushels of rice annually to each person over seventy or under fifteen years of age unable to work, and to foundlings until they reach the age of thirteen.

Latest reports place the number of paupers at 10,050, and expenditures at $88,975.

School attendance is compulsory. There are 30,275 schools in the empire, of which 71 are normal, 98 are technical, and 2 are universities; also, a military college and military school, with 1,200 students.. Latest reports give 82,213 teachers and 2,703,343 pupils. School age from 6 to 14. Public libraries, 21. Shintoism is the ancient religious faith; but Buddhism is the religion of nearly all the common people. The first railroad in the empire was opened June, 1875; it extended from Hiogo to Osaka, 25 miles. At the end of June, 1884, there were 236 miles of railway in the empire.

After a brief stay in Yokohama, I took passage on a steamer of the English Oriental and Occidental Steamship Company and started for another division of the globe, "America."

After a two weeks very agreeable sea voyage I arrived in the San Francisco bay on the evening of the 9th of November.

Already from a distance, San Francisco, amphitheatrically situated on the inner slope of a peninsula and on and at the base of high hills, is visible.

San Francisco, the chief city of California and commercial metropolis of the Pacific coast, is separated from the ocean by the above mentioned peninsula, which is 30 miles long and 6 miles across the city, at the northern end of which San Francisco stands, in lat. 37° 46′ N. and long. 122° 46′ W.

The greater part of the peninsula is hilly. In the N. E. corner of the city is Telegraph Hill, 294 ft. high; in the S. E. corner Rincon Hill, 120 ft. high; and on the W. side Russian Hill, 360 ft. high. The densely populated quarters are in the amphitheatre formed by the three hills.

The city is regularly laid out, the streets are broad and there are many handsome buildings.

The history of San Francisco is interesting on account of the rapid growth of the place. The first house was built in 1835, when the village was called Yerba Buena (Spanish " good herb "), so-named from a medicinal plant growing in abundance in the vicinity. In 1847 this was changed to San Francisco, and in 1848, the year that gold was first discovered in California by the white settlers, the population had increased to 1,000. The influx from the East then commenced, and in December, 1850, the population was about 25,000. According to the census of 1880 it amounted to 233,956, and it is now estimated as containing more than 300,000 population. The city was incorporated in 1850, and in 1851 and 1856, in consequence of bad municipal government and corrupt administration of the criminal laws, the people organized Vigilance Committees, and summarily executed several criminals and banished others.

This rough but wholesome discipline had its effect, and the city is now one of the most orderly in the country.

The commerce of San Francisco is very large, the chief articles of export being the precious metals, breadstuffs, wines, wool and fruits; and of import, lumber, coal, coffee, tea, rice and sugar.

The manufactures are important, including woolen and silk mills, and manufactories of watches, carriages, boots, furniture, candles, acids, wire-work, castings of iron and brass and silver ware.

The City Hall, in process of erection, will be a fine structure.

The U. S. Branch Mint contains the finest machinery, to be believed unapprochable in perfection and efficiency.

The Merchants' Exchange is one of the most costly and spacious buildings in the city. The Palace Hotel is a vast and ornate building, 9 stories high, and erected at a cost of $3,250,000.

Another palatial structure is the Baldwin Hotel. The Mercantile Library contains 50,000 volumes.

The finest and largest church edifice on the Pacific coast is that of St. Ignatius Church and College (Roman Catholic); the finest interior is that of St. Patrick's (Roman Catholic). The First Unitarian and Trinity churches are remarkably fine architectures, and the Jewish Synagogue of Emanu-El is a large, elegant and substantial structure, with two lofty towers and a richly decorated interior.

The University of California, near San Francisco, is the most important educational institution. The city also contains two Medical Colleges, an excellent School of Design, and three Academies.

Among the charitable institutions, the principal are the U. S. Marine Hospital, St. Mary's Roman Catholic, the City New Hospital, the State Woman's Hospital, the Protestant Orphan Asylum, the Almshouse, the Roman Catholic Orphan Asylum, the State Asylum for the Deaf, Dumb and Blind, near Oakland, and the Alameda Park Asylum for the Insane, on the Encinal, Alameda.

The Golden Gate Park comprises 1,043 acres. One of the features of the Park is a magnificent conservatory, in which, at the proper season, the only specimen of the Victoria Regia Lily in America can be seen; the building is modeled after the Royal Conservatories of Kew, England.

Laurel Hill Cemetry is a very beautiful burial-ground, with many fine monuments. In the vicinity is a singular, conically-shaped mountain, which rises up singly and alone to a considerable height above the surrounding tolerably level country. The great feature is Lone Mountain, with its unrivalled outlook, embracing views of the city, bay, ocean, Mount Diablo and the Coast Range.

There are about 40,000 Chinese in San Francisco, and the " Chinese Quarter " is worth a visit, especially the two theatres, in which the entire audience, even the women, who have a compartment to themselves, are found either smoking tobacco or opium, whilst the performance is carried on amidst the beating of gongs, the clashing of cymbals and other hideous kinds of noise. A visit to the opium cellars and gambling houses, and to the temples—open at all times—and in which joss-sticks smoke in front of the favorite Gods, will repay the curious traveler.

Of great interest is the Cliff House, in the vicinity of San Francisco, a low rambling building, set on the edge of some cliffs rising sharply from the ocean. The Seal Rock, close by, where the seals are basking in the sun or wriggle over the rocks, barking so noisily, is a beautiful sight.

Northward lies the Golden Gate, the beautiful entrance to San Francisco Bay. In front is the vast Pacific Ocean, on whose distant horizon, on a clear day, the peaks of the Farallone Islands are visible.

In the Southwestern part of the city is the old mission of San Francisco, Mission Dolores, it is an adobe building of the old Spanish style, built in 1778.

My next excursion was to the Yosemite Valley, and en route to it, to the Mariposa Grove of Big Trees.

The Grove is part of a grant made by Congress to be set apart for "public use, resort and recreation" forever. The area covered by the grant is 2 miles square and embraces 2 distinct groves which are about $\frac{1}{2}$ mile apart. The Upper Grove contains 365 trees, of which 154 are over 15 ft. in diameter. The largest tree in the Grove is the Grissly Giant (Lower Grove) which is still 94 ft. in circumference and 31 ft. in diameter, though much decreased by burning. The first branch is nearly 200 ft. from the ground, and is 6 ft. in diameter. The remains of a prostrate tree, now nearly consumed by fire, indicates that it must have reached a diameter of about 40 ft. and a height of 400 ft. The trunk is hollow, and will admit the passage of 3 horsemen riding abreast. There are about 125 trees over 40 ft. in circumference.

The Yosemite Valley is situated on the Merced River in the Southern portion of the county of Mariposa, about 220 miles from San Francisco. It is on the Western slope of the Sierra Nevada, midway between its E. and W. base. The valley is a nearly level area, about 6 miles in length and from a half to a mile in width, and almost a mile in perpendicular depth below the general level of the adjacent region, and inclosed in frowning granite walls rising with almost unbroken and perpendicular faces to the dizzy height of from 3000 to 6000 ft.

From the brow of the precipices in several places spring streams of water, forming cataracts of a beauty and magnificence surpassing anything known in mountain scenery. The valley is almost one vast flower garden, plants, shrubs and flowers of every hue cover the ground like a carpet, the eye is dazzled by the brilliancy of the color, and the air is heavy with the fragrance of myriads of blossoms. On every side are seen the beautiful and many colored Manzanita and Madrone and other beautiful trees.

The Yosemite was discovered in the Spring of 1851

by a party under the command of Captain Boling in pursuit of a band of predatory Indians, who made it their stronghold, considering it inaccessible to the whites. By an act of Congress passed in 1864, the Yosemite Valley and the Mariposa grove of Big Trees were granted to the State of California upon the express condition that they shall be kept "for public use, resort and recreation, inaleniable for all time."

The most striking feature of the valley scenery is "El Capitan," on account of its isolation, its breadth, its perpendicular sides and its prominence as it projects like a great rock promontory into the valley.

On the opposite side is the "Bridal Veil Fall," where the creek of the same name leaps over a cliff 900 ft. high into the valley below.

The "Sentinel Rock," 3043 ft. high, is one of the grandest masses of rock in the Yosemite.

The Yosemite Falls are regarded as the most wonderful feature of the scenery. The Fall has a total height of 2600 ft. which is not all perpendicular; there is first a vertical leap of 1500 ft., then a series of cascades down a descent equal to 626 ft. perpendicular, and then a final plunge of 400 ft. to the rocks at the base of the precipice. No falls in the known world can be compared with these in height and romantic grandeur.

The Half Dome is a crest of granite rising to the height of 4737 ft. above the valley.

The Mirror Lake, Vernon Fall and the Cap of Liberty are worth visiting, but the Nevada Fall is in every respect one of the grandest water falls in the world, in regard to the stupendous scenery by which it is surrounded, its vertical height and the purity and volume of the river which it forms.

It is almost impossible to describe all the wonders of this blessed spot and I will therefore proceed on my journey to Santa Cruz, one of the two famous Summer resorts of California. This city is attractively situated on the N. side of Monterey Bay, and nearby are Aptos and Soquel, popular sea-side resorts. Opposite Santa Cruz, at the S. extremity of the Bay, is the historic city of Monterey. Until 1847 this town was the seat of government and principal port on the California coast; but since the rise of San Francisco its commerce and business have dwindled away, and it is now one of the quietest places in the State. As a health-resort it has begun to attract attention within the last 4 or 5 years.

In the heart of the Santa Clara Valley—which lies between the coast and Santa Cruz Mountains, and is watered by the Coyote and Guadalupe rivers and by artesian wells, said to be the most fertile in the world—is the city of San José, with a population of 13,000. The main portion of the city occupies a gently rising plateau between the Coyote and Guadalupe Rivers, $1\frac{1}{2}$ miles apart. The most noteworthy features are: the Lick Observatory, in course of erection on the summit of Mount Hamilton, 4,443 feet high, 12 miles from the city and the Court House, the City Hall, the State Normal School and the Roman Catholic College of

Notre Dame. The famous Almaden Quicksilver Mines are about 14 miles from San José.

Santa Clara is a picturesque village with about 4,000 inhabitants and 3 miles from the former city.

Pacific Congress Springs with medicinal waters, recommended to sufferers with rheumatism, and Napa City, 46 miles from San Francisco, a thrifty place of about 4,000 inhabitants, with many beautiful drives in the vicinity, especially those to Santa Rosa and the famous wine cellars of Sonoma, are romantically situated.

Calistoga, a pretty town in a valley, encircled by forest-clad hills and mountains, has numerous mineral springs in the vicinity.

About 5 miles S. E. of Calistoga is the "Petrified Forest," one of the great natural wonders of California. Portions of nearly 100 distinct trees of great size, scattered over a tract of 3 or 4 miles in extent, have been found, the largest being 11 ft. in diameter at the base and 60 ft. long. They are supposed to have been silicified by an eruption of the neighboring Mount St. Helena, which discharged hot alkaline waters containing silica in solution.

The Geyser Spring, situated in Sonoma County in a lateral gorge of the Napa Valley, called the Devil's Cañon is near the Pluton River.

The approaches to the Springs are very impressive, the scenery being finer, according to Bayard Taylor, than anything in the Lower Alps. A multitude of springs gush out at the base of the rocks. Hot and cold springs, boiling springs and quiet springs lie within a few feet of each other.

They differ also in color, smell and taste. Some are clear and transparent, others white, yellow or red with ochre, while still others are of an inky blackness.

Some are sulphurous and fetid in odor, and some are charged with alum and salt. The surface of the ground is too hot to walk upon with thin shoes, and is covered with the minerals deposited by the waters, among which are sulphur, sulphate of magnesia, sulphate of aluminum and various salts of iron. They are recommended in rheumatism, gout and in skin diseases.

Among the health resorts of southern California, the most frequented is Santa Barbara, lying in a sheltered nook of the shore of the Pacific with an extremely equable and mild climate, the mean temperature in summer being 69, 58° and in winter 53, 33°.

The society of the place is exceptionally pleasant and refined. The town, with about 6,000 inhabitants, contains a Spanish quarter and a Chinese quarter, and the new American part of the town, especially the suburbs are handsomely built and tastefully adorned. Every plot of ground, no matter how small, has its row of orange trees, its exotics, and its bed of native perennials. Roses abound summer and winter. The Verbena beds are cut down like grass thrice yearly, and spring up again stronger than ever. Vines of every sort flourish luxuriantly, Heliotrope climbs 20 ft. high, Cacti of the rarest and most curious sorts grow freely, and a little shoot of the Australian blue-gum

(Eucalyptus globulus) becomes in 2 years a shade-tree 15 or 20 ft. high.

San Diego is another favorite resort, 460 miles S. E. of San Francisco. The climate is very salubrious, the thermometer seldom rises to 80°, or sinks to the freezing point, the usual mean being 62°.

482 miles from San Francisco lies the largest city in southern California, Los Angeles, on the W. bank of the Los Angeles river, a small stream, 30 miles above its entrance into the Pacific. The city was settled by Spaniards in 1780, and was called Pueblo de los Angeles from the excellence of its climate and the beauty of its surroundings. Its population by the census of 1880 was 11,311, and the adobe buildings of which it was originally composed are fast giving way to larger and more imposing structures. In the N. W. portion is a hill 60 feet high, commanding a fine view of the city, which lies in a sheltered valley, bounded on the W. by low hills that extend from the Santa Monica mountains, 40 miles distant, and on the E. by the San Gabriel plateau.

The climate is mild, the nights, however, are chilly. Along both banks of the river below the city extends a fertile plain, planted with vineyards and orange-groves, and there are also large vineyards within the city limits. Los Angeles is the center of the orange growing business of California, and lemons, olives, and other tropical fruits are cultivated in the vicinity.

About 60 miles E. of Los Angeles is San Bernardino. The view of Mount San Bernardino, the loftiest peak of the Coast Range, is exceedingly grand. San Bernardino is reached from Los Angeles by a stage-ride of 10 hours.

The Southern Pacific Railroad, between Los Angeles and Tucson, Arizona, leads through the famous Colorado Desert, 300 feet below the level of the sea, with no vegetation but snow-white sand on both sides, now and then interrupted by lonely Cacti—a very triste wearysome voyage. After Yuma is reached, there is a different atmosphere, and one feels greatly relieved. Yuma is near the junction of the Gila and Colorado rivers, and is the W. terminus of the Arizona branch of the Southern Pacific Railroad, and has a population of 2,500.

Tucson, with about 7,000 inhabitants, was, until recently, the capital of the territory and is an ancient city, founded in 1560 by Jesuits. It does a large business in exporting gold dust, wool and hides. Some sixty miles distant, near Casa Grande, is a remarkable ruin of an ancient Pueblo city, these interesting remains being preserved in a very perfect state, and extending $2\frac{1}{2}$ miles by $1\frac{1}{2}$ miles, showing that it must have had a population in olden times of at least 100,000 people.

Prescott, the capital of Arizona, is a small but very active place, and has an important commerce with mineral, agricultural and stock raising products.

Arizona was first visited by Spanish explorers as early as 1526, and is set off from New Mexico and became a territory in 1863. Area: 113,020 square miles; greatest length, 375 miles; greatest breadth, 340 miles. Country drained by Colorado and Gila, with their tributaries.

Temperature at Prescott: winter, $34°$ to $42°$; summer, $71°$ to $73°$. Rainfall at Fort Defiance, 14 inches.

Southern Pacific crosses from east to west near southern boundary, and Atlantic and Pacific north of the central portion, making ready communication with East and West. Wheat, barley, potatoes, hay and corn the chief crops. Soil fertile in river bottoms and among valleys of Middle and Eastern Arizona, corn planting following wheat or barley harvest, giving two crops yearly; oranges and other fruit produce well where there is water, the principal portion of irrigable land lies in the valley of the Gila and its northern branches; rich and abundant grasses, together with the mild climate, make much of the territory well adapted to stock raising; valuable timber is on the mountains and along the streams.

Abundant mineral wealth, which can now be developed with profit, owing to completion of railways; nearly all mountain ranges contain gold, silver, copper and lead; the gold production in 1882 was $1,065,000; silver, $7,500,000.

The Territory ranks second in silver. Superior quality of lime found near Prescott and Tucson; beds of gypsum in San Pedro valley; remarkable deposits of pure, transparent salt near Callville.

Population 40,440, including 155 Colored, 1,630 Chinese and 3,493 Indians.

School population, 10,283; school age, 6–21.

From Arizona I traveled directly to El Paso in Texas, staying there only a very short time. The Atchison, Topeka and Santa Fé R.R. connects here in its own depot with the Mexican Central R.R. The population of El Paso is about 1,500 and the city is growing very rapidly; a large retail and wholesale trade is done here, and its superior railroad facilities give El Paso merchants many advantages. Street cars run across the Rio Grande to the old Mexican town of Paso del Norte.

El Paso del Norte is built almost entirely of adobe, and the homes of its 6,000 people are scattered along a narrow, rambling, adobe-walled street running several miles down the river.

The ride to the city of Chihuahua introduces the traveler to the wide expanse of that high table-land which forms the greater portion of the interior of Mexico, but for variety it also includes a view of the beautiful valley of the Rio Carmen, with its green meadows and dark forests, while beyond, on the W., lie the Sierra Madre mountains.

Chihuahua, the capital of the state of the same name, is a beautiful city with 20,000 population. The city being the center of a rich mining, agricultural and stock-growing country has a great deal of wealth and refinement. Its magnificent cathedral is one of the most imposing edifices on the continent.

Returned to El Paso from this little and short Mexican excursion, I boarded the train for San Antonio in Texas.

San Antonio is the chief city of western Texas and has a population of about 22,000, one-third of whom are of German and one-third of Mexican origin. It is situated on the San Antonio and San Pedro rivers, and is divided into three quarters: San Antonio proper, between the two streams; Alamo, E. of the San Antonio; and Chihuahua, W. of the San Pedro. The former is the business quarter, and has been almost entirely rebuilt since 1860.

In the north part of the Alamo Plaza is the famous Fort Alamo, where in March, 1836, a garrison of Texans, attacked by an overwhelming Mexican force, perished to a man rather than yield. Missions San José, San Juan, and Concepcion, built by the Spaniards, who founded San Antonio in 1714, are interesting objects; and the market places and street scenes amuse the visitor as being so queer and foreign.

Austin was the next place I visited. It is the capital of Texas, has 11,000 inhabitants and is situated on the N. bank of the Colorado river, 160 miles from its mouth.

There are many fine buildings in Austin and several State charitable institutions. An artesian well has been sunk north of the Capitol, to the depth of 1,300 ft., from which a small stream constantly flows, discharging a medicinal, lime-impregnated water.

Houston, the third city of Texas in population and commerce and the first in manufactures, is situated at the head of tidewater on Buffalo Bayou, 45 miles above its mouth in Galveston Bay. By the census of 1880 it had a population of 18,646, and is the center of the railroad system of the State, with nine diverging railways which bring to it the produce of a rich grazing and agricultural region. Its manufactures are varied and extensive. The Bayou is navigable for vessels drawing 13 ft. of water.

Here also are several beautiful public and private buildings.

From Houston the Galveston, Houston and Henderson R. R. runs S. E. in 50 miles to Galveston, the largest city and commercial metropolis of Texas, situated at the N. E. extremity of Galveston Island, at the mouth of the bay of the same name. The city is laid out with wide and straight streets, bordered by numerous flower gardens, and contained 35,000 inhabitants in 1883.

The University of St. Mary (Roman Catholic) and the Galveston Medical College are flourishing institutions. Beside the handsome churches, the public buildings are beautiful and extensive. The Ursuline Convent has a female academy connected with it.

The Island of Galveston is about 28 miles long and $1\frac{1}{2}$ to $3\frac{1}{2}$ wide, bordered by a smooth, hard beach, and most all the streets in the city are lined with white and red Oleanders. The harbor is the best in the State, and the commerce of the city is very extensive, the chief business being the shipment of cotton.

Texas was first settled by the French on the Lavaca in 1685; admitted 1845; seceded February, 1861; re-admitted 1868.

Area, 265,780 square miles; extreme length, 825 square miles; extreme breadth, 740 miles; coast line, 400 miles.

Temperature at Galveston: winter, 53° to 63°; summer, 82° to 84°.

Rainfall at Fort Brown, 33 inches. Brownsville, El Paso, Indianola and Galveston are ports of entry.

Number of farms, 174,184; average value per acre, clear land, $8.98; woodland, $4.

Cotton most valuable crop.

Ranks first in cattle and cotton; second in sugar, sheep, mules and horses.

Population 1,591,749, among which, 393,384 Negroes, 136 Chinese and 992 Indians.

U. S. Army and paupers excluded from voting.

Number of colleges, 10; school population, 295,-344; school age, 8-14.

Bound for New Orleans in Louisiana; I arrived in this latter place in a considerably short time after leaving the State of Texas. New Orleans, the chief city and commercial metropolis of Louisiana, is situated on both banks of the Mississippi river, 100 miles above its mouth. The older portion of the city is built within a great bend of the river, from which circumstance it derives its name, Crescent City. It is built on land gently descending from the river toward a marshy tract in the rear, and considerably below the level of the river at high-water mark, which is prevented from overflowing by a vast embankment of earth, called the "Levee." This levee is 15 ft. wide and 14 ft. high, is constructed for a great distance along the river bank, and forms a beautiful promenade.

New Orleans was settled in 1718, but abandoned in consequence of overflows, storms and sickness; was settled in 1723, held by the French till 1729, then by the Spaniards till 1801; and by the French again till 1803, when with the province of Louisiana, it was ceded to the United States. It was incorporated as a city in 1804. The most memorable events in the history of New Orleans are the rebellion against the cession by France to Spain in 1763, the battle of January 8th, 1815, in which the British were defeated by Andrew Jackson, and the capture of the city by Admiral Farragut on April 24th, 1862. In 1810, seven years after its cession to the United States, the population of New Orleans was 17,243, and according to the census of 1880 it amounted to 216,140. In the value of its exports and its entire foreign commerce, New Orleans ranks next to New York. Not unfrequently from 1,000 to 1,500 steamers and other vessels from all parts of the world may be seen lying at the levee.

New Orleans is the chief cotton market of the world; and besides cotton, it sends abroad sugar, rice. tobacco, flour and pork in great quantities.

The manufactures of the city are not extensive.

New Orleans is not rich in architecture, but there are a few noteworthy buildings, chief among these are: the Custom House, the U. S. Branch Mint, the City Hall, the Cathedral of St. Louis (Catholic), the Church of St. John the Baptist, the Jewish Synagogue Temple

Sinai, the St. Paul's, and the First Presbyterian Church.

The University of Louisiana and the Straight University (for colored people exclusively) are of a high order.

Of charitable institutions New Orleans has an abundance.

Chief among the pleasure grounds of the city is Jackson Square, with the equestrian statue of General Jackson.

The French market is the great "sight" of New Orleans, and one of the most interesting spots in the vicinity is Battle-Field, the scene of General Jackson's great victory over the British, January 8, 1815. A marble monument will commemorate this victory. A National Cemetery occupies one of the corners of the field.

Lake Ponchartrin, 5 miles N. of the city, is famous for its fish and game. The swamps which lie between the city and the lake are covered with a thick growth of cypress and other trees.

Carrollton, in the suburbs, has many fine public gardens and private residences.

Algiers, opposite New Orleans, has extensive dry-docks and ship-yards.

An excursion to Baton Rouge, since 1881 capital of Louisiana, was well worth undertaking.

The road to this place, "The Coast," as it is called, is lined with plantations. Every spot susceptible of cultivation is transformed into a beautiful garden, containing specimens of all those choice fruits and flowers which flourish only in tropical climes.

Baton Rouge has 8,000 inhabitants, and is pleasantly situated on the last bluff that is seen in descending the Mississippi, and contains several public buildings.

Proceeding on my excursion, I reached Knoxville, in Mississippi, a small town, and afterwards Vicksburg, situated on the Walnut Hills, which extends for about two miles along the river, rising to the height of 500 feet, and displaying the finest scenery of the lower Mississippi. It is a well built city of 11,814 inhabitants. The view of the city from the water is in the highest degree picturesque. Vicksburg was founded in 1836 by a planter named Vick, members of whose family are still living there. As the chief commercial market on this portion of the river, it has long been a place of some note, but it is more widely known as the scene of one of the most obstinate and decisive struggles of the Civil War. After the loss successively of Columbus, Memphis and New Orleans, the Confederates made here their last and most desperate stand for the control of the great river. The place was surrounded by vast fortifications, the hills crowned with batteries, and a large army under General Pemberton placed in it as a garrison. Its capture by General Grant, after a protracted siege, on the 4th of July, 1863, cut the Confederacy in twain. Above Vicksburg, at the point where Sherman made his entrance from the " Valley of Death," is the largest national cemetery in the country, containing the remains of nearly 16,000 soldiers.

I extended my exploration to Jackson, the capital of Mississippi. It is regularly built upon undulating ground on the W. bank of Pearl River, and has about 6,000 inhabitants.

There are several exceedingly fine State Institutions, the State library containing 15,000 volumes. Jackson was captured by General Grant, on May the 14th, 1863, after a battle with General Johnston, in which the Confederates were defeated and valuable property destroyed.

On the road to New Orleans I stopped at Natchez, built mostly upon a high bluff, 200 feet above the level of the stream. This place was founded by d'Iberville, a Frenchman, in 1700, and is replete with historic associations. Here once lived and flourished the noblest tribe of Indians on the continent, and from that tribe it takes its name. Their pathetic story is festooned with the flowers of poetry and romance. Their ceremonies and creed were not unlike those of the Fire-worshippers of India. Their priests kept the fire continually burning upon the altar in their temple of the Sun, and the tradition is that they got the fire from heaven. Just before the advent of the white man, it is said, the fire accidently went out, and that was one reason why they became disheartened in their struggle with the pale-faces. The last remnant of the race were still existing a few years ago in Texas.

Mississippi, or the Bayou State, whose name is of

Indian origin, signifying, "Father of Waters," had its first permanent settlement at Natchez, 1716; admitted, 1817; seceded, 1861; re-admitted, 1870.

Area: 46,810 square miles, extreme length, 332 miles; extreme breadth, 189 miles; mean breadth, 142 miles; gulf frontage, including irregularities and islands, 287 miles; harbors at: Pascagoula, Biloxi, Mississippi City and Shieldsborough.

Temperature at Vicksburg: Winter, 47° to 56°; Summer, 80° to 83°. Rainfall at Natchez, 54 inches. Number of farms, 101,772. Average value per acre: clear land, $7.88; woodland, $3.78.

Forest area very large; pine, oak, chestnut, walnut and magnolia trees grow on uplands and bluffs, and long-leafed pine on islands and in sandy regions of the South; cotton lands mostly in Yazoo and Mississippi bottoms.

Ranks second in cotton.

Population, inclusive 650,291 Negros, 51 Chinese, 1857 Indians, 1,131,597. Slaves, in 1860, 436,631.

Number of Colleges, 3; school population 444,131, school age 5 to 21. Returned to New Orleans I began with the preparation for the statistics of the Creole State.

Louisiana, named in honor of Louis XIV, King of France, was first permanently settled by French, at New Orleans in 1718; admitted 1812; seceded January 1861; re-admitted June 1868.

Area: 48,720 square miles: greatest length, east and west, 300 miles; breadth, 240 miles; coast line, 1,256 miles.

Temperature at New Orleans; Winter, 53° to 61°; Summer, 81° to 83°. Rainfall 51 inches.

Number of Farms, 48,292. Average value per acre, cleared land, $14.36; wood land $3.53. 57 per cent. of laborers engaged in agriculture; rural income, per capita, $209.

Ranks first in sugar and molasses. Population, 939,946 including 483,655 Negroes, 489 Chinese and 848 Indians. Slaves in 1860, 331,726.

Sugar-cane first cultivated in the United States, near New Orleans, 1751 and first Sugar-mill used 1758.

I did not succeed in obtaining data about the school population.

Having procured my passport for the intended visit of the West Indies, I took passage for Havana. Key West was duly reached and a short stay made at this rather picturesque place. Key West, the second largest city in Florida, is situated upon an island of the same name. It is of coral formation and has a shallow soil, consisting of disintegrated coral, with a slight admixture of decayed vegetable matter. There are no springs and the inhabitants (about 7,000) are dependent on rain or distilled water. The natural growth is a dense, stunted chaparral, in which various species of cactus are a prominent feature. Tropical fruits are cultivated to some extent, the chief varieties being cocoanuts, bananas, pineapples, guavas, sapodillas and a few oranges.

A portion of the population are Cubans and natives of the Bahama Islands, and this place being the key to the best entrance to the Gulf of Mexico, is strongly fortified and has a fine harbor.

Among the principal industries are sponging, turtling, fishing and the manufactures of Cigars. The principal work of defense is Fort Taylor.

The weather favorable, Havana is reached from here in about 11 or 12 hours, where the traveler is subjected to a very rigorous examination on the part of the Duana (custom officers). The bay of Havana is extremely beautiful. To the right, the Castle Morro (the fortification of the bay) is a hilly range with many forts, towers, bastions and many noteworthy curiosities among which is the military prison, etc. On the left, lies the old city of Havana, built almost to the water's edge. The impression on entering the city at first is not very favorable, but the traveler soon finds himself in an attractive place, especially when visiting the public gardens and promenades. The city of Havana is of a very old date. Most of the public and a great many private buildings are built in the Moorish style. The commerce of the city is of colossal dimensions, and the shipping from here to other West Indian islands very large. During the winter months Havana is thronged with visitors, especially Americans, who come here to escape the northerly winds and inclemency of the weather, or to restore broken health. The drives in the vicinity are very beautiful. The old and brilliant edifice of the cathedral, with the ornamented interior and the precious gems, is worth visiting.

The principal industry is the manufacturing of

cigars and cigarettes. In these factories over 20,000 people find employment.

The Governor's garden, in the suburbs, contains beautiful specimens of palms and cocoanut trees and other exotic plants and flowers.

The yellow fever hospital proves to be a very beneficial institution, since this terrible scourge is raging here almost the whole year through, and the Observatory (meteorological) rather in an unfavorable condition. On the other side of the Bay is Regla, a small village, where, generally on Sundays, bull-fights take place.

The wonderful cave of Matanzas and the lovely Valley of Yumiri are accessible from the city in two and a half hours by rail, also several extensive sugar plantations.

I did not make any other excursions on the Island of Cuba, on account of the rather advanced period of the year and the prevalence of tropical maladies, and collecting all the possible data of this island I herewith reproduce the same.

Cuba, a Spanish colony in the West Indies, has an area of 43,220 square miles, and a population of 1,521,-684. 50 per cent. of the inhabitants are blacks and enfranchised slaves. The greatest length of the island is 760 miles; width varies from 20 to 135 miles; coast line about 2,000 miles. Surface is broken by a mountain chain running through the center from east to west; average altitude of summit is between 5,000 and 6,000 feet. Pico de Turquino, 7,670 feet, is the highest peak. There are over 260 rivers, all valueless for navigation purposes, except the Cauto. Mineral springs abound.

But little attention has been paid to the development of the mineral wealth. Gold was obtained by the early colonists, but for two centuries comparatively none has been found. There are extensive copper mines, and coal is abundant. Copperas and alum have also been obtained.

Rainfall at Havana: in the wet season, 27.8 inches; dry season, 12.7 inches. Average temperature: at Havana, 77°; at Santiago de Cuba, 80°. Yellow fever and earthquakes are frequent.

13 million acres of Cuban territory are uncleared forests; 7 million wild and uncultivated. Principal woods grown and exported are mahogany, rosewood, Cuban ebony and cedar.

Tobacco and sugar raising principal occupation of the people.

Many sugar plantations comprise 10,000 acres each.

Two crops of Indian corn grown per year; rice, cotton, cocoa and indigo also produced; most tropical fruits are abundant. Sugar product averages 520,000 tons per year. Total value of agricultural products over 90 million dollars. United States receives 80 per cent. of Cuban sugar. No manufactures deserving mention.

Roman Catholicism is the only religion tolerated. Education compulsory; school attendants, 34,812.

The government is administered by a Captain General, appointed by the Spanish crown.

The island is now represented in the Spanish Cortes, Madrid.

Thirty-six hours after leaving Havana, the first Mexican port (the proper seaport of the old capital of Yucatan), Progreso, is reached. Twenty-two miles distant from the latter is Merida, the capital of the State of Yucatan, a beautiful and quaint old city of about 55,000 inhabitants. The ride from Progreso to the capital is very interesting, leading through a laguna with brilliant aquatic and tropical plants and admirably fine scenery. The city and all the surrounding country abound in numerous picturesque ruins of great antiquity. Sixty-nine miles from the city are the celebrated ruins of Uxmal, and at seventy-five miles distant the famous cave of Sahachao, in the village of Tekox. The climate of Merida is very healthy, and deer shooting found in its neighborhood.

From Progreso the steamer proceeds to Frontera, remaining there but a few hours to transfer passengers, the mail and cargo, and then continues the route to Vera Cruz, about 200 miles from Frontera.

Approaching Vera Cruz, the Peak of Orizaba, covered with snow, is seen at a distance of 50 to 70 miles.

The old and historic city of Vera Cruz contains about 16,000 inhabitants, and is the commercial metropolis of Mexico.

In all commercial and social circles in this city, Spanish, English, German and French are freely spoken.

There are many old churches and chapels, monasteries and convents in Vera Cruz, and the tolling of church bells often deafening.

The commercial establishments are massive, fine structures, and the "Calle de la Independencia" a beautiful, long street, traversing the city. The bay of Vera Cruz is almost of an inkish hue. The gloomy looking fortification of the harbor, Fort Ullao, is of a very old date, and its subterranean, or rather sub-aquarian, prisons are, no doubt, remnants of Spanish inquisitory history. The partially rocky hills of the fort extend to a great length.

The Great Mexican Railway connects Vera Cruz with the City of Mexico, a distance of 260 miles.

This road has been justly considered one of the most wonderful engineering enterprises ever accomplished. Its construction occupied ten years, at a cost of $27,000,000. A great part of the road extends over the Sierra Nevada mountains, reaching at its highest point of elevation, Boca del Monte, 8,310 feet. The railroad trip is not only not tedious, though it takes about 18 hours to make it, but wonderfully grand. During one part of the trip the train rises 4,700 feet in a distance of 25 miles.

The scenery cannot be imagined, as the country through which it passes presents scenes of unparalleled grandeur and beauty, and on the journey every variety of climate is experienced, passing from the tropical climate of Vera Cruz and the cold winds from the snow peaks of the mountains, to the ever spring-like temperature of the City of Mexico, where sudden changes are unknown, the thermometer seldom, if ever, varying from 60° and 70° during the entire year.

This perfect spring-like climate makes it especially adapted to invalids. As the train advances over magnificent bridges and viaducts that span deep ravines and beautiful valleys, or plunges through tunnels and skirts the mountain side in great curves, it presents views of the grandest and most picturesque scenery of the world.

The principal cities on the road are Cordoba, a town of about 10,000 inhabitants, noted for its coffee plantations, where are located the principal workshops on the road.

In passing Orizaba the scene is beyond description, as the train curves around the Peak of Orizaba, which is 15,800 ft. high, covered with snow and ice. This peak supplies the City of Mexico and Vera Cruz with ice.

In the vicinity of Vera Cruz is the famous resort and rendez-vous of the elite, Medelin named after the great conqueror's birthplace.

I arrived in the evening in the City of Mexico and was greatly surprised to find the old home of Montezuma's brilliantly lighted by electricity.

Early the next morning I paid the Representative of the German Empire in Mexico, Mr. von Wecker-Gotter, my visit and to this gentleman as well as to the German Consul, Mr. Kossidowsky, I am greatly indebted for all the favors and kindnesses bestowed on me.

The Minister von Wecker-Gotter was leaving Mexico a short time after my arrival, and before starting, kindly accompanied me on my excursion from the City of Mexico to Orizaba. From this latter place I visited Atoyac, 29 miles distant, with an exceedingly rich "Flora" and where I made valuable collections.

In Cordoba I had the pleasure to form the acquaintance of the famous botanist, Fink, and over different detours, for instance, Huatusco, I proceeded to Mirador.

Furnished with recommendations to the Governor of Vera Cruz-Llave by the kindness of the Secretary of the Interior, the Governor Señor Castillo received me heartily in Orizaba. In Mirador I visited the extensive Hacienda of Señor Sartorius, a German.

Though only a very short time in the City of Mexico, I intended to explore the Republic in different directions and then return to the city, to stay there for some time.

I commenced with Guadalupe, with the old, noteworthy church of "Nuestra Señora de Guadalupe," San Juan Teotihuacan, Toluca, the capital of the State of Mexico, with 13,000 inhabitants, Cuantitlan and the historic City of Queretaro, which was the scene of the downfall and execution of the ill-fated Emperor Maximilian in 1867.

The city has 50,000 population and contains many important woolen mills, and is chiefly noticeable for its numerous ecclesiastical and religious structures, among the latter being the Franciscan Monastery, with its noble gardens and grounds.

Not far from this place and nearer from the City of Mexico is Polatitlan and Tula, on the banks of the river of the same name, famous as the ancient capital of the Toltecs.

At a more distant excursion, I visited Guadalajara, the capital of the State of Jalisco, with 93,875 inhabitants, a very important city, and Guanajuato with rich silver mines in its vicinity. Not far from Lagos there are also very productive mines.

Guanajuato is the capital of the State of Guanajuato, has a population of 73,500 and important cotton factories. In one of these latter is the greatest water-wheel in the world. There are also rich mines of silver in its neighborhood.

To Colima, the capital of the State of Colima, I started from San Marcos and was greatly pleased to witness the eruption of the volcano Colima, then active.

Once more in the City of Mexico, I enjoyed the valuable acquaintance of the well-known botanist Herera and intended to remain in the Metropolis, to recuperate from the wearysome travels, etc.

This ancient and interesting capital has a population of over 300,000, and was a seat of art, science and commerce long before the Spanish conquerers reached the shores of the New World. It is situated in the centre of the great valley of Mexico, which measures 45 miles long and 31 miles wide. Its elevation above the sea is 7,420 ft., which gives it a climate of remarkable uniformity, the range of the thermometer being from 50° to 70° F. The rainy season begins early in

June and continues until September, showers occurring usually in the afternoons and nights.

The city is built on a part of the old bed of Lake Texcoco, and tradition gives it a more romantic origin than it ascribes to the founding of Rome. Science and art have done much to make it a beautiful city, and there seems to be a disposition on the part of the people and the government to make their nation's capital compare favorably with the capitals of other countries. The city is encircled by walls and entered by gates. The residences are mostly of stone, 1 or 2 stories high, and built around court-yards. The public edifices are numerous and substantial.

Chief among the objects of interest is the Cathedral, 500 ft. in length, by 420 ft. in breadth, the largest ecclesiastical edifice in the western hemisphere. It is of mixed Gothic and Indian architecture, and is on the site of the chief temple of the Aztecs. The walls are gorgeously decorated, and the high-altar is a marvel of magnificence. The dress on the statue of the Virgin is incrusted with gems, the diamonds alone being worth \$3,000,000, it is claimed. The cathedral is on one side of the Grand Plaza, the other sides being occupied by the National Palace, comprising the government offices, mint and prison, the National Museum, in which the great Aztec Block of carved granite is shown, upon which were sacrificed, it is said, 10,000 persons in one year, and the Market Place. The Academy of Arts and Mining, the University of Mexico, the Public Library, containing 105,000 volumes, and the National Theatre, as well as numerous convents and churches are well worth visiting. The Government's Pawnbroker shop is a very useful and noteworthy institution.

Objects of great interest are found in the Botanical garden and the 2 aqueducts. The city is noted industrially for its manufacture of gold and silver lace, and of silversmiths' work.

Riding horse-back is one of the great amusements, and a ride along the canal, or over the hills to any of the adjacent villages is found very interesting.

Music is found in all the parks every afternoon and 3 times in the week also in the evenings.

Besides the many places of special note in the city, there are several interesting points within 2 or 3 miles distance.

At a distance of 2 miles is the old historic Castle of Chapultepec, which has, at different times, been the palatial residence of the Emperors Iturbide and Maximilian. The grand view from the tower of this old castle is unexcelled. The castle is surrounded by a dense park of ancient and immense trees, all draped in heavy moss. One mile from Chapultepec is Tacubaya, where are located some palatial country seats.

Other excursions were made to the volcano of Popocatapetl, 17,800 feet high, which is always covered with snow, and which produces large amounts of very fine sulphur; also to the extensive silver mines of Real del Monte and to the cities of Puebla and Jalapa, the former, the capital of the State of Jalapa, with 78,000 inhabitants, numerous fine church and convent edifices and fortifications and the ancient Pyramid in its vicinity.

Passing Meca-Meca on the journey to Morelia, the capital of Michoacan with 25,000 inhabitants and some commerce, the sacred mountain of the Aztecs comes in view.

During my stay in the city of Mexico I was also favored with the kindness of the Minister Señor Romero Rubio of the Cabinet of President Gonzales, having previously been introduced to the then Ex-President of Mexico, Señor Porfirio Diaz, by the late Ex-President of the United States, General Grant, at a banquet given in honor of these two gentlemen by the Mayor of the city of New Orleans.

My last trip to the coast was performed from Michoacan to Manzanillo, where I procured passage on one of the Pacific Mail Steamship Company's steamers for San Fransisco.

The Mexican Republic forms the southwestern boundary of the United States and has an area of 743,948 square miles, northern frontier, 1,400 miles, southern frontier, 345 miles; sea coast, 6,086 miles. Number of States, 27; Federal District, 1; Territories, 2; Population about 11,000,000. The chief exports are: Coffee, fruit, Brazil wood, silver ore, cattle hides and silver and gold bullion and silver coin.

The prominent agricultural products are: Cotton, Pulque (the juice of the Agave Magay, an Aloës), the **national beverage of the Mexicans,** Sugar, Wheat and Corn.

The mountains contain precious metals, but little attention is paid to the exploration of the bowels of the earth.

Other statistics I could not obtain.

I arrived in San Francisco just in time to witness the splendid procession of the North American Knights of Templars, who were assembled there in convention.

Here I received the much welcomed invitation to join the historic "Henry Villard" party en route for the far "Northwest."

I omit to specify the details of this journey, since they had been minutely described by almost all the leading newspapers on the continent, and continue to relate my experiences in the distant Northwest in the usual way. After a 60 hours sea voyage, I arrived in Portland, Oregon, staying there only a very short time and, with many of the invited guests, boarded the train of the new constructed Northern Pacific Railroad, for Deer Lodge, not far from Garrison, Montana, to witness the formal opening of this extensive line and to return to Portland, where the festivities took their brilliant course.

Portland is the commercial metropolis of the Pacific Northwest, and is situated on the Wilamette river, 12 miles above its confluence with the Columbia. Population, 40,000.

The city is handsome and has many fine public and private buildings.

There are many manufacturing establishments, and from every direction in the Pacific Northwest, railroads lead to Portland, making the city the grand terminus of a system which will completely develop the entire region. It lies in the heart of a great producing country, which has no other outlet, and for which it must serve as a receiver and distributor of exports and imports.

On my extravaganzas I visited Dalles, the second important city in Oregon, though only 4,000 inhabitants containing, a very lively place, with many manufactures. The water works are worth visiting.

Salem, the capital of the State, with only 3,000 population, is surrounded by a fertile prairie and situated on the Willamette river.

The Willamette University, the State institutions for the blind, the deaf and dumb, and the State Penitentiary are here located.

Tacoma, situated on Commencement Bay (Puget Sound, Washington Territory), has many fine buildings, public and private, and is the center of large trade and manufacturing interests, as well as of an important mining country.

This place is the N. terminus of the Northern Pacific Railroad on Puget Sound, as well as of the Cascade Division leading to valuable coal fields. Pacific mail steamships come up to the wharves.

Washington Territory is traversed by the Cascade and Coast Mountains, some of the peaks very high. The highest among these is the Mount Ranier, 14,444 feet above the level of the sea, and belonging to the Cascade Mountains.

Seattle on the Puget Sound, situated on Elliot Bay, is a very busy place, and is the seat of a university.

Port Townsend, W. of Townsend Bay, is the Port of entry of the Puget Sound custom district.

After visiting Victoria, the capital of British Columbia, situated in the southeastern part of Vancouver Island, on Victoria Harbor, immediately off the Strait of San Juan de Fuca, with 7,500 inhabitants, a large number of extensive mercantile houses, manufacturing establishments, several educational and religious institutions, and a garrison of British soldiers, I also proceeded to Esquimault, 3 miles from Victoria, where the headquarters of the English Pacific Squadron is, and where there is usually a fleet of from 3 to 5 ships, thus concluding my journeys in the far Northwest.

In Portland, where I was very well received, and where several compatriots of distinction had honored me with their acquaintance, I stayed about long enough to get familiar with the different circumstances concerning the State, etc.

Oregon, whose name derives from the Spanish word signifying, "Wild Thyme," on account of the abundance of the herb found by early explorers, was discovered by Captain Gray, of Boston, 1792. Fur Company's trading post at Astoria, 1811; organized as a Territory, 1848; admitted, 1859.

Area: 69,030 square miles; average length, 360 miles; breadth, 260 miles; coast line, 300 miles; Columbia river frontage, 300 miles.

Temperature at Portland: winter, 38° to 46°; summer, 62° to 68°.

Rainfall at Dalles, 22 inches, and at Fort Hoskins, 67 inches.

Portland, Astoria and Coos Bay are ports of entry.

Number of farms, 16,217; about 25 million acres arable land, and same of grazing land; forest, 10 million acres. Average value per acre, cleared land, $21.71; woodland, $4.50.

Wheat the staple; noted for superiority of its flour.

Cattle raising ranks second only to agriculture; wool is of fine quality. Extremely rich in minerals; gold found in Jackson, Josephine, Baker and Grant counties; copper in Josephine, Douglas and Jackson counties; iron-ore throughout the State; coal along Coast Range. Principal exports are wheat, flour, lumber and canned salmon. Over 10 million feet of lumber cut annually.

Population, 174,768, including 487 negroes, 9,510 Chinese and 1,694 Indians.

U. S. Army and Chinese excluded from voting.

Number of colleges, 7; school population, 65,216; school age, 4–20.

Resuming my journey on the Northern Pacific R.R., I arrived at Helena, the capital of the Territory of Montana, with a population of 8,000, where all routes of transportation converge. The public buildings and private residences are of a character to attract the eye of the stranger. The city is the center of important manufacturing interests, as well as of trade and commerce. Helena is situated in the very heart of a mineral region, unsurpassed either in Montana or elsewhere for the number and richness of its gold and silver bearing lodes, there being within 25 miles over 3,000 quartz lodes which have been claimed. The Drum-Lummon mine has recently been sold for $1\frac{1}{2}$ million dollars. Besides the gold and silver lodes, veins of galena, copper and iron are found in great numbers. Among the attractions of Helena are the noted Hot Springs, situated in a romantic glen, 4 miles W. of the town. The temperature of the water varies from 110° to 190° F. Eighteen miles N. of Helena is the great mountain-gate through which the waters of the Missouri plunge between walls 300 ft. wide and 1,000 ft. high. There are many cataracts, cascades, etc., around Helena, and it is almost impossible to describe them.

Revisiting Garrison, the northern terminus of the Utah and Northern Branch of the Union Pacific Railroad, thence passing through the Deer Lodge Valley, which spreads for a distance of 60 miles and a width of from 5 to 10 miles, and where there are found lofty peaks, beautiful mountain lakes, glittering cascades, mineral springs, and the Great Geyser Cone, which gives name to the river and valley, the road leads to Deer Lodge, a small place, with 1,500 inhabitants, 11 miles south from Garrison, and Butte City, 52 miles S. E. from Deer Lodge, with 9,000 inhabitants, both important mining centers on the Utah and Northern Railroad.

Missoula, a small but enterprising town, near the junction of the Hell Gate and Bitter Root rivers, has a noble outlook from the broad, high plateau. Bitter Root Valley is very picturesque, and the military post of Fort Missoula is 4 miles S. Following the Jocko river, the road traverses the Flathead Reservation. Here is Flathead Lake, wherein the Pend d'Oreille river takes its rise and winds for hundreds of miles through deep gorges and beautiful valleys, before discharging its waters into Lake Pend d'Oreille. About 40 miles from Flathead Lake, near St. Ignatius's Mission, are the Two Sisters cascades, of great beauty, which leap down from opposite walls of a great amphitheater, scooped out of the mountains, a sheer fall of 2,000 ft. They unite after their descent, and pass on as a single stream. The railroad now follows the charming valley of Clark's Fork of the Columbia river.

Heron is at the junction of the Idaho and Rocky Mountain Division, and there are railroad shops at this point. The road skirts Clark's Fork of the Columbia till it reaches the large opening in the river 45 miles long and from 3 to 15 miles in width, known as Lake Pend d'Oreille, whose beauty has made it notable. At Sand Point the road crosses one end of the lake.

Rathdrum, in Idaho, is a small town, which has recently come into notice as the main point of approach to the Cœur d'Alene mines in the Cœur d'Alene mountains. Some extraordinarily rich "Finds" are said to have been made.

Other excursions in the Territory brought me to Lewiston, Mount Idaho, Farmington and Louisville, small places with nothing of interest, and from here I returned to Butte City, where I expected to get all information regarding this Territory.

Idaho had already a white population previous to 1850, mainly trappers, prospectors and missionaries; the permanent settlement began with the discovery of gold in 1860; organized as a Territory, 1863.

Area: 84,800 square miles, length in W., 485 miles, and on Wyoming boundary, 140 miles; width, 45 miles in N. and nearly 300 miles in S. Drainage mainly by Salmon and Snake rivers and their tributaries.

Temperature at Boise City: winter, 30° to 40°; summer, 68° to 75°.

Florence and Silver City are flourishing mining towns.

Extreme north well timbered and much fertile land; extreme southeast populated almost entirely by Mormons, chiefly farmers.

Cash value per acre of corn in 1883, $18; wheat, $13.77; rye, $11.79; oats, $21.31; barley, $21.30; potatoes, $73.44; hay, $10.40.

Most of the gold is found in Idaho, Boise and Alturas Counties. Silver in Owyhee County, some of the mines being very rich. Coal in the vicinity of Boise City.

Manufactures, chiefly production of flour and lumber and smelting of ores.

Population, 32,610, inclusive 53 colored, 3,379 Chinese, and 165 Indians.

School population, 9,650 ; school age, 5 to 21.

Starting per Utah Northern Railroad, Ogden, in the Territory of Utah, was reached. This is a flourishing city of 6,000 inhabitants, and situated on a high mountain environed plateau. It is remarkably well built, and contains many fine buildings, among which is the Mormon Tabernacle.

Ogden is the junction between the Union Pacific and Central Pacific Railways, and of the Utah Central R. R., which extends to Salt Lake City and the Utah and Northern Division of the Union Pacific R. R. The machine and repair shops of the Central Pacific R. R. are located here.

Its streets are broad, with running streams of water in nearly all of them.

The country between Ogden and Salt Lake City is thickly settled, several Mormon villages have to be passed, with nothing particularly characteristic, except the co-operative stores, with an open eye and the legend, "Holiness to the Lord," printed over the doorways.

Salt Lake City, the capital of Utah Territory, is situated at the W. base of a spur of the Wahsatch Mountains, about 12 miles from the S. E. extremity of the Great Salt Lake. It lies in a great valley, extending close up to the base of the mountains; the gray and rugged mountain peaks, covered with perpetual snow, rising in the distance. The streets of the city are 128 feet wide. Shade trees and ditches filled with running water line both sides of every street. The dwellings and business structures are built principally of sun-dried bricks (adobe), but the newly built are of a modern pattern. The Great Tabernacle, of wood, except the 46 sandstone pillars supporting the immense dome-like roof, is oval in shape, inside and out, and will seat 15,000 persons, its organ is one of the largest in America.

The Temple, E. of the Tabernacle, in the course of erection when I was there, was estimated to cost 10 millions of dollars. Brigham's Block, enclosed by a high stone wall, contains the Tithing House, the Beehive House and the Lion House, the Assembly Rooms, the office of the Mormon newspaper, and various other offices, shops, dwellings, etc. Here was the residence of the late Brigham Young, and 18 or 20 of his wives lived in the Beehive and the Lion House. The handsome house, nearly opposite, supposed to belong to the prophet's favorite wife, and formerly known as Amelia Palace, is now known as the Gardo House.

In the Museum may be seen specimen ores from the mines, Indian relics, various products of Mormon industry and other curiosos.

Among the educational institutions are the Desert University, Hammond Hall, Collegiate Institute and St. Mary's Academy.

Fort Douglas, 2 miles E. of the city, overlooking the same, is garrisoned by a full regiment.

The Great Salt Lake is reached via Utah & Nevada

R. R. to Lake Point, and is one of the greatest natural curiosities of the West. It is 75 miles long and about 30 broad, is 4,200 feet above the sea, and contains six islands, of which Church Island is the largest. Several rivers flow into it, but it has no outlet. The water is shallow, the depth in many extensive parts being not more than two or three feet. Its water is transparent, but exceedingly salty and very buoyant; a man may float in it at full length upon his back, having his head and neck, his legs to the knee, and both arms to the elbow entirely out of the water. If he assumes a sitting posture, with the arms extended, his shoulders will rise above the water. Swimming, however, is difficult from the tendency of the lower extremeties to rise above the surface, and the brine is so strong that it cannot be swallowed without danger of strangulation, while a particle of it in the eye causes intense pain. A bath in it is refreshing and invigorating, though the body requires to be washed afterward in fresh water.

The Ontario mine, near Park City, and the Horn silver mine near Frisco, with smelting works of great dimensions, are noteworthy.

In the following, the reproductions of authentic statistic tables are given.

Utah was settled by Mormons under the leadership of Brigham Young, at Salt Lake, 1847, and the Territorial government formed in 1850.

Area, 84,900 square miles; average length, 350 miles; breadth, 260 miles. Largest rivers, Grand and

Green, together with the Colorado, which they unite to form.

Temperature at Salt Lake City: winter, 29° to 40°; summer, 69° to 77°; rainfall, 24 inches.

Number of farms, 9,452; land under cultivation, over 400,000 acres; value of farm products, $10,000,000. Valleys of the Cache, Salt Lake, Jordan, Sevier and Rio Virgin are irrigable, and produce fine crops of cereals and vegetables. Annual income from stock raising, about $2,000,000, though grazing interest not so important as in neighboring States and Territories.

Gold, copper and silver found in Wahsatch Mountains, the metal found being mostly silver. Gold production in 1882, $190,000; silver, $6,800,000.

Principal source of coal supply, in the valley of Weber river.

Ranks third in silver.

Population, including 232 negroes, 501 Chinese and 807 Indians, 143,963.

School population, 43,303; school age 6 to 18; number of colleges, 1.

Twenty-five miles from Ogden is Corinne, the largest Gentile town in Utah, having a large trade with the mining regions of eastern Idaho and Montana. Beyond Corinne the train winds among the Promontory Mountains, and skirts the N. shore of the Great Salt Lake, while the Mormon city lies near the S. end of it. Promontory Point is interesting as the spot where the two companies building the Pacific Railroad joined their tracks on May 10, 1869.

The last tie was made of California laurel trimmed with silver, and the last four spikes were of solid silver and gold. Beyond this the road enters upon an extended plateau, about 60 miles long and of the same width, known as the Great American Desert. Its whole surface is covered with a sapless weed five or six inches high, and never grows any green thing that could sustain animal life. The only living things found upon it are lizards and jackass-rabbits, and the only landscape feature is dry, brown and bare mountains. The earth is alkaline and fine, and is whirled up by the least wind in blinding clouds of dust. Rivers disappear in it, and it yields no other vegetation than the pallid Artemesia, or sage-brush.

At Humboldt Wells, farther on the road, are 30 springs in a low basin, some of which have been sounded to a depth of 1,700 feet without revealing a bottom, and it is supposed that the whole series form the outlets of a subterranean lake.

In a distance of 57 miles is Elko, with the State University of the State of Nevada, founded in 1875, and 1,200 inhabitants. Several important mining districts are tributary to Elko, and secure it a large trade. Winnemucca is another prosperous town with a large mining trade, 141 miles from Elko, and Humboldt, still farther on, affords a grateful if momemtary relief to the now wearied eye of the traveler. The desert extends from Humboldt in every direction, a pallid, lifeless waste, that gives emphasis to the word desolation; mountains break the level, and from the foot to the crest they are devoid of vegetation or other color than a maroon or leaden gray; the earth is loose and sandy; but here at Humboldt, irrigation compelled the soil to yield flowers, grass, fruit and shrubbery.

At Wadsworth the ascent of the Sierra Nevada is begun. The wearying sight of plains covered with alkali and sage-brush is exchanged for picturesque views of mountain slopes adorned with branching pine trees, and diversified with foaming torrents.

The ascent soon becomes so steep that two locomotives are required to draw the train. At short intervals there are strong wooden snow-sheds, erected to guard the line against destruction by snow-slides. These sheds, which are very much like tunnels, interrupt the view of some of the most romantic scenery on the line.

Reno, a busy town of 4,000 inhabitants, is situated on the Truckee river about five miles from the base of the Sierra. It has an immense trade with the mining districts, is in the heart of an agricultural and grazing valley, and contains the grounds of the State Agricultural Society, a Young ladies' seminary and several factories.

From Reno the Virginia and Truckee R. R. runs to Carson and Virginia City, in the great Nevada mining region. Carson is the capital of Nevada and is a thriving city of 4,500 inhabitants, containing the Capitol, the U. S. Mint and fine residences.

In the court-yard of the prison are shown footprints of human beings, birds and other animals on the sandstones (supposed to belong to the geological tertiary period).

From Carson 15 miles distant, and reached by stage, is the lovely Lake Tahoe, 35 miles long and 15 miles wide, 6,000 ft. above the sea, and surrounded by snow-capped mountain peaks, with marvellously clear water, whose depth has been sounded to 1,600 ft.

21 miles beyond Carson is Virginia City, completely environed by mountains, and containing 3,000 inhabitants, about one-fifth of whom are usually under ground. What is more surprising to the stranger is the proportions of the constant rushing crowd on the principal thoroughfare, and the cosmopolitan character of its elements. Piute and Washoe Indians, in picturesque rags, Chinamen in blue and black blouses, brawny Cornishmen, vehement Mexicans and many other people from far apart countries, mingle and surge along in the stream. Virginia City stands directly over the famous Comstock lode, and near by are the celebrated Big Bonanza mines, said to have been a few years ago the richest in the world. There are many more mines in the vicinity.

By stage from the Lake to Tahoe City, across the Lake, and thence to Truckee, the first important station in California, perched high up amid the Sierras, is reached.

Nevada, "The Sage Hen State," whose name derives from the Spanish, signifying "Snow Covered," had its first white settlements in Washoe and Carson Valleys, 1848; organized as a Territory from Utah,

1861; admitted, 1864. Area, 110,700 square miles; extreme length, 485 miles, length western boundary, 210 miles; extreme breadth, 310 miles. Humboldt is the longest river, its valley extending east and west, determined course of Central Pacific.

Temperature at Winnemucca, winter, 30° to 38°, summer, 66° to 73°.

Waters of rivers usually fresh and abound in fish. Number of farms, 1,404, many valleys easily cultivated, and crop yield good. Mineral resources of enormous value. Comstock lode, already mentioned, supposed to be the richest silver mine in the world; Eureka, one of the most productive. Amount of gold produced in 1882, $2,000,000; silver, $6,750,000. Rich lead and copper ores; also zinc, platinum, tin and nickel have been found. Extensive deposits of borax in Churchill and Esmeralda counties.

Ranks second in gold and fourth in silver. Population, 62,266, including 488 Colored, 5,416 Chinese and 2,803 Indians.

Number of Colleges, 1; school population, 10,483; school age, 6 to 18.

From Truckee, an excursion was made to Donner Lake, embosomed in the lap of towering hills and to Summit, situated on the line. Summit is the highest point on the Central Pacific road, 7,042 ft., and the scenery is indescribably beautiful and impressive. From Summit to Sacramento is a distance of 106 miles, and between these places the descent from that height to 56 ft. above the level of the sea has to be made.

Cape Horn and Colfax passed, and the train runs right through to the capital of California, Sacramento, the third city of the State in size, having a population of over 23,000, and second in commercial importance. It is built on an extensive plain on the E. bank of the Sacramento river, immediately S. of the mouth of the American river.

The city is very attractive, and of important public buildings there is only the State Capitol, one of the finest structures in the United States. The State Library in the capitol has over 35,000 volumes and the Sacramento Library about 15,000. The State Agricultural Society has a commodious and one of the finest race courses in the world. The Crocker Art Gallery is noteworthy, and is a present of the wife of Mr. S. B. Crocker. The through train from here to San Francisco pursues a very pleasant route, being for the most part through the valleys of the Sacramento and San Joaquin. Benicia, 57 miles from Sacramento, situated on the N. side of the Straits of Carquinez, contains the large depot and machine shops of the Pacific Mail Steamship Co., the United States Arsenal, and several noted educational institutions.

The train crosses the Straits on a mammoth ferry-boat, and in 27 miles reaches Oakland, a beautiful city of 35,000 inhabitants, situated on the E. shore of San Francisco Bay, nearly opposite San Francisco, of which it is practically a suburb. Oakland is luxuriantly shaded, is remarkably well built, and has a delightful climate. At Berkeley, 4 miles N., is the State University, which is open to both sexes, and whose tuition is free. At Oakland Point, where the railroad pier of the Company extends 2¼ miles into the Bay, the ferry-boat conveys the traveler to San Francisco, 3 miles distant.

As I intended to return to San Francisco, I only stayed there a very short time and procured passage for Hawai (Sandwich Islands), a regular line of steamers run between San Francisco and Honolulu. Honolulu, the capital of the Kingdom of Hawai, is situated on the island of Oahu, one of the group of the fifteen islands of which this Kingdom of Oceania consists.

Population, about 7,000, and with the exception of the botanical garden, laid out by the well known botanist Hildebrandt, and the Hospital for persons afflicted with Leprosy, situated in the suburb, Kakuato, has no other attractive points, but the excursions to the great volcanos are worth making. On one of these explorations I ascended the volcano Mauna-loa, erupting only every 5 or 6 years, but having for a neighbor the Kila-uea, 4,000 ft. high and in constant activity. The Mauna-loa is one of the highest valcanos.

Within the radius of the Kila-uea are two burning lakes: the Hali-mau-mau and the New Lake.

The circumference of the crater of this volcano measures 3½ miles.

Mauna-Kia is an isolated volcano and Hale-Kale, whose crater has a circumference of 35 miles, is undoubtedly the greatest crater of any volcano in the world. This volcano lies on the island of Maui, on which there is the most extensive sugar-plantation of the Sandwich Islands, Spreckelville, the property of the well known Mr. Spreckel from California, and where I was well received.

As the communication between these islands is very difficult, I was only able to visit 4 of the inhabited islands and tried to get every possible information concerning them.

My explorations lasted fully two months, and I was anxious to return to the United States viz. San Francisco.

Hawai, a Kingdom of Oceania, consists of a group of 15 islands of which 8 are inhabited. The Government is a limited monarchy.

Hawai is the largest island.

Area of the islands, 6,667 square miles.

At the last census, the population numbered 57,985, viz., 44,088 Natives, 5,916 Chinese, 4,651 white people, of whom 1,276 were Americans, 883 English, 272 Germans, 436 Portuguese, 81 French, and half-cast 3,420.

To a great extent the islands are mountainous, and there are numerous volcanoes, several of which are active.

The soil is exceedingly fertile and productive. Chief products, sugar and rice; but coffee, hides, bone, whale oil and wool are exported in considerable quantities. Value of exports in 1883, $8,121,200; imports, $5,624,240.

The islands of Hawai and Maui are provided with telegraphs and have about 32 miles of railway. Almost every house in Honolulu has its telephone.

There are numerous schools in the islands; the annual sum devoted to public instruction is $95,850. The King is a member of the Church of England; but all forms of religion are permitted and protected.

Landing in the Bay of San Francisco and resting myself from the tedious travels in the Sandwich islands, I proceeded to the State of Missouri, and direct to its greatest and most important city, St. Louis.

California derives its name from the Spanish word, signifying, "Hot furnace."

First settlement by Spaniards at San Diego, 1768, admitted 1850.

Area, 158,360 square miles, the second largest State; extreme length, 770 miles; extreme breadth, 330 miles; least breadth, 150 miles; coast line over 700 miles; San Francisco Bay, best harbor on western coast.

Temperature at San Francisco: winter, 50° to 55°, summer, 58° to 69°. Rainfall, Sacramento, 20 inches.

San Francisco, metropolis and only port of entry. Regular line of steamers to Australia, Panama, Mexico, China and Japan.

The U. S. Navy Yard is at San Pablo Bay. Number of farms, 35,934, average value per acre, cleared land, $27.16; woodland, $8.55.

One of the richest agricultural tracts in the Union; rich soil and favorable climate, often insuring two crops per year on same field; wheat the most valuable crop. Ranks very high as a fruit-growing State; fruits of temperate climates, the grape region, North.

Fine sheep-raising country, Cashmere goats have been introduced and are doing well.

Ranks first in barley, grape culture, sheep, gold and quicksilver.

Population, 864,694; with 6,018 Negroes, 75,132 Chinese, 86 Japanese, and 16,277 Indians.

Indians and Chinese excluded from voting.

School population, 216,330; school age, 5-17.

St. Louis is situated geographically almost in the centre of the great valley of the Mississippi, or basin of the continent, on the W. bank of the Mississippi river, 20 miles below the entrance of the Missouri, about 175 miles above the mouth of the Ohio, and 1,170 miles above New Orleans, in lat. 38° 37′ N. and lon. 90° 15′ W. It is built on three terraces. The corporate limits extend 11 miles along the river and about 3 miles back from it, embracing an area of nearly 21 square miles.

In 1762 a grant was made by the Governor General of Louisiana, then a French province, to Pierre Liguest Laclede and his partners, comprising the "Louisiana Fur Company" to establish trading-posts on the Mississippi; and on February 15, 1764, the principal one was established where the city now stands, and named St. Louis. In 1803 all the territory then known as Louisiana was ceded to the United States. In 1812 that portion lying N. of the 33d degree of latitude was organized as Missouri Territory. In 1822 St. Louis was incorporated as a city. The first census was taken in 1764, and the population was then 120. According to the Census of 1880 it was 350,522. The commerce of St. Louis, as the natural commercial entrepot of the vast Mississippi valley, is immense; the chief articles of receipt and shipment being breadstuffs, live-stock, provisions, cotton, lead (from the Missouri mines), hay, salt, wool, hides and pelts, lumber, tobacco, and groceries, but the prosperity of the city is chiefly due to its manufactures.

The city is mostly regularly laid out. Fourth and Olive streets contain the leading stores for retailing, and are fashionable promenades. The finest building in the city is the Court House. The Four Courts with the famous jail, semicircular in form and so constructed that all the cells are under the observation of one single jailer at once; the New Custom House with the Post-Office, the Chamber of Commerce, the Equitable Life Insurance Building, the U. S. Arsenal, in the extreme S. of the city and the Masonic Temple, are magnificent structures. Of churches, the Cathedral (Catholic), Christ Church, the First Presbyterian Church, the Jewish Temple, and the Pilgrim Congregational Church are the prominent. The Mercantile Library numbers 50,000 volumes, and contains paintings, coins, statuary and a sculptured slab from the ruins of Nineveh. The St. Louis University (Jesuit), is the oldest educational institution in St. Louis. Washington University embraces all the ranges of university studies except theological. Beside these, there are a great many educational institutions, public and private, and a number of charitable asylums, hospitals and such like institutions. Adjoining the Tower Grove Park, embracing 277 acres and beautifully laid out is Shaw's Garden, owned by Mr. Henry Shaw, who has opened it to the public and intends it as a gift to the city. The Garden contains 109 acres and is divided in the "Herbaceous and Flower Garden," the "Fruticetum," and the "Arboretum," all of miraculous beauty and grandeur. In the Fair Grounds of the St. Louis Agricultural and Mechanical Association is one of the best zoological gardens in America.

The Great St. Louis Bridge across the Mississippi, is regarded as one of the greatest triumphs of American engineering. The bridge is built in two stories, passes over a viaduct of five arches, and the lower roadway runs into a tunnel, 4,800 ft. long, passing under a large part of the city. The total cost of bridge and tunnel was over 10 millions of dollars. It was designed by James B. Eads, begun in 1869, and completed in 1874.

The City Water-Works, at Bissell's Point, on the bank of the river, are worth seeing.

Having had the pleasure to meet Professor Potter, the renowned Geologist, whom I had previously seen in the Mining Academy of the City of Mexico, my explorations in the most important iron regions, coal mines and lime-stone quarries of this State and other adjoining States were greatly facilitated, and to this gentleman I owe my success in obtaining all the desired informations, etc.

The next place visited was the "Queen City of the

West," Cincinnati, the chief city of Ohio, situated on the N. bank of the Ohio river, in lat. 39° 6' N. and lon. 84° 27' W.

Cincinnati is principally built upon two terraces, the first 60 and the second 112 ft. above the river. The central position of Cincinnatti has rendered it one of the most important commercial places of the West; but manufactures constitute its chief interest. Iron, furniture, boots and shoes, beer and whisky, machinery and steamboats, are leading items in the product; but pork packing is one of the principal industries.

The finest building in the city is the New U. S. Government Building, and the Masonic Temple, the Exposition Buildings with the Music Hall, and the Springer Music Hall, seating an auditorium of 5,000 persons and containing one of the largest organs in the world, are worth being visited. The Emery Arcade is said to be one of the finest and largest, and the Tyler-Davidson Fountain, surrounded by groups of statuary, is well worth seeing.

Among the Churches, the Roman Catholic St. Peter's Cathedral in pure Grecian style, and its altarpiece "St. Peter Delivered," by Murillo, one of the chief glories of art in America, and the Hebrew Synagogue, opposite the Cathedral, as also the St. Paul's Methodist are the most prominent.

The educational and charitable institutions of Cincinnati are numerous and important, and of these the University of Cincinnati, the School of Design, the Law and Art School, St. Xavier's College (Jesuit), the

Cincinnati Wesleyan and the Union Hebrew College, the Lane Theological Seminary, the Miami Medical College and the Medical College of Ohio, one of the most famous in the West, the Chickering Classical and Scientific Institute, the Woodward and the Hughes High School, the Mechanics Institute, with 6,500 volumes, the Cincinnati Hospital and the Longview Asylum for the Insane, are the most noteworthy.

More than a third of the residents of Cincinnati are Germans or of German parentage. The greatest part of them occupy the section of the city N. of the Miami canal, which they have named "The Rhine."

The Great Arbeiter and Turner Halls are worth visiting.

The Suspension Bridge over the Ohio, connecting the city with Covington, Kentucky, is the pride of Cincinnati. From tower to tower it is 1,057 ft. long; the entire length is 2,252 ft. and its height over the water 100 ft.

Well worth visiting are the United Rail Roads Stock Yards and the Price Hill, the Lookout House, Mount Auburn from whose summits, crowned by extensive music gardens, splendid views of the city, the river and the surrounding country are obtained.

Leaving Cincinnati for Louisville, Kentucky, by rail—the other route is on the river, per steamer—the city of Newport, connected with Covington by a bridge over the river Licking, and containing 20,433 inhabitants, beautiful gardens and imposing shade-trees, was first visited, and afterwards Covington.

Covington is a city of 29,720 inhabitants, the largest after Louisville and substantially a suburb of Cincinnati, whose business-men have here many costly residences. Except the Free Library, some educational institutions and the catholic St. Elizabeth Hospital, there are no other attractions in this place.

Louisville, the chief city of Kentucky, and one of the most important in the country, is situated at the Falls of the Ohio, where Beargrass Creek enters that river. Its site is one of peculiar excellence. The Falls are quite picturesque and can be seen from the town.

The first settlement of Louisville was made by 13 families, who accompanied Colonel George Rogers Clarke on his expedition down the Ohio in 1778. The town was established in 1780, and called Louisville in honor of Louis XVI. of France, whose troops were then aiding the Americans in their struggle for independence. It was incorporated as a city in 1828, when its population was about 10,000. In 1880 it had about 124,000. The trade of Louisville is immense. It is one of the largest leaf-tobacco markets in the world, the sales of this one article amounting to over $5,000,000 annually, and it is rapidly becoming one of the most important markets for live-stock in the country. Pork-packing is extensively carried on, and the sugar curing of hams is a special feature of the business. The annual production of iron foots up $5,000,000. Louisville is the great distributing market for the fine whiskies made in Kentucky. The manufacture of beer has also become a very important interest. Leather, cement, agricultural implements, furniture, and iron pipes for water and gas mains, are the other leading manufactures. The city is regularly laid out and has well paved streets.

The Court House, City Hall, the buildings of the Southern Exposition and some churches and colleges are of beautiful architectonic structures.

The Public Library, numbering over 35,000 volumes and connected with a museum and the natural-history department, containing also the celebrated Troost collection of minerals, one of the largest in America, are worth visiting. Louisville, being the centre of one of the finest fossiliferous regions in the world, there are numerous private collections, containing many excellent specimens elsewhere rare.

The University of Louisville is a flourishing institution, the Kentucky School of Medicine and Hospital College of Medicine, and the two High Schools, for males and females, as also the Colored Normal School are prosperous institutions of learning.

The State Blind School and many other charitable Homes and Hospitals are in this city.

On Cave Hill Cemetery is the monument of George D. Prentice, the poet, journalist and politician.

Opposite the W. end of Louisville is the finely-situated and handsomely-built city of New Albany, with 16,422 inhabitants and many pretty public and private buildings.

Jeffersonville, another flourishing town on the Indiana shore, lies opposite Louisville, and is connected with it by the great railroad-bridge across the Ohio, 5,219 ft. long.

Leaving Louisville for the world-wide known Mammoth Cave, the train passes Bardstown Junction, Lebanon Junction and Mumfordsville, a pretty village on the bank of Green River. This neighborhood was the scene of numerous encounters between Generals Buell and Bragg in the campaign of 1862. From Cave City a stage runs to the famous Mammoth Cave. The cave, which is the largest known, extends about nine miles; and it is said that to visit the portions already explored requires from 150 to 200 miles of travel. This vast interior contains a succession of marvelous avenues, chambers, domes, abysses, grottoes, lakes, rivers, cataracts, etc. Two remarkable species of animal life are found in the cave, in the form of an eyeless fish and an eyeless craw-fish, nearly white in color. Other animals known to exist in the cave are lizzards, frogs, crickets, rats, bats, etc., besides ordinary fish and craw-fish washed in from the neighboring Green River. The atmosphere of the cave is pure and healthful; the temperature which averages 59°, is about the same in winter and summer. It is a sheer impossibility to describe all the curiosities of this wonderful cave.

I did not travel considerably in this State, and had to collect Statistics, which I here reproduce.

Kentucky, the "Corn Cracker State," whose name signifies "dark and bloody ground," was the ancient hunting grounds of the Indians.

Earliest explorations made by John Finley and

others, 1767; Daniel Boone established himself there, 1769; admitted as a State, 1792.

Area, 40,400 square miles; greatest length, 350 miles; greatest breadth, 178 miles; river frontage, 812 miles; navigable waters, 4,000 miles.

Temperature at Louisville: Winter, 34° to 44°; summer, 75° to 80°. Rainfall at Springdale, 49 inches.

Frankfort is the capital, and has a population of 6,958. Lexington, the former capital, founded 1776, 16,656.

Louisville and Paducah are ports of entry.

Number of farms, 166,453; average value per acre, cleared land, $18.86; wood land, $12.82.

Ranks high as an agricultural State, has a worldwide reputation for thoroughbred horses and cattle, and is first in tobacco.

Population, 1,648,690 ind.; 271,451 negroes; 10 Chinese and 50 Indians.

Slaves in 1860, 225,483.

Colleges, 15; School age, 6-20.

Returning from the Mammoth Cave over the same road, I resumed my journey to Nashville, in the State of Tennessee, which I here describe.

Nashville is the capital of Tennessee and the largest city in the State in point of population (45,000), and is situated on the S. bank of the Cumberland river, 200 miles above its junction with the Ohio. It is well built and there are many imposing public and private buildings, among which deserve mention: the Capitol,

Vanderbilt University, the Court House, State Penitentiary, University of Nashville, Fisk University, Tennessee Central College, the State institutions for the Blind and Insane, the latter 6 miles distant, and several churches.

The Hermitage, the celebrated residence of Andrew Jackson, is 12 miles E. of Nashville.

In November 1864, the Confederate General Hood, having lost Atlanta, placed his army in Sherman's rear and began an invasion of Tennessee.

After severe fighting with General Schofield on November thé 30th he advanced upon Nashville and shut up General Thomas within its fortifications. For two weeks little was done on either side. When Thomas was fully ready, he suddenly sallied out on Hood, and, in a terrible two day's battle, drove the Confederates out of their entrenchments into headlong flight. The Union cavalry pursued them, the infantry following close behind, and the entire Confederate Army, except the rear guard, which fought bravely to the last, was broken into a rabble of demoralized fugitives, which at last escaped across the Tennessee. For the first time in the war an army was destroyed; and General Sherman, who had been awaiting in Atlanta the issue of Hood's maneuver, then started on his famous march to the sea.

Later on, I returned to this State once more, and now started for the East, the first place arrived at being Cleveland, in the State of Ohio.

Cleveland, the second city in size and importance

in Ohio, is situated on the S. shore of Lake Erie, at the mouth of the Cuyahoga river. The greater portion of the city stands on a gravelly plain, about 100 ft. above the lake. The new Breakwater W. of the river's mouth affords a safe harbor.

The city is tastefully laid out, the abundance of shade trees, chiefly elms, have given it the title of the "Forest City." The great stone viaduct which spans the river valley between the two divisions of the city, on a level with the plateau, is justly reckoned among the triumphs of American engineering, it is 3,211 ft. long and cost over $2,000,000. The population, in 1880, was 160,142. The commerce of the city is very large, especially with Canada and the mining regions of the Lake Superior.

The most important manufactures are of iron and coal-oil; in the production of refined petroleum, Cleveland is the first city in the world. Other important products are sulphuric-acid, wooden-ware, agricultural implements, marble and stone, railroad cars and white lead. Pork-packing is also carried on to some extent.

Euclid Avenue is undoubtedly the handsomest street of any city in the United States.

There are numerous fine public edifices and elegant private residences.

Of the 127 churches in the city, the most noteworthy are St. Paul's, the Old Stone Church, the Second Presbyterian, the Catholic Cathedral, etc. Of its educational institutions of which there are many, I will only mention the Adelbert College, or Western

Reserve University, the Case School of Applied Science, the Medical Department of the Western Reserve University, the Medical Department of the University of Wooster, the Brooks School and the Public Library, numbering 40,000 volumes.

The Marine, Charity, and Homoeopathic hospitals, the Hebrew Orphan Asylum and the City Infirmary are of great importance.

The Water-works of Cleveland near the lake are of great dimensions and the West-side Reservoir a very popular resort.

On **Lake View Cemetery**, containing 300 acres, lie the remains of the late President James A. Garfield. $2\frac{1}{2}$ acres on the highest point of the cemetery are being prepared for a monument beneath which his remains are to be placed.

Leaving Cleveland, the train passes the pretty villages of Berea and Elyria, and in 30 miles reaches Oberlin, noted as the seat of Oberlin College, from which no person is excluded on account of sex or color. This college, founded in 1834, combines manual labor with study, inculcates entire social equality between whites and blacks, and has a prosperous career.

The next important Station is Toledo, which within a few years has developed from an inconsiderable village into a large and rapidly growing city. Its population numbers 65,000 and its commerce is very large.

Situated on the Maumee river, 4 miles from a broad and beautiful bay, and 12 miles from Lake Erie, of which it is regarded as one of the ports, its manufactures are numerous and important, including car factories, iron works, locomotive shops, furniture factories, flour mills and breweries.

The commerce consists chiefly of the handling of grain. It has large and handsome public buildings, wide streets, several neat parks and costly water-works. Toledo is the converging point of 19 railroad lines.

Ohio, the "Buckeye State," has its name from the Indian, signifying "Beautiful River." First permanent settlement at Marietta, 1788; admitted as a State, 1802.

Area, 41,060 square miles, greatest length east and west, 225 miles; extreme breadth, 200 miles; Ohio river frontage, 430 miles; lake frontage, 230 miles.

Temperature at Cleveland: winter, 27° to 38°; summer, 68° to 73°. At Cincinnati: winter, 34° to 45°; summer, 74° to 79°. Rainfall at Cleveland, 38 inches.

Columbus, the capital of the State, is a great railroad center, and has 51,647 inhabitants (estimated now as over 75,000). There are many State institutions, several high-schools, medical colleges, and other Academies, etc., in Columbus, and the State Capitol considered to be one of the finest in the Union.

Near Dayton, in this State, is the greatest Soldiers Home in America, with numerous public and private buildings, a theater, and other places of resort for the invalid soldiers.

Number of farms, 247,189, of which 199,562 are occupied by owners; average value per acre, cleared land, $47.53; woodland, $41.37.

Dairy products are a source of great revenue. Ranks first in agricultural implements and wool; second in petroleum, iron and steel.

Population, 3,198,062, incl. 79,900 colored, 109 Chinese and 130 Indians.

Number of Colleges, 35; school population, 1,081,321; school age, 6-21.

My next aim was the wonder of the world, "The Falls of Niagara," and boarding a train for Buffalo, in the State of New York, I arrived there soon, and began with the usually first visited Goat Island, reached by a bridge 360 ft. long, the bridge itself being an object of interest, from its apparently dangerous position.

The view of the Rapids from the bridge is one of the most impressive features of the Niagara scenery.

The river descends 52 ft. in a distance of $\frac{3}{4}$ of a mile by this inextricable turmoil of waters. Below the bridge is "Chapin's Island." A short walk leads to "Luna Island," a huge rock-mass between the Center Fall and the American Fall, the width of this latter being over 1,100 feet, and the precipice over which it plunges is 164 ft. high. "Cave of the Winds" is a spacious recess back of the Centre Fall. The "Horseshoe Fall" is unsurpassingly grand and majestic. The mighty cataract here measures 2,200 ft. across, with a perpendicular plunge of 158 ft.

At the other end of Goat Island a series of beautiful bridges leads to the "Three Sisters," as 3 small islets, lying in the Rapids, are called.

These last named are rugged masses of rock, covered with a profuse and tangled vegetation. Among the many attractive points, which to describe, it is almost an impossibility, "Grand Island" above "Navy Island," deserves mention as the spot on which, in 1820, Major Mordecai M. Noah founded "Ararat," a city of refuge for the Jews, in the vain hope of assemblig there all the Hebrew population of the world.

The New Suspension Bridge, connecting with Canada, is 1,268 ft. from tower to tower, and 190 ft. above the river. The view of the falls and of the gorge below, from the bridge is admirably pretty. "Table Rock," formerly an overhanging platform, is still called so, though fallen long ago over the precipice.

The "Whirlpool," below the Falls, is occasioned by a sharp bend in the river which is here contracted to a width of 220 ft.

The appropriateness of the name Niagara (Indian: "Thunder of waters"), is very evident here.

The Falls of Niagara are situated on the Niagara River, about 22 miles from Lake Erie and 14 miles from Lake Ontario. The river is the channel by which all the waters of the 4 great upper lakes flow toward the Gulf of the St. Lawrence, and has a total descent of 333 ft., leaving Lake Ontario still 231 ft. above the sea.

With feelings of admiration and astonishment I left

this lovely and impressive spot—the thunder of its turmoil waters re-echoing in my ears—and returned to the city of Buffalo, the "Queen City of the Lakes."

Third in size of the cities in the State of New York, it is situated at the mouth of Buffalo Creek and head of Niagara River, at the E. end of Lake Erie. Its harbor is the largest and finest on the lake and it is the terminus of the Erie Canal, the New York Central, the Erie, the New York, West Shore and Buffalo, the Delaware, Lackawana and Western, and eight other railroads.

The city has a water-front of about 5 miles, half upon the lake and half upon Niagara River. Its commerce is very large, its position at the foot of the great chain of lakes makes it the entrepot for a large part of the traffic between the East and the great Northwest. The population, 1880, was 155,134. The lake navigation of the city is the most important element of business; the manufactures are also large, the chiefest being of iron, tin, brass, and copper-ware. Malting and brewing, for which the climate is very favorable, are extremely carried on.

Buffalo was first settled in 1801; it became a military post during the war of 1812, and was burned by a force of Indians and British in 1814; and it was incorporated as a city in 1832. Since the completion of the Erie Canal in 1825 its growth has been very rapid.

Buffalo is handsomely built. The prominent public buildings are: the Custom House and Post Office, the

State Arsenal, the State Armory, the Erie County Penitentiary, the Court House and the City Hall.

The most notable churches are: the Episcopal, St. Paul's Cathedral, and the Catholic St. Joseph's Cathedral.

The leading educational institutions include: the Medical College of the University of Buffalo, the Jesuit Canisius College and several female academies.

The Buffalo Historical Society, with a large library and cabinets, and the Society of Natural Sciences, with a very valuable collection of minerals. and a good botanical and conchological cabinet, and a complete set of Professor Ward's fossils casts, are located in the same building.

The Grosvenor Library numbers 12,000 volumes, and of the many charitable institutions, the State Insane Asylum is one of the largest in the Union.

Of great curiosity are also the extensive canal basins, the piers, the grain-elevators and some of the iron works.

The International Bridge crosses the Niagara river to the Canadian village of Fort Erie.

By way of Suspension Bridge I continued my travels in the State of New York, and visited Rochester, with 89,366 population, situated on both sides of the Genesee river, 7 miles from its mouth in Lake Ontario. Soon after it enters the city the river makes a rapid descent, there being a perpendicular fall of 96 ft. near the center, and two others of 25 ft. near the northern limit. It is to the prodigious water-power thus afforded that much of the prosperity of the city is attributable, and it contains several of the largest flour mills in the country. Other important industries are the production of clothing, boots and shoes, engines and boilers, agricultural implements, trees and garden and flower seeds. The nurseries are worth paying a visit.

There are a number of exceedingly fine buildings in Rochester, as for instance, the City Hall, Powers Buildings, the University of Rochester with the finest geological cabinets in the Union, collected by Professor Henry A. Ward, and Warner's New Building. There also are several good educational academies and charitable institutions.

The Genesee Falls have several falls, the first of which is 96 ft. high, the second 25 ft. and the third 84 ft.

Charlotte, 7 miles distant, on Lake Ontario, is the port of Rochester.

The route from Rochester to Syracuse, not far from where the Aqueduct, 848 ft. long and with a canal-width of 45 ft., carries the Erie Canal over the Genesee river, has nothing noteworthy. Syracuse has 68,192 inhabitants and very important Salt springs, the most extensive in America. Of the leading High-schools, the University of Syracuse (Methodist) is most prominent. Manufactures and trade in this city are also of a grand scale.

Rome is a thriving city of 12,045 population, and the large railroad-shops and rolling-mills are located here.

Rome is one of the best lumber-markets in the State, and there is excellent water power, the city being situated at the Junction of the Erie and Black River Canals.

The last important town en route for Albany is Utica, situated on the S. bank of the Mohawk. The city has 33,913 inhabitants, extensive and varied manufactures, and is the center of an important railway and canal system. Here is the State Lunatic Asylum and several spacious and pretty buildings.

From Utica the train runs for some time parallel with the Lake Erie, who traverses the State of New York from Buffalo to Albany, and afterwards through the picturesque Mohawk Valley, and alights in the capital of the State of New York, the beautiful city of Albany.

The capital of New York State is finely situated on the W. bank of the Hudson, at the head of the sloop navigation and near the head of the tide water. It was founded by the Dutch as a trading post in 1614, and next to Jamestown in Virginia, was the earliest European settlement in the original 13 States. Its present name was given it in 1664, in honor of the Duke of York and Albany, afterward James II. It was chartered in 1686, and made the State capital in 1798, since which time its population has increased from 5,349 in 1800, to 90,903 in 1880, estimated now, to over 100,000.

Albany has a large commerce, as the entrepot of the great Erie canal from the W. and the Champlain canal from the N., and as the center to which several important railways converge.

The New Capitol, begun in 1871, now nearly finished, is the largest and most splendid edifice in America, the Federal Capitol excepted. Of granite, in Renaissance style and standing on the most elevated ground in the city, with a tower, 320 ft. high, it is visible for miles around. The structure is 300 ft. N. and S. by 400 ft. E. and W.

The State Library in the Capitol numbers 150,000 volumes, and contains a collection of curiosities and historical relics.

The State Geological and Agrictural Hall has valuable collections in Natural History, Geology and Agriculture and many curious relics. The Medical College is a prosperous institution with an extensive Museum, and the Law School of the University of Albany is of great importance. The Dudley Observatory, founded and endowed by Mrs. Blandina Dudley, stands on Observatory Hill, near the limits of the city and has a valuable special library, and some fine apparatus.

The educational institutions of Albany are numerous and efficient, its hospitals and charities noteworthy.

Of the 50 churches in the city, the Cathedral of the Immaculate Conception, seating 4,000 persons, is the pre-eminent.

6 miles above Albany, on the E. bank of the Hudson, and at the head of river navigation is Troy,

with 56,747 inhabitants, containing extensive manufactures of iron, steel, cars, cotton and woolen-goods, hosiery and shoes, and with a large commerce.

The Athenæum, St. Joseph's Theological Seminary, the Rensselaer Polytechnic Institute, this latter, one of the leading schools in America for instruction in civil engineering, are excellent schools of learning.

In West Troy is the great Watervliet Arsenal, with 40 buildings in a park of 105 Acres.

From Albany to New York the trip was made down the Hudson river, the "Rhine" of America.

The beauty and grandeur of the stream; the picturesque sceneries on its banks; the wooded mountains and the hills crowned with pretty villas, and thousand other attractions, make this majestic river to one of the finest in the world. The greater variety, and its superior breadth as well as its stately flow to the sea make it somewhat equal if not superior to the Rhine.

I will only mention a few of the many lovely spots on both sides of the river as coming down from the place of my departure.

The scenery from Albany to Hudson, though pleasing, is somewhat monotonous until Catskill Landing is reached, where there is a little more variety. At Rhinebeck-Landing, opposite Kingston and Rondout, is the Beekman House, 200 years old and the best specimen of an old Dutch Homestead. From New Paltz-Landing, 14 miles distant, I visited Lake Mohonk, a delightful summer resort, situated near the summit of

Sky-Top, one of the loftiest of the Shawangunk Mountains, 1,243 ft. above the river. The largest city between Albany and New York, Poughkeepsie, is reached by ferry from New Paltz-Landing. Built on an elevated plain, nearly 200 ft. above the river, it is backed by high hills. This city has several fine churches, numerous and elegant residences, and no less than eight important educational institutions, including Vassar College, one of the leading female colleges of the world. The buildings of this college, with the main building, 500 ft. in length, are modeled after the Tuileries. North of the city are the vast buildings of the Hudson River State Hospital for the Insane.

Opposite Fishkill-Landing is the handsome built city of Newburg, containing 18,000 inhabitants. Here the Highlands begin. Newburg was the theatre of many interesting events during the Revolution, and Washington's Headquarters, an old gray stone mansion S. of the city, is still preserved as a museum of historical relics. On the W. bank of the river is the picturesque village of Cornwall-Landing. Between the latter place and West Point, in the Highlands, respectively Breakneck and Bacon Hill, 1,187 and 1,685 ft. in height, the mountains are among the most commanding features of the river scenery, and from the summit of the latter New York City may be seen.

West Point is one of the most attractive places on the river. It is the seat of the National Military Academy. Of the most noteworthy buildings, the Cadets' Barracks, the Academy, the Mess Hall and the

Library, containing 26,000 volumes, deserve mention. The Observatory is in the Library Building. The Chapel and the Museum of Ordnance and Trophies are interesting.

From Fort Putnam, on Mount Independence, 600 ft. above the river, fine views are obtained.

The scenery to where the Highlands come to an end is of striking beauty.

Passing the Buttermilk Falls and arriving at Iona Island in whose neighborhood is Sugar-loaf Mountain, at the foot of which is Beverly House, where Benedict Arnold was breakfasting when news came to him of André's arrrest, and whence he fled to the British vessel Vulture, anchored in the stream below, Caldwell's-Landing is reached by ferry. This place is memorable for the costly but futile search after the treasures which the famous pirate, Captain Kidd, was supposed to have secreted at the bottom of the river here.

Peekskill, opposite Caldwell's-Landing, is one of the prettiest towns on the Hudson. Beyond, the former remains of a small Revolutionary fort are seen, and Verplanks Point is notable as the spot where Henry Hudson's ship, the "Half Moon," first came to anchor after leaving Yonkers.

At Croton Point, a prominent head-land, projecting into the river, the Croton River enters the Hudson, and 6 miles down this stream is Croton Lake, which supplies the Metropolis with water. The lake is formed by a dam 250 ft. long, 40 ft. high and 70 ft. thick, and the **water is conveyed to New York by the famous Croton**

Aqueduct, which is over 40 miles long, with 16 tunnels and 24 bridges. Sing Sing occupies an elevated slope, and makes a fine appearance from the river. The State Prison is located here, and its vast stone buildings are conspicuous objects from the steamer. Many fine villas crown the heights above and around the village, looking down upon the Hudson, which at this point attains its greatest breadth.

Nyack, a popular suburban place is opposite Tarrytown, which has many scenic and historic attractions.

By an inscription in the village the spot is marked where André was arrested, and Tarrytown witnessed many fights between guerillas during the Revolution.

It takes its chief interest, however, from its association with Irving's life and writings. Here is the church which he attended, and of which he was warden at the time of his death; here he is buried, and near by are the scenes of some of his happiest fancies, including the immortal Sleepy Hollow and the bridge rendered classic by the legend of Ichabod Crane.

26 miles distant from New York is the village of Irvington, named in honor of Washington Irving, whose unique little cottage at Sunnyside is close by, upon the margin of the river, but hidden from the traveler's view by the dense growth of the surrounding trees and shrubbery. The cottage is a quaint and picturesque structure, and the E. front is embowered in ivy, the earlier slips of which were given to Irving by Sir Walter Scott, at Abbotsford, and planted by Irving himself. In the vicinity of Irvington are many fine

residences, the most conspicuous of which is the Paulding Manor, situated on a high Promontory, and said to be the finest specimen of the Tudor architecture in the United States.

Tappan Zee, 10 miles long and 4 miles wide at the widest part, is a widening out of the river, beginning at Piermont. Tappan, an old town, is interesting as one of Washington's headquarters during the Revolution and as the place where the unfortunate Major André was imprisoned and executed, October the 2d, 1780.

Yonkers, an ancient settlement, was the home of the once famous Phillipse family, of which was Mary Phillipse, Washington's first love.

The desolate and lonely appearance of the cliffs, the so-called Palisades looming up: the distance of New York City is only short.

These Palisades, a series of grand precipices, rising in some places to the height of 300 ft., stretch along the river-bank in unbroken line, for more than 20 miles. The rock is trap, columnar in formation, and the summit thickly wooded.

Passing Fort Washington and affording fine views of the Jersey shore, the northern suburbs, the harbor and the city, the steamer lands in the metropolis, thus ending the brilliant trip.

After a brief stay in New York, making this city my headquarters, I started direct for Chicago, the principal city of Illinois, the metropolis of the West, and the greatest railway centre on the continent. It is situated on the W. shore of Lake Michigan, at the mouth of the Chicago River, in lat. about 41° 50′ N., and lon. 10° 33′ W. from Washington. The city stands on the dividing-ridge between the basins of the Mississippi and St. Lawrence, and is surrounded by a prairie stretching several hundred miles S. and W.

The first white visitors to the site of Chicago were Joliet and Marquette, who arrived in August, 1673. The first permanent settlement was made in 1804, during which year Fort Dearborn was built by the U. S. Government. At the close of 1830, Chicago contained 12 houses and 3 country residences, with a population, composed of whites, half-breeds and blacks, of about 100. It was organized in 1833 and incorporated as a city in 1837. At the first census taken, on July 1st, 1837, the entire population was found to be, 4,170, at the census in 1880, 503,304.

The present population is estimated to exceed 600,000.

Chicago was visited by two conflagrations of enormous dimensions, but one year after the first fire, 1871, a large part of the burned districts had been rebuilt, and the second fire in 1874, though it destroyed 18 blocks in the heart of the city, left no marks after a few months.

Chicago ranks next in commmercial importance to New York among the cities of the Union. As early as 1854, it had become the greatest primary depot for grain in the world; and since then it has also become the greatest grain, live-stock, and lumber market in the world.

The manufactures of Chicago are extensive and important, employing about 150,000 persons, and including iron and steel works, factories of car-wheels, cars, and other railroad appliances, flour mills, furniture-factories, manufactories of boots and shoes, and tanneries. They number about 4,000, the annual product being over 300 millions of dollars worth.

There are 25 elevators of enormous storage capacity and 26 railways enter the city.

Most of the public buildings were burned down in the great fire, and have not been replaced as rapidly as the business structures. The New City Hall and County Court House, nearly completed, is estimated to $5,000,000. The Custom House and Post Office, the Board of Trade Building and the Exposition Building are among the finest in the city.

There are over 300 churches in Chicago, of which are the most prominent: Unity Church, Twelfth Street Church and the Roman Catholic Cathedral.

The Public Library contains 92,000 volumes. The Academy of Sciences established in 1857, has lost a valuable collection of 38,000 specimens in the fire. The Art Institute, the University of Chicago, Dearborn Observatory, the Baptist Theological Seminary, the St. Ignatius College, the Presbyterian Theological Seminary, Rush Medical College, the College of Physicians and Surgeons, Woman's Medical College, Chicago Medical College and the Hahnemann College, are the most famous literary and educational institutions.

Among the many hospital and charitable establishments, the following deserve special mention: Cook County Hospital, Mercy Hospital, Michael Reese Hospital, maintained by the United Hebrew Relief Association, the Newsboys' Home, Foundlings Home, Home for the Friendless, Protestant Orphan Asylum, St. Joseph's (male) and St. Mary's (female) Orphan Asylums and the Old People's Home.

The U. S. Marine Hospital is one of the largest and costliest in the United States.

The Public Parks of Chicago are nicely laid out and the Lincoln Park contains the Zoological Garden.

The Water Works of Chicago are worth being inspected.

The intercourse between the three divisions of the city is effected by 35 bridges, which span the river at intervals of two squares, and swing on central pivots to admit the passage of vessels, These bridges, however, are a serious impediment to navigation, as well as to vehicles and pedestrians; and in order to obviate the inconvenience, a tunnel was constructed under the South Branch. It is 1,608 ft. long, with a descent of 45 ft. Another similar tunnel, whose total length is 1,890 ft. was constructed under the main river in 1870, connecting the North and South Division.

The Union Stock Yards where the vast live-stock trade of the city is transacted, comprise 345 acres, of which 146 are in pens and have 32 miles of drainage, 8 miles of streets and alleys, 2,300 gates. They have capacity for 25,000 cattle, 100,000 hogs, 22,000 sheep, and 1,200 horses. Connected therewith are the Packing and Slaughtering houses, whence are shipped annually ten million pounds of hog product alone.

The Grain Elevators are a very interesting feature, all situated on the banks of the river.

About 16 miles S. of Chicago is the unique city of Pullman. It is named after the inventor of the Pullman Sleeping Cars. From 5,000 to 6,000 workers are employed in the shops, where the cars are manufactured. Adjoining Pullman are S. Chicago and Grand Crossing, which contain rolling-mills, iron and steel-mills, and many of the larger manufactures.

The distance between Chicago and Milwaukee, in Wisconsin, is 85 miles.

The road via Milwaukee Division of the Chicago and Northwestern R. R. runs along the W. shore of Lake Michigan, through a rich farming, well-cultivated and populous country. A few miles beyond Waukegan the train crosses the boundary line and enters Wisconsin, soon reaching Kenosha, with 8,000 inhabitants, important manufactures and a large trade in the products of the surrounding country. 11 miles from here is the academic city of Racine, the second city of the State in population and commerce. Situated on the mouth of Root river, its harbor is one of the best on the lake, its commerce very large and the varied and extensive manufactures are the chief source of the city's wealth. Racine College (Episcopal), is one of the most prominent in the United States.

Milwaukee, the commercial capital of Wisconsin, and next to Chicago the largest city in the Northwest, is situated on the W. shore of the Lake Michigan, at the mouth of Milwaukee river.

This river flows through the city, and with the Menomonee, with which it forms a junction, divides it into 3 nearly equal districts.

The climate is peculiarly bracing and healthful and the atmosphere remarkably clear and pure. The city is regularly laid out.

Milwaukee was settled in 1835, and incorporated as a city in 1846. Its population in 1880, was 115,-578. The Germans constitute fully one half of the entire population.

The commerce of Milwaukee is very large, wheat and flour being the most important articles. There are six grand grain elevators and the flour mills are on an immense scale. Butter, wool, hides and lumber are also important articles of trade. Its manufactures are extensive and embrace the highly esteemed and widely exported Lager-bier, pig-iron and iron castings, leather, machinery, agricultural implements, steam-boilers, car-wheels, furniture, and tobacco and cigars. Pork-packing is extensively carried on.

Most all streets are well shaded. The County Court House and the U. S. Custom House with the Post-Office are exceedingly fine structures.

The Northwestern National Asylum, for disabled soldiers, is an immense building. The Academy of Music, with seats for 2,300 persons, owned by the German Musical Society, and the Opera-House are handsome edifices.

The Grain-Elevator of the Chicago, Milwaukee and St. Paul and the Chicago and Northwestern Railways, is well worth a visit, since it is considered to be the largest in the Union.

The Rolling-mill at Bay View, outside the city limits, is one of the most extensive in the West.

Two of the flour-mills in Milwaukee manufacture daily 1,200, respectively 1,000 barrels of flour.

Leaving Milwaukee, via La Crosse and St. Paul Division of the Chicago, Milwaukee and St. Paul R. R., the first city on this route, Portage City, an important place, with 5,000 inhabitants, large manufactures, and containing a High-school and the workshops of the R. R. Company, was reached. I passed Tomah and Sparta, on the La Crosse river, two flourishing villages in a fertile valley and arrived at La Crosse, on the E. bank of the Mississippi, at the mouth of the Black and La Crosse rivers. It is finely situated on a level prairie, has many handsome buildings, a High-school, flourishing graded schools and an extensive trade in lumber, contains 9 saw-mills, 3 foundries and machine-shops, a large factory of saddlery and harness and various other establishments. Population, 15,000.

On the same line lies the small, but prosperous city of Winona. The First State Normal School is located here, as is the High-School. Winona is one of the most important lumber-distributing points on the Upper Mississippi, and as a grain-shipping-point it ranks among the first in the Northwest. Manufacturing is also extensively carried on in this little city with 10,208 inhabitants.

Madison was my next stopping-point. This capital of the State has about 12,000 inhabitants and is a flourishing commercial centre. It lies in the very heart of the "Four-Lake Country," so called from a chain of beautiful lakes which extend over a distance of 16 miles, and discharge their surplus waters into Yahara or Catfish River, a tributary of Rock River. They are named: Mendota, or Fourth Lake, Monona, or Third Lake, and Lakes Wanbesa and Kegonsa. The city lies between Lakes Mendota and Monona. It contains the State Capitol, the Court House and Jail, the Post Office and U. S. Court House, the University of Wisconsin, the Washburn University, (with a telescope whose glass is second only to that in the National Observatory), the State Hospital for the Insane, the Wisconsin Historical Society, (with an interesting collection of relics and a valuable library of 110,000 volumes), and many handsome churches.

Beyond Madison, the St. Paul train passes many small places of no interest, until Prairie du Chien, a town of about 3,000 inhabitants, situated on the E. bank of the Mississippi, 2 miles above the mouth of the Wisconsin is reached. This place is in the midst of a beautiful prairie, 9 miles long, and 1 mile wide, bordered on the E. by high bluffs.

It is an important local shipping point and has varied and important manufactures. The St. John's

College and St. Mary's female institute are under control of Roman Catholics.

Faribault, one of the most populous and prosperous interior towns in the State, was the last place in Wisconsin which I visited. In 1853 it was the site of Alexander Faribault's trading-post. Its population in 1880 was 5,500, and here are the State Asylum for the Deaf and Dumb and Blind, an Episcopal Academy, several flour-mills, foundries and saw-mills.

Between Faribault and St. Paul, Minnesota, in Northfield, are located, Carlton College, (Congregational) and St. Olaf's College, (Lutheran).

The "Badger State," Wisconsin, has its name from the river, an Indian word signifying "Wildrushing River." First settled by French at Green Bay, 1669; organized as a Territory, 1836; first territorial legislature at Belmont, September 1st, 1836; admitted as a State, 1847.

Area, 56,040 square miles; greatest length, 300 miles; greatest breadth, 260 miles; Mississippi River navigable throughout south-west boundary; excellent harbors in Lake Superior on north, and Lake Michigan on east.

Port Washington one of the finest natural harbors in the world.

Temperature at Milwaukee: winter, 19° to 31°; summer, 63° to 70°; rainfall, 30 inches.

Population of Eau Claire, 21,668, and of Fond du Lac, 12,726.

Number of farms, 102,904; average value per acre,

cleared land, $26.27; woodland, $19.55. Wheat most valuable crop; cultivation of flax increasing; many acres devoted to culture of cranberries.

Extensive lead mines in Grant, Lafayette and Iowa counties; native copper in the north, in Crawford and Iowa counties. Milwaukee clay famous for making cream-colored brick. Iron ores in Dodge, Sauk, Jackson and Ashland counties.

Ranks second in hops.

Population, inclusive 5,576 Colored and 2,695 Indians: 1,563,423.

Betters and duelists excluded from voting.

Number of colleges, 7; number of public schools, 6,588; school population, 495,233; school age, 4–20.

St. Paul, the capital of Minnesota, with 125,000 inhabitants, is a beautiful city and is situated on both banks of the Mississippi River.

The streets are well graded and partially paved. The principal public buildings are the State Capitol, the U. S. Custom House, containing the Post Office, and the Court House and City Hall, in progress. The Grand Opera House has seats for 2,300 persons, and the Exposition Building is, like the former, a fine place of amusement. There are 75 churches in the city, 4 public and as many private libraries, those of the Historical Society and Library Association comprising together about 24,000 volumes. The Academy of Sciences contains about 126,000 specimens in natural history. There are three free hospitals, and a Protestant and Roman Catholic Orphan Asylum.

Carver's Cave is a great curiosity of nature, containing a lake which may be crossed in a boat, and Fountain Cave, about 2 miles above the city, was apparently hollowed out of the rock by a stream which flows through it. It contains several chambers, the largest being 100 ft. long, 25 wide and 20 high. White Bear Lake and Bald-Eagle Lake are popular resorts with picturesque sceneries.

Minnehaha Falls, immortalized by Longfellow's poem, are romantically situated. The commerce of the city is very extensive.

10 miles above St. Paul, is Minneapolis, on both sides of the Mississipi, built on a broad esplanade overlooking the famous falls of St. Anthony. The city is regularly laid out, has wide and straight streets, with 2 rows of trees on each side and many substantial business blocks and elegant residences. The City Hall, Court House, Chamber of Commerce, the Lumber Exchange and the Minneapolis Exposition are noticeable structures.

The Athenæum Library contains 8,000 volumes and that of the University of Minnesota, 13,000. The last named and the High-School are important institutions, but there are numerous good public and private schools.

The prosperity of the city is owing to the abundant water-power, for manufacturing purposes, from the Falls of St. Anthony. The fall is 18 ft. perpendicular, with a rapid descent of 82 ft. within 2 miles. The rapids above the cataract are finer than the fall itself.

Minneapolis is the center of immense lumber and flour interests, being the largest flour-manufacturing place in America. Its population is about 129,000. The value of the flouring-mill products is estimated at about $22,000,000 annually.

I extended my explorations in this State as far as to the boundary-line between the United States and Canada via St. Paul and Duluth R. R. and visited en route the city of Duluth.

The commercial importance of this place, which has about 17,500 inhabitants, derives from its situation at the extreme west point of the Great Lakes, lying on the shore of Lake Superior, near the mouth of the St. Louis river. It is the terminus of 5 rail roads. The city is well-built and contains many fine public buildings; its manufactures, especially in lumber, are extensive.

The North Shore of Lake Superior is comparatively an unknown region. North of Duluth the shore rises into grand cliffs of greenstone and porphyr, 800 to 1,000 ft. in height. The Palisades, 58 miles from Duluth, are a remarkable rock formation, presenting vertical columns from 60 to 100 ft. high, and from 1 to 6 ft. in diameter.

Near by, Baptism river comes dashing down to the lake in a series of wild water-falls. At a distance of 53 miles from the Palisades, Pigeon River is the boundary-line between the United States and Canada; and here begins the "Grand Portage," a series of lakes and streams, beyond which are Saskatchewan and Manitoba.

The "Gopher State," Minnesota, named from the river; term of Indian origin, signifying "Whitish or Sky-colored water." Explored by Hennepin and La Salle, 1680; Fort Snelling, built 1819; organized as a Territory, 1849; admitted, 1858.

Area, 83,365 square miles, extreme length, 380 miles; breadth near north line, 337 miles; near middle, 183 miles; and on the south line, 262 miles.

Temperature at St. Paul: winter, 11° to 30°; summer, 67° to 74°. Rainfall at Fort Snelling, 25 inches.

Pembina, port of entry on Red river.

Number of farms, 140,000; value per acre, cleared land, $20; woodland, $15.

Total acreage of the State, 53,353,600; in farms, 16,000,000; in forests, 1,800,000.

Wheat the staple, and milling the great industry, giving employment to 4,000 people.

Ranks fourth in wheat and barley.

Dairy interests increasing in value, production of butter and cheese becoming one of the great industries.

Population, 1,118,486, inclusive 1,814 Colored, 99 Chinese, and 1,215 Indians.

Number of colleges, 5; school population, 400,000; school age, 5-21.

Resuming my journey on the Northern Pacific R. R., I reached Moorhead, a town of 5,000 inhabitants on the Red River and the centre of an important trade and thriving manufactures, also the seat of an Episcopal

College. Fargo, on the opposite side of the Red River, is the first station in Dakota, has a population of 10,000, and is regarded as the future commercial center of Dakota. Fargo and Moorhead base their prosperity on the fact that they are the entrepots of the wheat-growing interests. Brick is manufactured here extensively, and there are many other manufactures and the car-shops and round-houses of the R. R. Company.

Bismarck, the territorial capital, situated on the E. bank of the Missouri River, has a population of 5,000. Many fine public buildings and a Catholic seminary are in this city, and there is a lively trade carried on by four lines of steamers with the region of the Upper Missouri.

Mandan on the W. bank of the Missouri, has 2,000 inhabitants. The Missouri River is spanned by a fine iron railroad bridge, and another iron wagon bridge gives access to Fort Abraham Lincoln. Reaching the twin towns of Medora and Little Missouri, lying on the E. and W. banks of the Missouri, 240 ft. apart, the headquarters of several large stock-raising companies are found to be located there as well as the Northern Pacific Refrigerator Car Company's shops, and the extensive abattoirs of the Marquis de Mores, a young French gentleman, who has thousands of cattle on the range and is doing an extensive trade in shipping dressed beef. In the vicinity are valuable coal mines. This is also the central point of Pyramid Park, being but 4 miles distant from Cedar Cañon, and 6 miles from the burning coal-mines.

Between here and the boundary of Montana is the geologically interesting region of the so-called "Bad Lands."

From Glendive, on the Yellewstone River, a distance of 80 miles, Fort Budford is reached by stage.

Miles City, on the Yellowstone, at the mouth of Tongue River, has many fine buildings and 3,000 population. There is a 14 mile ditch for irrigation and valuable lignite mines in the near vicinity. 2 miles farther on the railroad is Fort Keogh, a military post of 10 companies, and passing a number of stations, among which is Custer, deriving its name from Fort Custer, the largest post in the territory, 30 miles S., reached also by stage, Billings, on the Yellowstone River, with 1,500 population, is entered into. Here are the R. R. Company's repair-shops, and from here large shipments of cattle, wool, hides, and bullion are made. The Maginnis Mines, Fort Benton and other important points of valuable grazing, mining, and agricultural regions are reached by stages.

At the fort of the Belt Mountains, about midway between the Great Lakes and the Pacific Coast and at the last crossing of the Yellowstone River, is Livingston, with a population of 2,600.

It has the largest railroad round-house and machine-shops between Brainerd and Portland. Large deposits of iron, lime and sand-stone, silver ore, and bituminous coal exist in close proximity. Lumber, lime and brick are manufactured in the town. White Sulphur

Springs are 65 miles to the N. These Springs contain remarkable medicinal qualities.

The Yellowstone Park Branch diverges here and runs to Cinnabar and from the end of the railway the "Wonderland" of the United States is reached by stage, in 6 miles.

Dakota, so called from a tribe of Indians of the same name had its first settlements at Pembina, made by Lord Selkirk, 1812. It was organized as a Territory, 1861, and had its first legislature at Yankton, March 1862.

Area, 149,100 square miles; average length, 450 miles; breadth, 350 miles; ranks in size next to Texas and California.

General elevation, 1,000 to 2,500 ft.; Red River frontage, about 250 miles; the Missouri navigable throughout the territory.

Temperature at Bismarck: winter 4° to 27°; summer, 63° to 71°. Climate dry, and cold not so penetrating as in moister regions further east. Rainfall at Fort Randall, 17 inches; 73 per cent. of year's rain falls in spring and summer.

Yankton is the chief town of the South.

Dakota is the finest wheat-growing country on the continent. Nutritious grasses at all seasons and abundant water offer remarkable advantages for stock-raising; wool growing an important industry; climate especially favorable for sheep. Ranks fourth in gold, and mineral wealth centred in Black Hills; coal found in workable quantities west of the Missouri.

Population, 135,177 in 1880, with sufficient increase since then to entitle her to admission as a State. In the population are included 401 Negroes, 238 Chinese, and 1,391 Indians.

The Yellowstone National Park, which Congress has set apart as a public park for the benefit and enjoyment of the people, is situated partly in Wyoming and partly in Montana.

It is 65 miles N. and S. by 55 miles E. and W., comprises 3,575 square miles, and is all more than 7,000 ft. above the sea. Yellowstone Lake has an altitude of 7,788 ft.; and the mountain-ranges that hem in the valleys on every side rise to the height of 10,000 and 12,000 ft. and are covered with perpetual snow.

The entire region was at a comparatively recent geological period the scene of remarkable volcanic activity, the last stages of which are still visible in the hot springs and geysers. In these the Park surpasses all the rest of the world. There are probably 50 geysers that throw a column of water to a height of form 50 to 200 ft. and nearly 10,000 springs, chiefly of 2 kinds, those depositing lime and those depositing silica. There is every variety of color, and the deposits form around their borders the most elaborate ornamentation. The temperature of the calcareous springs is from 160° to 170°; that of the others rises to 200° or more.

The chief points of interest are, the Mammoth Hotel Terraces, the Norris Geyser Basin, extending from the Lake of the Woods to Madison river, the

Mammoth Paint-Pots, at the foot of Mount Johnson, the Monument Geyser Basin, on the top of Mount Schurz, in which is the Prismatic Cañon, the Ebony Basin, containing Walpurgia Lake, and the Black Warrior Geyser. On the N. of the park are the sources of the Yellowstone; on the W. those of the principal forks of the Missouri; on the S. W. and S. those of Snake river, flowing into the Columbia, and those of Greene river, a branch of the Great Colorado, which enters into the Gulf of California; while on the S. E. side are the numerous head-waters of Wind river.

The Yellowstone River, a tributary of the Missouri, is the most extraordinary river on the American continent; its source is near S. E. corner of the park in the Yellowstone Lake, 12 miles long and 10 to 15 wide, 7,788 ft. above the sea, and nearly inclosed by snow-clad mountains, rising 3,000 to 5,000 ft. higher. 15 miles below the lake are the Upper Falls, and $\frac{1}{4}$ of a mile farther down the majestic Lower Falls, which are 360 ft. high.

Below the Lower Falls the river flows for 20 miles through the Grand Cañon, whose perpendicular sides, from 600 to 1,500 ft. apart, rise to the height of 1,200 to 1,500 ft. Below the Grand Cañon, the river receives Tower Creek, which flows for 30 ft. through a gloomy and pretty deep cañon, the Devil's Den, 600 ft. above its mouth the creek pours over an abrupt descent of 156 ft., thus **forming a most beautiful and picturesque fall.**

The most remarkable group of hot springs in the world is the Mammoth or White Mountain Hot Springs. Many of these springs are dead, but the calcareous deposits from them cover an area of about 2 square miles. The springs in activity extend from the river's edge to nearly 1,000 ft. in elevation. The Sulphur Mountain, rising from an almost level plain to a height of 150 ft., is perforated with numerous fissures and craters, from which sulphurous vapor pours forth in abundance.

Close by are some Boiling Mud Springs, and a few miles above the Sulphur Mountain is the Mud Volcano, which has broken out from the side of a well-timbered hill. This volcano is in a constant state of ebullition, throwing up masses of boiling mud and sending up dense columns of steam which rise several hundred feet and are seen for miles around.

The Great Geysers of the Yellowstone region are situated on the Fire-Hole river, the middle fork of the Madison in the W. portion of the park. They form 2 large groups, the Upper and Lower Geyser Basins. Most of the Springs and Geysers are near the river. Their average temperature is over 170°, that of the air 67°. Among these, the "Old Faithful," the "Giantess," the "Grand Geyser" and "Giant Geyser," are the most prominent, the waters of which are thrown up in columns to a height of from 100 to 250 ft. The Castle, the Grotto, the Punch-bowl, the Riverside, the Soda, and the Fan Geysers, and numerous others which have not been named, are worthy of notice.

Passing Bozeman, with 2,500 population and several

flour and plaining mills, and where coal, gold, silver, iron and copper are found nearby, the military post of Fort Ellis is 3 miles E. on the railroad, and after Gallatin, at the head of the Missouri river and Townsend are passed, Helena, the territorial capital, is reached, already described by me. An excursion to the Gregory mine district, one of the most productive in the world, was worth making.

Montana was formerly a part of Idaho; became a Territory, 1864; and received about 2,000 square miles from Dakota in 1873.

Area, 146,080 square miles; length, east and west, 460 to 540 miles; average breadth, 275 miles. Drained by the Missouri and its tributaries and the tributaries of the Colorado. Through the E. portion run the small tributaries of the Missouri and the Yellowstone in every direction, while a great number of small rivers, tributary to Flathead and Missoula rivers, forming one of the forks of the Columbia, water the W. section of the territory.

Temperature at Virginia City: winter, 17° to 30°, summer, 55° to 65°; rainfall seldom exceeds 12 inches per annum. Immense area of cultivable land; cereal productions are very large, some varieties of corn grown in portions of Territory, but generally too cold.

Grazing interest of value; estimated area of valuable grazing land, 100,000 square miles; great extent of plains and mountain valleys yet untouched by herdsmen.

Montana is one of the richest mining countries in

the world; mineral wealth almost inexhaustible; the production in 1882 amounted to about 7 millions of Dollars, of which $\frac{2}{3}$ was silver and $\frac{1}{3}$ gold.

Manufacturing interests mainly smelting works, and flour and lumber mills.

Ranks fifth in silver and in gold.

Population, 39,159, including 346 Negroes, 1,765 Chinese, and 1,663 Indians.

School population, 10,482; school age, 4 to 21, graded schools in Deer Lodge City, Virginia City and Helena.

Resuming my journey to Denver, Colorado, by way of Salt Lake City, on the Union Pacific R. R., I intended to stay in Denver for some time and to explore the interior of Colorado, but especially to study the Geology of the Rocky Mountains. After the required rest, I started first to Central City, a prosperous mining-town with 2,500 inhabitants, beautifully situated on mountain slopes, at an elevation of 8,300 ft. There are a number of quartz-mills here, and being in the centre of a very rich gold-mining region, it has great business. From here I travelled through Clear Creek Valley to Idaho Springs, a nice little village, beautifully situated in a lovely valley, among lofty mountain-ranges, 7,800 ft. above the sea. The chief attractions are the hot and cold mineral springs containing magnesia, soda, iron and lime, considered to be remedial in rheumatic diseases, and as they are chiefly for bathing there are extensive bathing establishments.

12 miles beyond the Springs is the important

mining town of Georgetown, situated on S. Clear Creek, at a height of 8,412 ft., one of the highest towns in the world. It is surrounded by hills and has many interesting spots in the neighborhood and is the starting point for Gray's Peak, 14,251 ft. above the sea. The mountain view from the Peak is undescribably grand.

En route for Graymont, and just before Silver Plume, the R. R. (Colorado Central, branch of the Union Pacific) describes a double curvature, the so-called Loop, considered to be one of the wonders of American railroad-engineering, without any other equal in the world than the railroad line between Vera Cruz and Orizaba in Mexico. Graymont is at the foot of the aforesaid Gray's Peak.

On the second excursion, Colorado Springs, whose name is misleading, since the Springs are 5 miles distant from here, in Manitou Springs, was visited. Colorado Springs is a flourishing village, situated on the plains, with a fine view of the mountains.

Manitou Springs, the "Saratoga of Colorado," are situated among the foot-hills at the base of Pike's Peak, and on the banks of the beautiful Fontaine Creek. The waters, containing sulphur, soda and iron, have great tonic effects. The romantic Ute Pass and the Ute Falls are in the nearest neighborhood, the latter descending in an unbroken sheat over a precipice 50 ft. high. The picturesque Williams Cañon, 15 miles long with rocky-walls, rising 6 to 800 ft. above a very narrow pass below, are also in the vicinity.

Manitou is on the trail to Pike's Peak, reached on

horse-back in about 11 to 12 hours. The view from its summit, 14,300 ft. high, embraces many thousand square miles of plain and mountain, and it stands on the edge of a great mountain-range. Here is a station of the Weather-Signal Bureau, occupied summer and winter.

A few miles E. of Manitou Springs, on the plain, the so-called Mesa (table), are wonderful formations of sandstone.

2 miles from Manitou is the "Garden of the Gods," a little mountain-valley. The road enters it through the "Beautiful Gate," a narrow passage-way between two high ledges of cliffs, in whose center a rock pillar, 30 ft. in height, stands, thus still further narrowing the passage-way. The garden consists of a tract of land of about 450 acres in extent, hemmed in by mountains and bordered by red sandstone cliffs and is almost shut in from the plains.

1 mile from the Garden, at "Glen Eyrie," are similar formations of isolated rocks, one of these, the Major Domo, rising to a height of 120 ft., while at its base, it is not more than 10 ft. in diameter.

Glen Eyrie is a beautiful mountain-gorge, and closed in on every side by cliffs, whilst a lovely mountain-brook traverses it from one end to the other. Up the rugged Queen's Cañon is the Devil's Punch Bowl, romantic cascades and rapids. Cheyenne Cañon, 9 miles from Manitou, has picturesque cascades and beautiful rock-formations.

The most visited spot in Colorado, also 9 miles from

Manitou Springs, "Monument Park," is very striking, and filled with phantastic groups of eroded sandstone, from 5 to 50 ft. high, almost a unique in the West. They are on each side of the Park, which is not quite one mile in length, and mostly ranged along the low hills of the same.

Caves with peculiar interior formations of stalactites and stalagmites are also here to be found, the Grand Cavern, 9,000 ft. above the sea, has magnificent detail-formations.

Pueblo, the most important city in South Colorado, was my next aim.

This city is situated at the confluence of Arkansas River and Fontaine Creek. It is the center of a vast and rich agricultural and grazing region, does a very large trade, and has a population of about 4,000, there are several extensive iron-smelting-works.

From Pueblo the Leadville Division of the Denver and Rio Grande R. R. runs N. W. to Cañon City, near which is Talbott Hill, where Professor Marsh has excavated some of the most remarkable fossils ever discovered. Beyond Cañon City, the Grand Cañon of the Arkansas is entered. The Arkansas river cuts here its way for 8 miles through mountain walls of granite, in some places 3,000 ft. perpendicularly. The beauty of the scenery at the Royal Gorge is of an extraordinary brilliancy, and here the track runs for 200 ft. along an iron bridge suspended over the river by steel girders fastened in the rocks on both sides. Beyond the Royal Gorge the land widens and offers magnificent views of the Sangre de Christo mountainchain in the S. flanking the "Sierra Blanca," the highest point in the Rocky Mountains, 14,650' above the level of the sea.

Between Cañon City and Salida nothing noteworthy is found, except a insignificant little place, bearing the somewhat strange name Cotopaxi.

I stayed one day in Salida and ascended the following day the famous "Marshall Pass," 10,800' above the sea, and forming the natural divide between the Atlantic and Pacific Ocean. E. of the Pass the waters flow toward the Arkansas river who discharges into the Mississippi, and on the W. toward the Gunnison, the latter emptying in the Grand river. The Grand river in junction with the Green river forms the Colorado river who discharges in the Gulf of California.

The view from this Pass is exceedingly fine, especially to the Mount Ouray in the Sangre de Christo mountains. There are many snow-sheds on the Pass to prevent snow-slides. The most important place on the other side of the mountain-chain (the continental divide), is Gunnison, with about 5,000 inhabitants. It is the great outfitting center of the region, and the trade growing out of mining interests is very large. It is very cold here in winter, already in November 26° below Zero=$25\frac{1}{2}$ (cold) R.

About $1\frac{1}{2}$ hours by rail, W. of Gunnison, is the famous Black Cañon of the Gunnison river. Of all the accessible cañons in the country, this is the grandest, the almost perpendicular descent is 2,000 ft. and the river which penetrates this cañon is very rich in mountain-trouts.

After visiting the Cañon I returned to Gunnison.

A lake, on a mountain S. of Cimaron, has disappeared the year previous my arrival in consequence of an earthquake and even the mountain itself had been transformed; this must have caused great sensation, since concussions of the earth in this high-plateau, averaging 7,000′, are very rare.

I started from Gunnison by the South Park Branch of the Union Pacific R. R. in a northeasterly direction and arrived in Leadville the next morning.

On this road lies the highest railroad pass in the country, the Alpine Pass, 11,650 ft. above the sea. The view from this Pass exceeds all others in the State and is almost beyond description.

The city of Leadville is 10,200 ft. above the ocean, considered to be the highest town in the world, and is in the very heart of the Silver El Dorado, discovered 1878. It has over 18,000 inhabitants, and is the most celebrated mining-camp in the West.

The mineral wealth promises to last for an indefinite period of time. The city itself has more of a prosaic than a romantic character, but the surroundings are marvellously pretty, especially the mountain chain of the Divide, W. of the city, with the picturesque Mount Elbert. E. of the city is the Mosquito Range, most of the mining works at its western slope. Here are Fryer Hill, Carbonate Hill, and Yankee Hill. All the mines in this region are known as the Carbonate Camp, on account of the silver found with carbonate of lead.

The mountains in which silver is found are of the lime formation and in the fissures are the ores, and the silver is between a whitish Porphyr and dolomitic lime-stone.

Long before the discovery of the Carbonate Camp, gold was found in the neighborhood, and the place named by California prospectors and diggers, the California Gulch, and another place above the former: Oro.

Here it was, where the Governor and Senator Tabor of Colorado—the same man, whom the State of Colorado owes a great deal of its devolopment and its consequent progress and prosperity—had been digging gold.

The total value of ore produced for 1880, the last census year, was $15,025,153. 14 miles from Leadville are the celebrated twin Lakes, nearly 2 miles above the sea-level.

There are but a few lakes in the Rocky Mountains.

The smelting-works are of gigantic dimensions, rivaling with those of Pueblo and Denver. The refining is done in Omaha (Nebraska) and in Baltimore (Maryland); copper-ores are sent to Swansea, England.

The climate of Leadville is very agreeable, cool in summer and not very cold in the winter, the temperature of Denver lower than that of Leadville, but there is more snow in winter in the latter.

After close inspections of the prominent mines, as for instance, the Galena and Carbonate mines, etc., I returned to Denver by way of the South Park line, on which the two mountain-chains of the Mosquito and Park ranges, running parallel, and a Pass, 11,000 ft. in height, have to be crossed. Up to Breckenridge, in the valley, there is nothing of extra ordinary note, but when Como is reached, the mountain scenery is of unusual splendor and brilliancy.

Beyond this place, the lovely South Park (one of the many parks in the interior of the Rocky Mountains) has to be traversed. North, Middle, South and San Luis Parks are the most prominent of them. San Luis Park lies in a region where many Mexican live and where Spanish predominates.

All these Parks are dryed-out lake bottoms, and are variously situated, some at an altitude of from 7,000 to 9,000 ft. above the sea.

E. of the South Park, the so-called Kenosha range, 10,000 ft. high, has to be crossed and on the other side is the Platte cañon, very picturesqe, and the risingpoint of the South Platte river, the same on which the city of Denver is situated, and who, in junction with the North Platte, empties into the Missouri.

Once in the plains, the beautiful city of Denver was soon reached, and a Siesta taken.

The Southwest of the State has a great future, though the mining interest undeveloped and almost in its infancy. The beauties of Nature are of marvelous splendour, and it is surprising to find the means of communication and transportation by rail in such a neglected and pitiable condition.

Denver, the capital and largest city of Colorado, is

situated on the S. bank of the South Platte river, at the junction of Cherry Creek, 15 miles from the E. base of the Rocky Mountains, and about 500 miles W. of the Missouri river. It occupies a series of plateaus, facing the mountains, and commanding a grand and beautiful view. Pike's and Long's Peaks, as well as the snow-covered summits of the range, extending more than 200 miles are seen from here. Denver is the commercial center of Colorado, and beautifully built, mostly of brick, manufactured in the vicinity. The trade of the city is very large, and from it 5 railways radiate. The public buildings are handsome and extensive and the private residences very beautiful.

Denver possesses the Denver University, the U. S. Branch Mint, and among its chief structures are: the Court House, City Hall, Chamber of Commerce, the Tabor Opera House, the Railroad depot, several breweries and factories and a few good hotels. The Denver Smelting and Refining Works occupy a very large building, with a capacity of 40 tons of ore per diem.

According to the census of 1880, it had a population of 35,630, but estimated now to have 80,000 inhabitants.

Intending to return to Denver later on, I started for Santa Fé, in New Mexico.

La Junta, situated on the Atchison, Topeka and Santa Fé R. R., is the junction with the main line which extends to all points of New Mexico and Arizona. The next important place is Trinidad, lying at the foot of the Raton Mountains, with a population of 5,000.

It is the center of a large mining business and cattle trade. The city presents a true Mexican type with its mixture of brick and adobe houses. 14 miles distant from here, at Morley, the road climbs through the Raton Pass on the mountains on a grade of 185 feet to the mile. Ascending the "Devil's Cañon," as it is called, the Spanish Peaks, 100 miles to the N., are distinctly visible, and 5 miles further up the mountain, at a height of 7,688 ft., the train suddenly plunges into a tunnel, ½ a mile in length.

While coming through the tunnel the border has been crossed and one finds himself in the territory of New Mexico.

Las Vegas, in that territory is reached, and the brightness of sunny New Mexico manifests itself at once. Las Vegas, on a branch of the Pecos River, has 1,500 inhabitants and is the trade-centre of the great sheep-ranches of New Mexico.

A branch line connects the city with Las Vegas Hot Springs, the attractive sanitarium. It is situated at the mouth of a beautiful cañon, and the Springs have an altitude of 6,400 ft. At Lamy, named in honor of the Archbishop of New Mexico, etc., the railroad branches to the interesting and historic city of Santa Fé. This place is the oldest town in the United States, has a population of 5,500, and is the seat of an archiepiscopal diocese, a convent and of 2 ancient Roman Catholic churches, of which the Church of "Nuestra Señora de Guadalupe" is very famous. It is a center of mining interests. Among the great curiosities of its relics is the ancient Governor's Palace, a long and low structure, built of adobe, extending on one side of the Plaza, where the Soldiers' Monument stands, and which was erected in honor of those who fell in the Indian and the late civil wars. On the N. E. outskirts of the city is the military post of Fort Marcy. Santa Fé is mostly built of adobe and its streets present a very picturesque commingling of Americans, Mexicans and Indians.

Resuming my journey from Lamy, I arrived at Albuquerque, a town of over 4,000 population, situated on the Rio Grande River, at an elevation of 5,000 ft. above the sea. This place, with its modern structures and its extensive trade in wool and hides, etc., is one of the most flourishing and prosperous cities in New Mexico. The vineyards of the Jesuits are well cultivated and the grand Cathedral in the old part of the city, 2 miles distant, is a beautiful edifice. Not far from here is the famous institution in which children of different Indian tribes are educated.

The train runs through a region full of fine sheep and cattle ranches till it reaches the great mother ridge of the Rocky Mountains at Continental Divide (a station). Wingate, 3 miles from Fort Wingate, is a busy little town, and from here stages run to the Indian village of Zuni, 45 miles N., famous through the researches of Mr. F. Cushing, who has found among these Indians relics of a high and mysterious civilization.

Passing Manuelito, where a stage-line runs to Fort Defiance, the headquarters of the Navajo Agency, Holbrook, is reached. I visited the Moqui Indian Village, 70 miles away, and found the same well worth a visit. These Indian towns, built on eminences, are so situated that they can only be approached through a narrow defile. The houses are 2 or 3 stories high, built of mud and stone, and ranged in the form of hollow squares. Access can only be had by ladders to the second stories, the first being built solid without any opening. There are seven of these Moqui Pueblos, or Dying Cities, as they have been called, and of which Zuni is the chief, and the inhabitants have often and deeply excited the curiosity of archaeologists. They are skilled in pottery, weaving and mural decorations, and their religious rites are of a very strange nature.

At Cañon Diablo, the scenery is very sombre and impressive, and the railroad spans the mighty chasm by a bridge 500 ft. long and 225 ft. high.

From Peach Springs is the departing point for the Grand Cañon of the Colorado, one of the greatest natural wonders in the world.

The Grand Cañon of Colorado was made known to the world only a few years ago by the adventurous voyage of my worthy friend, the Major Powell, down the river. The Colorado river is formed by the Grand and Green rivers, which unite in Utah, and flows southward into Arizona. It passes through a succession of remarkable cañons, but all of these preliminary wonders sink into insignificance before the Grand Cañon, which is more than 300 miles long. The Cañon opens all the series of geological strata down to the granite foundation.

The walls are from 3,000 to 7,000 ft. in height. The plateau adjacent to the cañon is said to be about 7,000 ft. above the level of the sea.

The river, looking up the cañon, is magnificent and beyond the most extravagant conception of the imagination.

Continuing my journey on the Atchison, Topeka and Santa Fé R. R., I reached Socorro, which has a population of about 5,000, and is one of the principal mining towns of the territory. Mining, grazing, and fruit-growing are the principal industries. Socorro has a stamp milll, and famous smelting-works (Billings). The Socorro mining district contains the famous Torrence and Merrit Mines, within 3 miles. The ores are mostly carbonate of lead, carrying silver, some of which runs as high as $28,000 to the ton. Situated in the Rio Grande valley, the city is beautiful, and in addition to the above named industries does a great trade in agricultural and stock-raising products, and has many fine ranches in its vicinity. San Marcial has about 1,200 inhabitants, is a thriving place, and here are the repair-shops of the R. R. company. In 1862, the battle of Valverde, named after a little Mexican village across the river, was fought here between the Federals under General Canby and the Confederates under General Sibley.

New Mexico is named in honor of one of the Gods of the Aztecs, the ancient inhabitants of Mexico. Colonized by Spaniards, 1582; organized, 1850.

Area, 122,580 square miles; length, eastern boundary, 345 miles; western, 390 miles; average breadth, north of 32°, 335 miles; altitude, 3,000 to 4,000 ft.

Temperature at Santa Fé: winter, 27° to 37°; summer, 66° to 70°. Rainfall at Fort Marcy, 17 inches.

Las Vegas, Silver City and Albuquerque are growing in importance.

Crops abundant wherever water can be obtained, and corn will ripen almost anywhere; 6,660 square miles irrigable land; number of farms, 5,053. Total acreage of the territory, 78,451,200; in farms, 631,131; in forests, 219,224; unoccupied, 77,820,069.

Grazing interest extensive and valuable.

Mineral wealth is rapidly developing. Gold is found in Grant, Lincoln, Colfax and Bernalillo counties; rich copper mines on the San Pedro Grant, in Bernalillo county and in the Pinos Altos region. Zinc, quicksilver, lead, manganese, and large deposits of coal have been found. Gold production in 1882, was $150,000; silver, $1,800,000.

Population, 119,565, including 1,015 colored, 57 Chinese and 9,772 Indians.

School population, 20,255; school age, 7-18.

By way of Fort Worth, on the Texas Pacific R. R., with 8,000 inhabitants and extensive farms in its neighborhood, and Lampasas, famous for the gigantic ranches in the vicinity, I proceeded to the already described city of Houston, thence to New Orleans, where the International Exposition was held.

Arrived in New Orleans toward the end of March,

I prolonged my stay in that city till the close of the Exhibition, on the 1st of May, 1884, and started for the State of Alabama, viz.: Mobile.

Mobile, the largest city and only seaport of Alabama, is situated on the W. side of Mobile river above its entrance into Mobile Bay. It was the original seat of French colonization in the Southwest and for many years the capital of the colony of Louisiana. Historians differ as to the precise date of its foundation, though it is known, that as early as 1702, there was a settlement, a little above the present site of the city. In 1780, England surrendered it to Spain, and that Government made it over to the United States in 1813. It was incorporated as a city in 1819, the population being then about 800.

Mobile was one of the last points in the Confederacy occupied by the Union forces during the late war, and was not finally reduced until April 12, 1865, three days after the surrender of General Lee. On August 5, 1864, the harbor fortifications were attacked by Admiral Farragut, who ran his fleet past the forts, and closed the harbor against blockade-runners, though he failed to capture the city itself.

The trade of Mobile is much hindered by the shallowness of its harbor.

The manufactures include carriages and furniture, paper, foundries and machine-shops, the chief business is the receipt and shipment of cotton, coal and lumber.

Its population is nearly 32,000. The city is laid out beautifully, the streets adorned with shade-trees.

Fort Morgan, formerly Fort Bowyer, on Mobile Point, and Fort Gaines, on the S. extremity of Dauphine Island, command the entrance to the harbor, which is about 30 miles below the city. Remains of batteries, erected during the war, are still seen in and about the harbor, and on the E. side of the Tensas river are the ruins of Spanish Fort and Fort Blakely. There are some costly public edifices, *f. i.*, the Custom House, which contains the Post Office, several fine churches, hospitals, the Barton Academy, the Medical College, and 6 miles W. of the City, the famous College of St. Joseph, a Jesuit institution, in which is a valuable collection of scientific apparatus, and a library with 8,000 volumes.

Montgomery, the capital of the State, is not very far from here, and is situated on the left bank of the Alabama river, has 19,500 population, and from February to May, 1861, was the first Capital of the Confederate States. The principal buildings are; the U. S. Court House and Post Office, the State House, the City Hall and the Court House. The train passes many nice villages, and crosses one of the most productive portions of Alabama on its course from Mobile, 180 miles distant.

Other excursions I did not make in this State, and therefore reproduce the collected statistics of it.

The name of Alabama derives from an Indian word, signifying, "Here we rest." Settled near Mobile Bay by French, 1702, admitted as a State, 1819; seceded 1861; re-admitted 1868.

Area, 52,250 square miles; length, 330 miles; average breadth, 154 miles; seacoast, 60 miles. Inland steam navigation about 1,500 miles. Mobile is the only seaport.

Temperature at Huntsville; winter, 46° to 52°; summer, 79° to 83°, rainfall 55 inches. July is the hottest month. Fruit trees blossom February 1st to March 1st.

Huntsville, with 4,977 population, is the northern trade center, Selma, an important railroad center, and the two cities Birmingham and Bradford, very important manufacturing centers, especially of iron, etc., and a great coal trade is carried on in them.

Number of farms, 135,864. Average value per acre, cleared land, $6.53; woodland, $4.08. Number of industries, 2,070; flour and grist mills, 807; sawmills, 354. Mineral regions in northeast corner, extending southwest, about 160 miles, with average width of about 80 miles, contains 3 distinct coal fields, area over 5,000 square miles, and beds, 1 to 8 ft. thick; limestone, sandstone and iron near the coal.

Population, 1,262,505, inclusive 600,107 Negroes and 213 Indians. Slaves, in 1860, 435,080. Number of colleges, 4; school population, 401,002; school age 7–21.

En route to Florida, the city of Jacksonville was reached. This is the largest city in Florida and is situated on the left bank of the St. John's River.

Its population is 17,698, and with the suburbs, about 22,000. The bluffs on the N. E. and N. W. of the city are picturesque, and the commerce of some importance.

Cotton, fruit, sugar, fish, and vegetables are shipped to northern and foreign ports. The main temperature, 69.6°; the coldest month (January), 52.7°; the hottest month (July), 83.4°. There are several fine drives to Moncrief's Spring and on the shell-road, to the Fair Grounds.

Sanford, on the St. John's River, lies in a distance of 16 hours steamship ride from Jacksonville and near this young, but rapidly growing city are a number of fine orange-groves. Opposite from Sanford is Enterprise, one of the most popular resorts in southern Florida for invalids. Frederick De Bary, the well known importer of New York, and the founder of the De Bary Steamship Line on the St. John's, has his country-seat here.

The St. John's River has its sources in a vast elevated savanna midway down the peninsula, flows almost directly N. for 300 miles to Jacksonville, and then turning E. empties into the Atlantic.

Its banks are lined with a luxuriant tropical vegetation, orange-groves, shade-trees and picturesque villages. For hundreds of miles one passes through a grand forest of cypresses robed in moss and mistletoe; of palms towering gracefully far above the surrounding trees, of water-oak, poplar and pine trees, and where the hammocks rise a few feet above the water-level, the olive, cotton tree, juniper, cedar, the sweet-bay and live-oak shoot up their splendid stems; while among the inferior growths and shrubbery, the azalea, agave, poppy, the mallow, sumach, the sensitive plant and the nettle are noted. Vines, the wood-bine and, bignonia and the fox-grape ran in these thickets and clamber along the branches. For its whole length the river affords glimpses of perfect beauty.

Green Cove Springs takes its name from a sulphur spring, and is one of the favorite resorts, 3 miles above Magnolia.

Palatka, admirably situated on the elavated W. bank of the river is the largest city on the river above Jacksonville, its population is 5,000. Above Palatka the vegetation becomes more characteristically tropical, and the river narrows down to a moderate-sized stream, widening out at last only to be merged in Grand and Little Lake George, Dexter's Lake, Lake Beresford, and Lake Monroe, at Enterprise.

Lake George is one of the most beautiful lakes in the world, 6 miles wide and over 13 miles long, and from here to the already described Sanford, Drayton, an island in the lake, and embracing, 1,700 acres, and Volusia, 5 miles above Lake George, a landing station, and Orange Grove, Hawkinsville, Blue Spring and Lake Monroe are the most prominent features.

On another excursion from Jacksonville, I visited St. Augustine, situated on the Atlantic coast of Florida and occupying a narrow peninsula formed by the Matanzas River and the St. Sebastian. All the old Spanish residences in this place, which contains a resident population of 2,200 (increased in the winter by from 8,000 to 10,000 visitors) are built of coquina-stone, those of the American residents in the modern style.

The most interesting feature of St. Augustine is the old Fort of San Marco, built of coquina, a unique conglomerate of fine shells and sand found in large quantities on Anastasia Island, at the entrance of the harbor, and quarried with great ease. The Fort was 100 years in building and was completed in 1756, as is attested by the following inscription over the gateway: "Don Fernando being King of Spain, and the Field-Marshal Don Alonzo Fernando Herida, being Governor and Captain-General of this place, St. Augustine of Florida and its provinces, this Fort was finished in the year 1756. The works were directed by the Captain-Engineer Don Pedro de Brazos y Gareny."

Its dark passages, gloomy vaults and recently-discovered dungeons impress the visitor, and bring one to ready credence of its many traditions of inquisitorial tortures; of decaying skeletons, found in the latest opened chambers, chained to the rusty ring-bolts, and of alleged subterranean passages to the neighboring convent. The Sea-Wall and the City Gate are imposing structures in a fair state of preservation.

In the old Catholic Cathedral, one of the bells bears the date of 1682, and there are several convents, and the Governor's Palace, formerly the residence of the Spanish Governors.

The old Huguenot Burying-Ground, and the Military Burying-Ground where the remains of those who fell in the prolonged Seminole war rest, are interesting.

The Soldiers' Monument, in honor of the Confederate dead, was erected in 1871.

The climate of St. Augustine is singularly equable both winter and summer; the mean annual temperature being 70°.

A third excursion from the starting-point Jacksonville was to the Ocklawaha River. The river empties into the St. John's about 25 miles S. of Palatka, opposite the diminutive town of Welaka after flowing for about 250 miles through different counties. This excursion was made up the Ocklawaha to Silver Spring and well worth making. Alligators of immense size are numerous, and birds of the most curious forms and brilliant plumage are seen everywhere on this trip. Silver Spring, said to be the traditional "Fountain of Youth," has wonderful clear waters, and on the bottom, 80 ft. below, the exact form of the smallest pebble is visible. By the water of this spring, a deep river, 100 ft. wide, is formed, and known as Silver Spring Creek.

Of other curiosities in Florida is the Indian River Country, a long lagoon, beginning near the lower end of Mosquito Inlet. The water of this lagoon or sea-arm is salty, though it receives a considerable body of fresh water through Santa Lucia River, an outlet of the Everglades. The adjacent lands are mostly fertile, producing abundantly oranges, lemons, limes, bananas, pineapples, guavas, grapes, sugar-cane, different berries and garden vegetables.

The climate is excellent and the tropical scenery delightful. It was by one of the many southern outlets of Indian River that General Breckenridge escaped to Nassau after the collapse of the Confederacy.

155 miles W. of Jacksonville is the beautifully located capital of the State, the city of Tallahassee. The abundance and variety of its flowers and shrubs give it the appearance of a garden.

There are some fine public buildings in which is included the Capitol, the Court House, and the West Florida Seminary. The climate is very healthy, and the Lakes Bradford, Jackson and Lafayette very attractively situated in its neighborhood.

The Wakula Spring, an immense lime-stone basin, 106 ft. deep, with crystalline clear water, and so copious that a river is formed at its very start, is reckoned among the chief wonders of Florida.

The Gulf coast of Florida has already been partially described by me, and after leaving this State, I entered an other southern State: the "Empire State of the South," Georgia.

The discoverer of Florida, the "Peninsula State," landed on Easter Sunday, or "Flowery Easter," hence the name.

Settled by Spaniards at St. Augustine, 1565; organized as a territory, 1822; admitted as a State, 1845; seceded 1861; re-admitted, 1868.

Area, 58,680 square miles; coast line, 1,146 miles, 472 being on Atlantic; length, north and south, 350 miles; length, east and west, 340 miles; mean width of peninsula, 100 miles; greatest elevation, 250 ft.

Temperature at Jacksonville: winter, 55° to 61°; summer, 80° to 83°. Rainfall at Fort Myers, 57 inches.

Pensacola has a population of 6,845. Number of farms, 23,438; owned by State, 15,000,000 acres; value per acre, cleared land, $9.48; woodland, $3.03; swamp, $1.00; school lands, $1.25.

Corn most valuable crop. Over three million orange trees planted since 1870 and millions of oranges exported yearly.

Population, 269,493, inclusive 126,690 negroes, and 180 Indians. Slaves, in 1860, 61,745.

Betters on elections and duelists excluded from voting.

School population, 88,677; enrolled in public schools, 39,315; school age, 4-21.

Per steamship I arrived in the city of Savannah, the chief city and commercial metropolis of Georgia, situated on the S. bank of the Savannah river. Its streets are broad and beautifully shaded, and contain at many of the crossings small public parks, of which there are 24 in the city. It is universally conceded that Savannah is one of the handsomest cities in America.

The chief business of the place is in cotton, though the trade in lumber is also considerable. As a cotton port it ranks second in the Union. The chief manufacturing establishments are plaining mills, foundries, and flour and grist mills.

Of noteworthy buildings, Savannah possesses several, among these are the Custom House, the Court House, the Post Office, Exchange, the U. S. Barracks, the Police Barracks, Artillery, Armory and Jail. Chatham Academy and St. Andrews Hall are conspicuous structures. The Masonic Hall building is interesting as the place where the Ordinance of Secession was passed, January 21st, 1861. Four years later, on December 28th, 1864, a meeting of citizens was held in the same apartment to commemorate the triumph of the Union arms. The Georgia Historical Society has a fine library and some interesting relics. The Telfair Academy of Arts, McCarthy's Business College, and the Savannah Medical College are famous educational institutions, there are also several very fine churches in the city.

The most attractive place of public resort is Forsyth Park with a handsome fountain and the stately Confederate Monument. The Pulaski Monument is one of the most perfect specimens of monumental architecture in the United States, and appropriately covers the spot where Pulaski fell, during an attack upon the city while it was occupied by the British, in 1779.

The drives are of great beauty, the most prominent: to Bonaventure Cemetery with its magnificent scenery. 1 mile beyond Bonaventure is Thunderbolt, also a popular drive, and according to local tradition, deriving its name from the fall of a thunderbolt which caused the issue of a spring of water from the spot, flowing ever since.

Augusta, with a population of 32,000, is one of the most beautiful cities in the South. It is situated on the Savannah river and contains the finest monument in the South, the Confederate Monument, another monument is that which was erected in 1849, to the memory of the Georgian signers of the Declaration of Independence. Augusta has very fine buildings and a prosperous commerce and extensive manufactures. A fine view of the city is obtained at Summerville, a suburban town, where the U. S. Arsenal and the range of workshops, built and used by the Confederates during the war, are located. An excursion trip brought me to Macon, a very prosperous and picturesque city with 20,000 inhabitants, on the Ocmulgee river. Here are several important iron-foundries, machine-shops, cotton and carriage manufactures, and flour-mills. The Mercer University is a prosperous institution, and the Pio Nono College, the Wesleyan Female College, and the State Academy for the Blind are spacious and imposing buildings. Rose Hill Cemetery is considered one of the finest burial-grounds in America.

Atlanta was the last place in the State which I visited. It is the capital and the most important commercial city in the State, except in the cotton-trade, and has a population of 50,000 (in 1880). It is the great center of railroads, is picturesquely situated upon hilly ground, 1,100 ft. above the sea, and is laid out in the form of a circle. Its public buildings are of immense proportions and beauty.

Its position made it of vital importance to the

Southern cause, and with its capture by General Sherman, September 2d, 1864, the Confederacy's doom was sealed. Before abandoning the city, to fall back on Macon, General Hood set fire to all machinery-stores, and war munitions which he could not remove, and in the conflagration the greater part of the city was reduced to ashes. In 1868 Atlanta was made the State capital.

Georgia, the Empire State of the South, is the farthest south and latest settled of the 13 original States, named in honor of George II., King of England; settled by English at Savannah, 1753; seceded, January, 1861; re-admitted, December, 1870.

Area, 59,475 square miles; extreme length, 320 miles; extreme breadth, 254 miles; coast line, 480 miles; number of harbors, 3. Savanna, Ogeechee, Altamaha, Satilla, St. Mary's, Flint, Chattahoochee and Upper Coosa are navigable rivers.

Temperature at Augusta: winter, 46° to 52°; summer, 79° to 83°. Rainfall at Savannah, 48 inches.

Savannah, Brunswick and St. Mary's are ports of entry. Columbus contains the largest cotton-mill in the South. Andersonville was the seat of the largest rebel prison during the civil war.

Number of farms, 62,003 in 1860, and 138,626 in 1880. Average value per acre, cleared land, $6.93; woodland, $5.45. 72 per cent. of laborers engaged in agriculture; rural income, $155 per individual. Ranks second in rice and sweet potatoes. Latest mining reports give 100,000 tons of coal and 91,416 tons of iron ore.

Population, 1,542,180, incl. 725,133 colored; 17 Chinese and 124 Indians.

Non-taxpayers are excluded from voting.

I could not obtain the School Statistics of this State.

From Atlanta I proceeded to Charleston, which was settled in 1679 by an English colony under William Sayle, who became the first Governor.

It played a conspicuous part in the Revolution, having been the first among the chief places of the South to assert a common cause with and for the colonies. It was thrice assaulted by the British, and only yielded to a 6 weeks siege by an overwhelming force, May 12th, 1780. It was the leading city, both in the nullification movement during Jackson's administration and the incipient stages of Southern secession. Open hostilities in the civil war began at Charleston, with the bombardment of Fort Sumter, on April 12th, 1861; and for the next 4 years it was one of the chief points of Federal attack, without being lost by the Confederates, however, until General Sherman's capture of Columbia, on February 17th, 1863. During the war many buildings were destroyed, and the towers and steeples of churches riddled with shot and shell. Since its close, rapid progress has been made in the work of rebuilding, and Charleston is now more prosperous than ever. It has about 50,000 inhabitants. The commerce of the city is very large, the chief exports being cotton, rice, naval stores and fertilizers. The manufacture of fertilizers from the valuable beds of marl and phosphates (fossiles), discovered in 1868, is now one of the principal industries. There are also flour and rice mills, bakeries, carriage and wagon factories and machine-shops. Lumber is taking a place among the leading articles of exports. Ever since my stay in Charleston, the city has been visited by several earthquakes which were very detrimental, and nearly the whole region along the river was inundated and the houses destroyed.

Charleston is situated at the confluence of the Ashley and Cooper rivers, in lat. 32° 45′ N., and lon. 79° 57′ W.

Of the public buildings of Charleston, several are, or were of imposing beauty, viz.: the U. S. Custom House, the City Hall and the Old Orphan House. The College of Charleston, the Medical College and Roper Hospital, the City Hospital, the Chamber of Commerce, the Masonic Temple, the U. S. Court House, the Charleston Library, Academy of Music, the County Jail, and the South Carolina Society Hall are more or less handsome structures. St. Michael's and St. Philip's Church, the former a venerable old structure, are very famous. In the portion of the grave yard lying across the street is the tomb of John C. Calhoun. In the old Huguenot Church, the quaint and elegant mural entablatures with which its walls are lined can be seen.

15 miles from here is the old Church of St. James, on Goose Creek, built in 1711. The harbor of Charleston is a large estuary, extending 7 miles to the Atlantic.

The passage to the inner harbor is defended by 4 fortresses.

Fort Sumter, rendered famous by the part which it played in the opening scene of the Civil War lies upon a shoal in the harbor, covering the channel. Sullivan's Island, the "Long Branch" of South Carolina, and Mount Pleasant, in the vicinity, are public resorts and much frequented.

Aiken is among the most famous and frequented winter-resorts in America. It lies on an elevated plateau, about 700 ft. above the sea and the land consists of almost unmixed sand, covered by a scanty crust of alluvium, which bears but little grass, only the great southern pine grows here abundantly and pine-forests encircle the town.

The natural barrenness of the soil has been overcome within the city by careful culture and liberal use of fertilizers, and every house has its garden with trees and southern plants. Inside the white palings are dense thickets of yellow jasmine, rose-bushes, orange, wild-olive, and fig trees, bamboo, Spanish bayonet, and a great many vines and creepers, but, without the palings, the soil is as dry and white as it is upon the sea-shore. The air is remarkably pure and dry, and the average temperature is $63.1\frac{1}{2}°$. In this place I had the honor to form the acquaintance of the botanist Ravenel.

The capital of the State, Columbia, is a beautiful city, situated on the bluffs of, and 15 ft. above the Congaree, on an elevated level plateau, a few miles below the charming falls of the river.

During the occupation by Sherman's forces in February 1865, the city was considerably changed through the unfortunate conflagration which destroyed a large part of it. There are several handsome public and private buildings, 2 Seminaries, the University of South Carolina, the Executive Mansion and the State House (unfinished), the Lunatic Asylum, State Penitentiary, the U. S. Court House and Post Office, the City Hall, several Academies, and the Market-House, in Columbia. The car-shops of the R. R. Company cover 4 acres of ground and there are other large manufacturing establishments. In the N. W. of the city are the Fair Grounds of the South Carolina Agricultural and Mechanical Society.

The "Palmetto State," South Carolina, was named in honor of Charles II. of England, by whom the province was created in 1663. It is one of the 13 original States. First permanent settlement made by the English at Port Royal, 1670. Famous nullification troubles occurred 1832–33; led by J. C. Calhoun, and opposed vigorously by President Jackson, during which his famous expression "by the Eternal" was first used.

Seceded November, 1860; re-admitted June, 1868.

Area, 30,170 square miles; extreme length, 275 miles; greatest breadth, 210 miles; coast line, 200 miles. Largest rivers, Savannah, Great Pee Dee, Santee and Edisto.

Temperature at Charleston: summer, 79° to 83°; winter, 50° to 54°; rainfall, 43 inches; frosts seldom occur.

United States customs districts at Beaufort, Charleston and Georgetown.

First railroad to use American locomotives, the South Carolina, built 1830–33.

Number of farms, 93,864. Average value per acre, cleared land, $6.24; wood land, $3.65.

Number of flour and grist mills, 720.

Ranks first in phosphates. Gold mines in Abbeville, Edgefield and Union Counties. White and variegated marbles' found in Spartanburgh and Laurens Counties.

Population, 955,577, including 604,332 Colored, 9 Chinese, and 131 Indians.

Slaves, in 1860, 402,406.

U. S. Army and duelists excluded from voting.

Number of colleges, 9; school population, 262,279; school age, 6–16.

On the road to the Lookout Mountain—my next exploration-tour—I visited Chattanooga, a city of 30,000 inhabitants, situated on the Tennessee River near where the S. boundary of Tennessee touches Alabama and Georgia. 7 railroads converge here. Chattanooga is a very important shipping-point and contains a number of iron-mills, blast-furnaces and cotton factories. It is the seat of the Methodist University. During the war Chattanooga was an important strategic point for the operations in Tennessee and Georgia, and played a prominent part in most of the campaigns in this region. Above the city the celebrated Lookout Mountain towers to the height of 2,200 ft. above the sea. It was on this

Mountain that the battle was fought "above the clouds." The points on the Lookout worth visiting are Lake Seclusion, Lulah Falls, Rock City and the Battle-field.

I next put up at Knoxville, a city of 12,000 population, situated on the Holston River, 4 miles below the mouth of the French Broad. It is built on a healthy and elevated site and is the principal commercial place in E. Tennesee, with some manufactures. The East Tennessee University, with which is connected the State Agricultural College, the Knoxville University, the Freeman's Normal School, and the State Institution for the Deaf and Dumb are located here. The Cranberry-Region Magnet-iron-works, close to the boundaries of North Carolina, are almost uniques in the world, and offered me many interesting features.

On account of the far advanced season I was unable to visit the city of Memphis and gathered all possible data concerning this city, which I here cite as they were given to me officially.

Memphis is the second city of Tennessee, it is situated on the fourth Chickasaw bluff, and had in 1880 a population of 33,593. Memphis has an immense railroad—and on the Mississippi an important steamboat-traffic, and is regularly laid out. The cotton trade and its manufactures are very large. In the center of the city is a handsome park, and the public buildings and private residences of exceedingly pretty forms.

Memphis was captured by the Federals early in the war (June 6, 1862), and was never afterward held by the Confederates. A short distance below Memphis the Mississippi turns toward the W., and crosses its valley to meet the waters of the Arkansas and White rivers. The latter enters the Mississippi 161 miles below Memphis, and the former about 15 miles further down. The Arkansas river is 2,000 miles in length, for 800 of which it is navigable by steamers. It rises in the Rocky Mountains, and, next to the Missouri, is the largest tributary of the Mississippi.

The capital and largest city in the State in point of population (45,000), is Nashville, on the S. bank of the Cumberland river, 200 miles above its junction with the Ohio, and built on irregular gradual rising land. It has numerous imposing buildings, among which the Capitol, constructed inside and outside of a beautiful variety of fossiliferous lime-stone is pre-eminent.

The University of Nashville, with a fine museum, the Fisk University, the Tennessee Central College, Vanderbilt University, etc., are fine educational institutions, and there are numerous others. The State Penitentiary is located here and the manufactures are varied and important. 12 miles E. of Nashville is the "Hermitage," the celebrated residence of Andrew Jackson.

In November, 1864, the Confederate General Hood, having lost Atlanta, placed his army in Sherman's rear and began an invasion of Tennessee. After severe fighting with General Schofield on November 30, he advanced upon Nashville and shut up General Thomas within its fortifications. For two weeks little was done on either side. When Thomas was fully ready, he suddenly sallied out on Hood, and, in a terrible two day's battle, drove the Confederate forces out of their intrenchments into headlong flight. The Union cavalry pursued them, the infantry following close behind, and the entire Confederate Army, except the rear-guard, which fought bravely to the last, was broken into a rabble of demoralized fugitives, which at last escaped across the Tennessee. For the first time in the war an Army was destroyed; and General Sherman started on his famous march to the sea.

The "Big Bend State," Tennessee, whose name derived from "Tannassee," Indian name for Little Tennessee River, was first settled permanently, on Tennessee river, in 1756, about 30 miles from present site of Knoxville; first Anglo-American settlement west of the Alleghanies and south of Pennsylvania; admitted, 1845; seceded, February, 1861; re-admitted, 1868.

Area, 42,650 square miles; greatest length, east and west, 432 miles; greatest breadth, 109 miles.

Temperature at Nashville: winter, 37° to 48°; summer, 75° to 81°. Rainfall at Memphis, 45 inches.

Memphis, principal grain and cotton market between St. Louis and New Orleans. Number of farms, 165,650. Value per acre, cleared land, $13.00; woodland, $7.28. Most valuable minerals are iron, copper and coal; area coal fields, over 5,000 square miles;

copper region in southwest; excellent marbles and limestones.

Ranks second in peanuts. Hemp, broom corn and flax are also valuable products. Population, 1,542,-359, incl. 403,151 colored, 25 Chinese and 352 Indians. Slaves in 1860, 275,719.

Non-payers of poll-tax excluded from voting. School population, unknown.

I now started for the mountain region of North Carolina where the Appalachian system reaches its loftiest altitude, presents scenes of beauty and sublimity unsurpassed by anything E. of the Rocky Mountains. It consists of an elevated table-land, 250 miles long and about 50 broad, encircled by two great mountain-chains, the Blue Ridge on the E. and the Great Smoky on the W., and traversed by cross-chains that run directly across the country, and from which spurs of greater or lesser height lead off in all directions. Of these transverse ranges there are four: the Black, the Balsam, the Cullowhee, and the Nantahala.

Between each lies a region of valleys, formed by the noble rivers and their minor tributaries.

Clingman's Dome rises to the height of 6,660 ft. Mount Mitchell, the loftiest summit E. of the Mississippi, is the dominating peak of the Black Mountain group of the colossal heights, the most famous of the transverse ranges. With its two great branches it is over 20 miles long, and its rugged sides are covered with a wilderness of almost impenetrable forest. Above a certain elevation, no trees are found save the balsam-fir, from the dark color of which the mountain takes its name. N. of the Black Mountain stand two famous heights, these are the Grandfather Mountain in the Blue Ridge and Roan Mountain in the Smoky.

The Balsam, which in length and general magnitude is chief of the cross ranges, is 50 miles long, and its peaks average 6,000 ft. in height. From its S. extremity two great spurs run out in a northerly direction; one terminates in the Cold Mountain, which is over 6,000 ft. high, and the other in the beautiful peak of Pisgah, which is one of the most noted landmarks of the region.

Asheville, situated in the lovely valley of the French Broad River, 2,250 ft. above the sea, surrounded by an amphitheatre of hills, commands one of the finest mountain-views in America.

Morgantown is a popular resort, and is situated on the slopes of the Blue Ridge, 1,100 ft. above the sea. About 15 miles W. of Morgantown on the Glen Alpine Springs with Lithia waters, and 25 miles from the former is the Grand Linville Gorge, where the Linville River bursts through the massive barrier of the Linville Mountains.

Resuming my journey per Western North Carolina R. R., I arrived at Raleigh, the capital of the State, with 8,000 inhabitants, situated on an elevation 6 miles W. of the Neuse River and a little N. E. of the center of the State.

The State House is built after the model of the Parthenon. The U. S. Custom House and Post Office, the State Geological Museum, the Institution for the Deaf and Dumb, the State Insane Asylum, and the Penitentiary are fine structures.

North Carolina, the "Old North State," or "Tar State," is one of the 13 original States and was discovered by Lord Raleigh, 1584, settled by the English at Albemarle, 1650; seceded, May, 1861; re-admitted, June, 1868.

Area, 52,250 square miles; length, 450 miles; breadth, 185 miles; coast line, over 400 miles; area dismal swamp, 150,000 acres.

Temperature at Wilmington: winter, 46° to 51°; summer, 76° to 80°. Frost seldom occurs before November. Rainfall at Gaston, 43 inches. Deaths by consumption, 1.5, per 1,000 of population.

Wilmington, principal seaport and chief city, with 13,446 population. Charlotte contains assay office.

Farms in 1860, 75,203, increased to 157,609 in 1880; average value per acre, cleared land, $9.77; woodland, $5.53.

Agriculture the leading industry; corn the most valuable crop; tobacco the leading product, and orchards very productive. Ranks first in tar and turpentine, and second in copper. Number of different industries, 3,802; flour and grist-mills, 1,313; sawmills, 776. About 3,000 boats are engaged in general fisheries.

Population, 1,399,750, with 531,278 Colored, and 1,230 Indians. Slaves, 1860, 331,059.

Public school system adopted 1840; at present

over 2,000 public schools in operation; school age, 6-21.

The road to Richmond, Virginia, is admirably pretty. The scenery and the distant mountain ranges, changing their contures, the farther one proceeds, is of an extraordinary brilliancy, and many lovely little places, dense forests, and well-cultivated fields and meadows are passed before Richmond is reached.

This metropolis of the State of Virginia and its capital is situated on the N. bank of the James river, about 100 miles from Chesapeake Bay. It is built on several eminences, the principal of which are: separated by Shockoe Creek, Church and Shockoe Hills, surrounded by beautiful scenery.

Richmond was founded 1737, incorporated 1742, and became the State capital in 1779, when it was a small village.

In 1861 great prominence was given to it as the capital of the Southern Confederacy, and one of the great aims of the Federal authorities, throughout the war, was to reduce it into their possession. Strong lines of earth-works were drawn around the place by the Confederates, and are yet to be seen. When General Lee evacuated Petersburg, April 2d, 1865, the troops defending Richmond on the E. were withdrawn, and to prevent the tobacco warehouses and public stores from falling into the hands of the Federals, the buildings, together with the bridges over the James river, were fired. This resulted in the destruction of a large part of the business section of the city, the number of buildings destroyed having been estimated at 1,000, and the loss at $8,000,000.

With the cessation of hostilities, the burned quarters were rebuilt, and at present Richmond is surpassing its former prosperity,

In 1880, the population was 63,803. The commerce is very large, the chief articles of export being tobacco and flour. The manufactures include ironworks, machine-shops, foundries, sugar-refineries, cigar-factories, furniture, sheetings and shirtings, coach and wagon-factories and stoneware.

The most conspicuous object in the city, is the State Capitol. The plan for the building was furnished by Thomas Jefferson, and is after the Maison carrée at Nismes, in France. In the State Library are 40,000 volumes. The equestrian statue of Washington, surrounded by bronze figures of famous Americans is of a colossal size and is one of the finest bronzes in the world.

The Historical Society Collections, and not far from it, the life-size marble statue of Henry Clay, and the statue of General "Stonewall Jackson, of heroic size, are well worth seeing.

The Medical College, Richmond College and the Southern Female Institute, are famous schools of learning. The Brockenbrough House, formerly the residence of Jefferson Davis, President of the Southern Confederacy, is now used as a school-house. The Almshouse, State Penitentiary and the Mozart Academy of Music are fine edifices, as are the Churches St.

John's (Episcopal), Monumental Church and St. Paul's (also Episcopal).

Libby Prison and Belle Isle retain some interest as military prisons during the late civil war.

Of the several cemeteries of Richmond, Hollywood is the principal, in it lay the remains of President Monroe and of President Tyler. In the soldiers section rises a monumental pyramid in honor of the dead. 5 bridges across the river connect Richmond with Spring Hill and Manchester, the latter a pretty town with 2 fine cotton-mills. The Tredegar Iron-Works, which were the great cannon manufactory of the Confederacy, are worth a visit, covering over 15 acres of ground, and the Gallego and Haxall Flour-Mills are among the largest in the world.

A few hours ride from the city bring the traveler to several battle-fields and National Cemeteries.

Boarding a train of the Wilmington and Florence R. R., and crossing the James River, the well built city of Petersburg was reached. It it situated at the head of navigation on the Appomattox River, 12 miles above its entrance into the James. Its trade is large; tobacco, wheat, corn, cotton and general country produce, the chief business. In 1880, Petersburg had 23,000 population. There are some fine public buildings.

Petersburg was the scene of the last great struggles during the late civil war and is now prospering.

Norfolk was next visited. The city is pleasantly situated on the N. bank of the Elizabeth River, 8 miles from Hampton Roads and 32 miles from the ocean.

After Richmond it is the most populous city in the State, with 26,000 inhabitants and a large trade. Oysters, early fruits and vegetables arrive here in large quantities, and are shipped to Northern ports. Its harbor is defended by Fortress Monroe and the Rip Raps, this Fortress being the largest in America and having Hampton in its vicinity, where the National Soldiers Home and the Normal and Agricultural Institute for colored people and Indians, the most interesting institutions in the country, are located. 9 miles from Fortress Monroe, on Hampton Roads, is Newport News, famous for the great historic interest in connection with the Revolutionary War and the late Civil War.

The city of Norfolk is irregularly laid out, but the streets are generally wide and the houses well built; some of its churches very fine structures. Norfolk was founded in 1682, incorporated in 1705 and burned by the British in 1776. In 1855 the city was severely visited by yellow fever and played a prominent part in the first year of the civil war, when it was captured by Virginians and became the chief naval depot of the Confederacy. Off Norfolk, on March 8, 1862, was fought the memorable engagement between the Confederate iron-clad Virginia and the Federal iron-clad Monitor, which marks one of the most notable epochs in naval warfare and changed the course of naval construction throughout the world. Opposite Norfolk, connected by ferry, is Portsmouth, a city of 11,388 inhabitants, and one of the best harbors on the Atlantic.

coast. At Gosport, the S. extremity of the city, is a U. S. Navy Yard, and near by is the U. S. Naval Hospital. At the time of the secession of Virginia, April 18, 1861, nearly 1,000 men were employed at the Navy Yard. Two days afterward it was destroyed by fire, with property valued at several million dollars, including 11 war-vessels.

On a rather wearysome journey I arrived at Lynchburg, important from the lines of railway which center here. The city has 15,000 inhabitants and does a great business in tobacco and other manufactures. It lies on the S. bank of James river and has an inexhaustible water-power. About 20 miles in the background rises the Blue Ridge, together with the Peaks of Otter, which are in full view. In the neighborhood are vast fields of coal and iron-ore, and the celebrated Botetourt Iron-works are not far distant.

On the pretty long tour from here to Fredericksburg, I passed well cultivated and rich agricultural regions and mining districts. The city, quaint and old, is situated on the S. bank of the Rappahannock river, and is noted as being the scene of one of the severest battles of the civil war, fought December 13, 1862, in which General Burnside was defeated by General Lee. 11 miles W. of Fredericksburg, on the E. edge of "The Wilderness," the battle of Chancellorsville, in which "Stonewall" Jackson lost his life, was fought May 2-4, 1863. Southward from Chancellorsville is Spottsylvania Court-House, where in May, 1864, were fought some of the bloodiest battles of General Grant's campaign on his way to Richmond.

Just outside the limits of Fredericksburg an unfinished monument, begun in 1833, marks the tomb of the mother of Washington, who died here in 1789. It was in the vicinity of Fredericksburg that Washington himself was born, and here he passed his early years. At Hanover Junction, 37 miles from Fredericksburg, another battle was fought between General Grant and General Lee in May, 1864.

At Alexandria, 7 miles below Washington, on the S. side of the Potomac, I received the sad news of the death of the Ex-President of the United States, General Grant, and having had the honor to be personally acquainted with the "Hero" of many battles, I hastened to New York to attend at his funeral.

The city of Alexandria dates from 1784 and is intimately associated with the life and name of Washington. In Christ Church the pew No. 59, in which he sat, is an object of much interest. Pew No. 46 was occupied by General Robert E. Lee when he resided at Arlington before the war. The Museum, Court House and Thelogical Seminary are among the prominent buildings, and on the outskirts of the city is a National Cemetery, in which nearly 4,000 soldiers are buried.

The State of Virginia, "The Old Dominion," was named in honor of Elizabeth, the Virgin Queen. It is one of the 13 original States. Settled by the English at Jamestown, 1607. Slavery introduced 1619. Seceded

May, 1861; re-admitted, January, 1870. Area, 42,450 square miles; greatest length, east and west, 440 miles; greatest breadth, 190 miles. Coast line, about 120 miles, or tidal frontage, 1,500 miles.

Temperature at Norfolk: winter, 40° to 48°; summer, 75° to 80°. Rainfall at White Sulphur Springs, 38 inches.

Number of farms, 118,517; 51 per cent. of laborers are engaged in agriculture. Average value per acre, cleared land, $9.42; woodland, $7.48.

Marble quarried on Potomac. Number of sandstone quarries, 10; ship-building establishments, 65; saw-mills, 907; flour and grist-mills, 1,385.

Gold produced 1882, $15,000. Ranks first in peanuts, and second in tobacco.

Population, incl. 631,616 colored, 6 Chinese and 85 Indians, 1,512,565.

U. S. Army and non-taxpayers of capitation tax excluded from voting.

Number of colleges, 7; school population, 555,807; school age, 5-21.

The "Pan Handle State," West Virginia, has only been slightly explored by me, the few cities and other places which I visited did not offer any important features, and I was compelled to rely on the informations received from various sources.

West Virginia is composed of northern and western counties of the original State of Virginia; denounced passage of secession ordinance, April 22, 1861, and became a State, 1863.

Area, 24,780 square miles; greatest length, north and south, about 240 miles; greatest breadth, 160 miles. Big Sandy, Great and Little Kanawha, Guyandotte, and Monongahela are navigable rivers.

Temperature at Morgantown: winter, 34° to 42°; summer, 70° to 75°. Rainfall at Romney, 45 inches.

Charleston, capital, has 4,192 inhabitants and some trade. The metropolis of the State is Wheeling, its population about 35,000. The trade on the Ohio river is very important in this city and there are many manufactures of iron-works, nail-mills, and glass-works. The National Road crosses the Ohio here by a graceful suspension bridge, 1,010 ft. long, and the railroad bridge below the city is one of the finest in the country. There are several fine buildings, formerly occupied by the State Government, in Wheeling.

Parkersburg is a port of delivery, and has 6,500 inhabitants and an important trade especially in petroleum.

The bridge crossing the Ohio, 1½ miles long, to Belpré, is said to be one of the most magnificent bridges in the United States.

Martinsburg, with 6,335 inhabitants, is pleasantly situated on an elevated plateau above Tuscarora Creek, which affords a fine water-power. Much fighting occured in this vicinity during the civil war, and in June, 1861, the Confederates destroyed 87 locomotives and 400 cars belonging to the railroad company.

Number of farms, 62,674. Average value per acre, cleared land, $21.05; woodland, $9.39. 61 per cent.

of laborers engaged in agriculture. Staples are tobacco, wheat and corn, the last being the most valuable crop. Iron ore yields 50 to 80 per cent. pure metal. Petroleum is extensively produced in Ritchie, Pleasants, Wood and Wirt counties.

Population, 618,457, including 25,886 Colored, and 29 Indians. Slaves in 1860, 18,371.

Flourishing free school system; school population, 216,605; school age, 6–21.

After a brief stay in New York I started anew, to explore the State of Connecticut, and visiting Bridgeport, a prosperous city of 30,000 population, situated on an arm of the Long Island Sound, and famous for its many manufactures in sewing machines, leather, carriages, arms, cutlery and locks, I proceeded to New Haven, the largest city of Connecticut, at the head of the New Haven Bay, on a broad plain surrounded by rolling hills. It is the centre of 5 railroads, has a large coasting trade and considerable foreign commerce, chiefly with the West Indies. Its manufactures are very large, including hardware, locks, clocks, machinery, firearms, carriages, jewelry, pianos, and India-rubber goods.

Population, 62,882. New Haven contains a great many charitable institutions.

The Medical College is considered to be of high standing. Yale College is one of the most important and oldest educational institutions in America, founded in 1700 and established at New Haven in 1717. The Gothic library in the College contains 140,000 volumes. The Winchester Observatory contains a 6-inch heliometer, and an 8-inch equatorial instrument. In the Peabody Museum are the collections of the University in geology, mineralogy, and the natural sciences, including the famous collection of Professor Marsh.

There are very handsome public and private buildings in this city.

Beyond New Haven, 37 miles distant, is the capital of Connecticut, Hartford, situated on the Connecticut River. Its population in 1880 was 42,553 and it is the centre of fire and life insurances in the Union. The manufactures are very extensive, and include brassware and iron, steam-engines, tools, machinery, sewing-machines, fire-arms, silver-plated ware, woolens, etc. The State House is marvellously pretty, and the State library in that building is one of the largest law-libraries in America. The Asylum for the Deaf and Dumb, founded 1817, was the first institution of the kind in America, and the other State and Municipal charitable institutions in the city are also famous. The Connecticut Historical Society has a good collection of paintings, statuary and books. Some of the churches in the city are very pretty. Trinity College, (in the course of erection when I was there) will be a handsomely adorned architecture. In the S. E. portion of the city, located on the banks of Connecticut River, is the famous Colt Fire-Arms Manufactory. "Mark Twain's," residence is also here.

After a few more excursions to almost all parts of the State, I continued my voyage to the smallest State in the Union, Rhode Island.

Connecticut, the "Nutmeg State," has its name from the Indian word, signifying "Long River." It is one of the 13 original States, the first settlement (permanent) was made by the English at Hartford, 1635.

Area, 4,990 square miles; average length, 86 miles; average breadth, 55 miles; sea-coast, over 100 miles. Principal river valleys: Thames, Connecticut and Housatonic. Most important harbors: Bridgeport, New Haven, New London, Saybrook and Stonington.

Temperature at New Haven: winter, 27° to 40°; summer, 68° to 74°; rainfall, 44 inches.

Waterbury is an important manufacturing city with 17,806 inhabitants. Fairfield, Middletown, New Haven, New London and Stonington are ports of entry.

Number of farms, 30,598; average value per acre, cleared land, $29.00; woodland, $24.50. Number of different industries, 4,488. Ranks first in clocks, third in silk goods.

Population, 622,700, incl. 11,547 Colored, 123 Chinese, 6 Japanese and 225 Indians.

Those unable to read are excluded from voting. Number of colleges, 3, having about 160,000 volumes in their libraries. School age 4-16.

I found myself now in Newport, one of the two capitals of the State of Rhode Island; the other being Providence. Newport is one of the most fashionable and frequented of all the American summer resorts, it is situated on the W. shore of Rhode Island and on Narragansett Bay, 5 miles from the ocean. It is a port of entry and was settled in 1637, incorporated in 1700. Sumptuous mansions and charming villas lie along the terraces which overlook the sea.

Of curiosities there are too many in this place to describe them minutely and I will only mention a few, *f. i.*, the Touro Park with the Old Stone Mill, also called the Round Tower, the old State House, founded in 1739, the Jewish Synagogue, erected in 1762, the venerable Trinity Church, the Redwood Library, containing 20,000 volumes, paintings and statuary, the Historical Society, with a fine collection of colonial relics, and the Free Library, containing 15,000 volumes.

The surf-bathing in Newport is unsurpassed and there are 3 fine beaches.

The drives in and around Newport are of unusual elegance, and numerous lovely spots, such as caves, glens, ponds and hills ornament the place. $3\frac{1}{2}$ miles from the city is Fort Adams with 460 guns, one of the largest and strongest fortresses in America.

Goat Island, opposite the city wharves, is the headquarters of the torpedo division of the U. S. Naval Service. Lime Rock, in the harbor beyond Goat Island, is famous as the home of Ida Lewis.

In Narragansett Pier I found the same sea-sight life as in Newport, and made a trip to the second capital of the State, Providence. In wealth and population, Providence is the second city of New England and the chief in the State.

It is picturesquely situated on the northern arm of

Narragansett Bay, known as Providence river. Providence was founded in 1636 by Roger Williams, who had been banished from Massachusetts on account of his religious opinions. In 1880 the population was 104,-850. The manufacturers in this city are very extensive, including cotton and woolen goods, iron, prints, and jewelry, some of these are of world fame, as for instance, the Gorham Company's silver-ware factory, the Providence Tool Company's works, and the Steam Engine Company's, and Corliss Steam Engine Works. 60 wool and 100 cotton mills centre in this city.

Of public buildings worth mentioning, are the City Hall, the County Court House, the Brown University, founded in 1764 and containing over 50,000 volumes, and many others. The Rhode Island Historical Society has a valuable library and some interesting historical relics.

The Athenaeum contains a library of 38,000 volumes and some valuable paintings.

The Soldiers' and Sailors' Monument erected by the State in memory of its 1,741 citizens who fell in the civil war is an exceedingly fine structure. Of charitable and educational institutions there is an abundance in Providence. The drives in the suburbs, etc., are very pretty. On the State Farm in Cranston are the State Prison, Workhouse, House of Correction, Almshouse and the Hospital for the Insane.

Rhode Island, "Little Rhody," is one of the 13 original States and smallest in the Union; supposed temporary settlement by Icelanders as early as 1000;

settled by Roger Williams at Providence, 1636; last of the 13 colonies to ratify the Constitution, which it did in 1790.

Area, 1,250 square miles; extreme length, north and south, 47 miles; extreme width, 40 miles. Good harbors at Providence, Bristol, Warren and Newport, the latter one of the finest in the world.

Temperature at Newport: winter, 29° to 43°; summer, 64° to 71°; rainfall, 42 inches.

U. S. customs districts at Newport, Providence, Bristol and Warren. Population of Lincoln, 17,269; of Pawtucket, 22,894; of Warwick, 13,284, and of Woonsocket, 16,145.

Number of farms, 6,216. Hay is the most valuable crop. It outranks, in proportion to its size, all other States in value of manufactures. Number of looms, 30,274; spindles, 1,649,295, using 161,694 bales of cotton and giving employment to 22,228 persons. Ranks second in cotton, flax and linen goods.

Population, 303,816, incl. 7,127 Colored, 27 Chinese, and 77 Indians.

Persons without property to the value of $134, excluded from voting.

Number of colleges, 1; Browns University, at Providence, founded 1764; common school system excellent; school age, 5–15.

Resuming my journey, I arrived at the capital of Massachusetts and chief city of New England, the pretty city of Boston, situated at the W. extremity of

Massachusetts Bay, in latitude 42° N. and longitude 71° W.

The first white inhabitant of Boston was the Rev. John Blackstone, arrived in 1623. In 1635 Mr. Blackstone sold his claim to the peninsula, on which Boston proper stands, to John Winthrop, afterward the first Governor of Massachusetts for £30, and removed to Rhode Island. The first church was built in 1632; the first wharf in 1673.

The city was incorporated in 1822, with a population of 45,000, which had increased to 362,839 (including the suburbs of Brighton, Charleston and W. Roxbury) in 1880. On the 9th of November 1872, one of the most terrible conflagrations ever known in America, swept away the principal business portion of Boston. The district burnt over extended from the heart of the city to the harbor. About 775 of the finest buildings were destroyed, causing a loss of $70,000,000.

The Indian name of the peninsula was Shawmut, meaning "Sweet Waters." It was called by the earlier settlers Trimountain or Tremont. It embraces Boston proper, East Boston, South Boston, Roxbury, Dorchester, Charleston, Brighton and West Roxbury, containing in all about 22,000 acres. The city is connected by several bridges with the above mentioned places. The harbor is a spacious indentation of Massachusetts Bay, embracing 75 square miles, including several arms. There are more than 50 islands or islets in the harbor.

The Common, a park in the heart of the city, considered to date from 1634, is a very attractive spot with the ancient and historic Frog Pond, the Soldiers monument, and several fine fountains on the grounds. The Public Garden contains Washington's noble equestrian statue, the statues of Edward Everett, Charles Sumner, and of "Venus rising from the Sea," and the monument in honor of the discovery of ether as an anæsthetic.

The State House, on whose terrace in the front are statues of Daniel Webster and Horace Mann, and on the entrance floor the statue of Governor Andrew, busts of Samuel Adams, Lincoln and Sumner and a collection of battle-flags, and in the Rotunda the statue of Washington, copies of the tombstones of the Washington family in Brington church-yard, England, is a very fine building.

The Anthenæum is one of the best endowed institutions in the world, and the library of the American Academy of Arts and Sciences, in the same building, contains 15,000 volumes. On Louisburg Square are statues of Columbus and Aristides, and the Park Square contains the bronze group, "Emancipation."

The Society of Natural History has valuable cabinets and a library of 12,000 volumes, the Boston Public Library 450,000, and the famous Tosti collection of engravings. The Museum of Fine Arts contains Egyptian antiquities, statuary, casts and one of the richest collections of paintings and engravings in the country. The Masonic Temple, the Massachusetts

Charitable Mechanics' Association Building, and the New England Manufacturers' and Mechanics' Institute, and the Institute of Technology, deserve to be mentioned.

There are numerous churches in Boston, and the Trinity Church (Episcopal), is one of the largest, finest, and most splendidly decorated churches in America, the Catholic Cathedral of the Holy Cross, and the old and new South Churches rank next to it.

Faneuil Hall is the most interesting building in the Union, next to Independence Hall, Philadelphia. This famous edifice, the "cradle of liberty," was erected in 1742 and presented to the town by Peter Faneuil, a Hugnenot merchant. Destroyed by fire in 1761, it was rebuilt in 1768 and enlarged to its present dimensions in 1805. In it are the portraits of the founder, Washington, Samuel Adams, J. C. Adams, Webster, Everett, Lincoln, Governor Andrew, Henry Wilson, Charles Sumner. The U. S. Custom House, the City Hall, with statues of Benjamin Franklin and Quincy, the New Post Office and Sub-Treasury, not yet completed, Horticultural Hall, Odd-Fellows' Hall, Music Hall, with 3,000 seats, and several business buildings are fine and spacious structures. There are a great many public and private educational institutions in Boston.

Boston University, founded in 1869 by Isaac Rich, bequeated by this Philanthropist with $2,000,000, is well-known, and the new building of the Young Men's Christian Association is considered to be the finest of its kind in the world. The Massachusetts Historical

Society has a library of 25,000 volumes, manuscripts, coins, maps, charts, portraits and historical relics.

On the old North Burying-Ground, on Copp's Hill, lie the three fathers of the Puritan Church, Drs. Increase, Cotton, and Samuel Mather.

Of charitable institutions there are too many in Boston to be specially named.

The Soldiers' Home is located in Chelsea, and near by is the U. S. Naval Hospital.

The environs of Boston are remarkably artractive. Charlestown, Brighton, Jamaica Plain, and W. Roxbury, Dorchester and Roxbury were annexed and now form part of the city. At Charlestown is the famous "Bunker Hill Monument," commemorative of the eventful battle fought on the spot, June 17, 1775. The U. S. Navy-Yard is also located here. .Nantasket Beach is a celebrated summer resort in the vicinity.

In Brookline is the Brookline Reservoir, and about 1 mile distant from here, the Chestnut Hill Reservoir, both with colossal capacities.

Cambridge, one of the two most renowned of the American academic cities, contains the Harvard University, the oldest and most richly endowed institution of learning in the United States. Its library numbers 160,000 volumes. Near the college yard are the Zoölogical Museum, the Botanical Garden, containing a valuable herbarium and the Observatory.

On the Common, near by, stands a monument in honor of the soldiers who fell in the civil war, and not far from it, the Shepard Memorial Church, erected in honor of Thomas Shepard, who was pastor at Cambridge from 1635 to 1649.

In front of the latter is the famous Washington Elm, beneath which Washington assumed the command of the American army in 1775, and which is thought to be 300 years old. Many structures built before the Revolution are still standing, among them the house used by Washington for his headquarters and recently inhabited by the poet Longfellow, and Elmwood, the home of James Russell Lowell. Mount Auburn Cemetery is one of the most beautiful and ancient burial-places in America.

Waltham, 10 miles distant from Boston, a flourishing manufacturing village, of 11,711 inhabitants, on the Charles River, is noted as the site of the Waltham Watch Company's Works, which are the most extensive in the world. The first cotton-mill in the U. S. was erected at Waltham in 1814.

I made Boston my headquarters for the frequent excursions to different parts of this State and the neighboring State of New Hampshire, beginning with the exploration of the cotton-manufacture region.

After visiting Lowell with 59,485 inhabitants, situated on the Merrimac, at the mouth of the Concord, and one of the most noted manufacturing cities in the Union and whose prosperity is ascribed to the water power from the Pawtucket Falls in the Merrimac, I started for Lawrence, also a very prosperous large manufacturing city with 39,178 inhabitants and great water power from the Merrimac. Its leading manufactures are cotton cloth, woolens, shawls, paper, files and flour. The vast mills are separated by a canal which distributes the water power.

South Lawrence across the river is a busy manufacturing suburb.

Fall River was next visited. It contains 49,006 population and extensive manufactures of cotton-cloth, there being more spindles in operation than in any other American city.

Taunton, another flourishing manufacturing city with 21,213 inhabitants, and Quincy, a beautiful old town, noteworthy as the home of the Adams and Quincy families, followed, and after collecting authentic statistics about the cotton and wool industries in that region, I travelled to the boot and shoe manufacturing district.

Lynn, with 45,861 inhabitants, situated on the shore of Massachusetts Bay and surrounded by pleasing sceneries, is famous for its extensive manufactures of boots and shoes, it also contains a costly Soldiers' Monument and a very fine City Hall.

Worcester, the second city in Massachusetts in wealth and population, is a vast manufacturing centre, also a great railroad centre. Its population is now estimated at 75,000. Its principal manufactures are of boots and shoes, machinery and tools, a great variety of metal and wood products, stone-ware, jewelry, carpets, etc.

The principal staple is iron and steel wire, which in 2 establishments alone gives employment to over 4,000 workmen.

The city is regularly laid out with wide streets and the Union R. R. Depot is one of the largest in New England. The American Antiquarian Society contains a library of 60,000 volumes and a valuable cabinet of antiquities, and the Free Public Library 70,000 volumes.

The Lyceum and Natural History Society has interesting collections. The Worcester Academy, the Oread Institute for young ladies, the Highland Military Academy, the State Normal School, the Catholic College of the Holy Cross, and the Free Institute of Industrial Science are institutions of great fame, and the State Lunatic Asylum, a vast stone structure of great dimensions.

The beautifully situated city of Haverhill ranks in its leading industry of shoemaking next to Lynn. The city contains 18,475 inhabitants and a library of 20,000 volumes. 1 mile N. E. of Haverhill is Lake Kenoza, a pretty little lake, named and celebrated by the poet Whittier, who was born in Haverhill in 1807.

After a brief stay in Boston to which I had returned, I went to Springfield, noted for its great variety of its industries. In 1880 its population was 33,340, it is situated on the Connecticut river, is well built, and its wide streets are shaded with elms and maples. The U. S. Arsenal, the Court House and the building of the City Library (with 48,000 volumes, and a Museum of Natural History), and the City Hall, containing a public hall seating 2,700 persons, are well worth visiting. The Arsenal is the greatest in the United States.

There are also some fine churches in Worcester.

From Boston, 16 miles distant, is the venerable town of Salem with 28,000 inhabitants, the site of the first permanent settlement of the old Massachusetts colony. The year 1692 is remarkable in the history of the city, being the date of the witchcraft delusion at Salem village, now a part of Danvers, for which several persons were tried and executed. In the Court-House are deposited the documents that relate to these curious trials. The house is still standing in which some of the preliminary examinations were made. The place of execution is in the western part of the city, an eminence overlooking the city, harbor and surrounding shores, and known as Gallows Hill. Plummer Hall is a handsome building, containing the library of the Salem Athenæum (14,000 volumes), and that of the Essex Institute (25,000 volumes, and a large collection of manuscripts, pamphlets, and various historical relics). East India Marine Hall contains the large and rare ethnological museum of the East India Marine Society, and rare natural history collections of the Essex Institute. Peabody Institute, in which are deposited many interesting works of art, and the various memorials of the founder, the great Philanthropist, George Peabody, of which may be mentioned the portrait of Queen Victoria, the Congress Medal, etc. A short distance from the Institute is the house in which Mr. Peabody was born, and in Harmony Grove Cemetery not far from there is his grave.

Amherst, noted for its college, is charmingly situated. Its population is 4,000, and the leading interest paper manufacturing. Amherst College was founded in 1821, and is one of the high-standing institutions of New England. The college collections in zoölogy, botany, geology, mineralogy, etc., are among the richest in the country. The Shepard cabinet of minerals is of immense value and is said to be surpassed only by those of the British Museum and the Imperial Cabinet at Vienna; and the collection of 20,000 specimens of ancient tracks of birds, beasts and reptiles in stone is without a rival. The Massachusetts Agricultural College possesses the famous Durfee Plant-House, containing many rare and beautiful plants. It was founded in 1866 and has become the most successful agricultural school in the United States.

On a side-excursion I arrived at Mount Holyoke, the "Gem of the Massachusetts Mountains." From the Prospect House, on the top of this mountain, 1,120 ft. above the sea, and where an observatory is, the view is magnificent.

Per Boston, Hoosac Tunnel and Western R. R., the famous Hoosac Tunnel, 136 miles from Boston, was reached. It is next to that under Mt. Cenis, the longest in the world, and is one of the most wonderful and costly engineering.

New Bedford, the greatest whaling port in the world, with 33,393 inhabitants, and Plymouth, a manufacturing village, with 7,000 inhabitants, on Cape Cod Bay, were also visited. The interest of Plymouth is chiefly historical, and it will be forever famous as the landing place of the Pilgrim Fathers, on December

22, 1620, and as the site of the first settlement made in New England. Plymouth Rock, on which the Pilgrims first landed, is covered by a handsome canopy of granite, in the attic of which are inclosed the bones of several men who died during the first year of the settlement. A portion of the rock has been placed in front of Pilgrim Hall, and surrounded by an iron fence. Pilgrim Hall contains a large hall, the public library, busts and portraits, and many interesting relics of the Mayflower Pilgrims and other early settlers of Massachusetts. The National Monument to the Pilgrims consists of a granite pedestal 40 ft. high, surrounded by statues 20 ft. high, and is surmounted by a colossal granite statue of "Faith," 40 ft. high.

The environs of Plymouth are very attractive.

On this occasion—I was then in Boston—I consider it my sacred duty to pay my tributes of everlasting gratitude to the than Mayor of the City of Boston, Mr. O'Brien, to Ex-Governor Robinson, Legislator Resinovsky, Reverend Schindler, author of several important works, to Professor Morse, whom I had already seen in Japan, to the Secretary of the Imperial German Consulate, Mr. Lagrege, and to several Professors of the Harvard University, especially Professor Asa Gray, whose death is a great loss to the scientific world.

I cannot find words for the interpretation of my feelings toward these generous and kind-hearted men, for the hospitality and the many favors shown to me during my stay in Boston.

Massachusetts, the "Old Bay State," is one of the

13 original States. First settlement made by English Puritans, at Plymouth 1620.

Area, 8,315 square miles; length, northeast and southwest, 160 miles, breadth, 47 to 100 miles.

Temperature at Boston: winter, 27° to 38°; summer, 66° to 71°; rainfall, 45 inches.

Number of farms, 38,406; average value per acre, cleared land, $85; woodland, $43.25.

Hay, the most valuable crop. Ranks first in cotton, woolen and worsted goods, and in cod and mackerel fisheries, owning over half of the fishing vessels of the U. S., and second in wealth and commerce.

Population 1,941,465, including 20,361 Colored, 229 Chinese, 8 Japanese and 369 Indians.

Number of quarries, 113; ports of entry, 9; customs districts, 11. First American newspaper, Boston, 1690; first freight railroad in United States, Quincy; first American library at Harvard College. Number of colleges, 7; education compulsory; schools excellent; school age, 5–15.

Nashua was the first place visited in the State of New Hampshire. It it a pretty manufacturing city of 13,397 inhabitants, situated at the confluence of the Merrimac and Nashua Rivers.

17 miles distant from Nashua is the largest city of New Hampshire, Manchester, with a population of 32,630 and extensive manufactures, chiefly of prints.

The immense factories are on the canal and the water-power is furnished by this canal around the Amoskeag Falls of the Merrimac. The public library contains 20,000 volumes. In the city are a number of neat public squares and several fine churches.

9 miles beyond Manchester is Hooksett, with extensive brick-yards and several cotton-factories, and at the same distance from the latter, Concord, the capital of New Hampshire, on the sloping W. bank of the Merrimac River, handsomely built and with wide streets and an abundance of trees. Concord is famous for the superior quality of the granite quarried in its vicinity, and its celebrated carriage-manufactories. It contains 18,838 inhabitants, and the State Capitol, City Hall and Court House, the State Prison and the Insane Asylum are beautiful structures.

The seat of Dartmouth College, one of the most famous institutions of learning in America, is in Hanover. It was founded in 1769; and Daniel Webster, Rufus Choate and Chief Justice Chase were among its alumni. The Reed Hall, one of the group of buildings of the college, contains 50,000 volumes. The college includes, besides the literary department, a medical school and the New Hampshire College of Agriculture and the Mechanic Arts.

I returned from an excursion to Portsmouth, the only seaport of New Hampshire, standing upon a peninsula on the S. side of Piscataqua river, and excepting the narrow strip connecting it with the mainland, is entirely surrounded by water. The harbor is very deep and in it are several islets. The city is an old tranquil place with beautifully shaded streets and some old and venerable churches and residences.

The tomb of Sir William Pepperell is here. On Continental Island is the U. S. Navy Yard, admirably located. The population is about 13,000.

The road leading to the neighboring State of Maine, has densely populated districts and well-cultivated farmlands on both sides, as well as factories, etc., and the scenery around Portland has been declared by travelers to be among the most enchanting in the world.

Portland, the commercial metropolis of Maine, picturesquely situated on a high peninsula at the S. W. extremity of Casco Bay, is one of the most beautiful cities in America. It was settled in 1632, and has had a steady growth; but on the 4th of July, 1866, a great fire swept away half the business portion, destroying over $10,000,000 worth of property. The entire disdrict destroyed by the fire has since been rebuilt. The streets are profusely embellished with trees and the population in 1880, was 33,810. The City Hall is considered one of the largest and finest municipal structures in the country.

The Post Office, Custom House, Marine Hospital and some of the churches are imposing edifices. The Society of Natural History has a fine collection of fishes, birds, reptiles, shells and minerals; the library, 15,000 volumes. From the Observatory, on Munjoy's Hill, fine views are obtained and the drives around the city are excellent. The harbor is deep and spacious and is dotted with lovely islands, and defended by 3 powerful forts.

From here, the capital of Maine, **Augusta,** is 62

miles distant, and reached per Main Central and Knox and Lincoln Railway. The first important place on this road is Brunswick, a thriving town at the head of tide-water on the Androscoggin river, noted as the seat of Bowdoin College, whose gallery of paintings is famous.

Beyond Brunswick the train crosses the Androscoggin and runs into the center of the lumber industry, Gardiner. On the banks of the Kennebec, 4 miles from Gardiner, is Hallowell with extensive granite quarries in the neighborhood and 2 miles distant, at the head of navigation on the Kennebec, is Augusta, the capital of the State of Maine. This city is beautifully situated and has an abundance of shade-trees and shrubbery.

The State House, Court House, the State Insane Asylum, and the Kennebec Arsenal are noteworthy buildings.

I continued my travels in this State to Bangor, the second city of Maine, and one of the greatest lumber-markets in the world. Situated at the head of navigation on the Penobscot river, 60 miles from the ocean and containing 18,000 inhabitants, the city is very wealthy and handsomely built. Ship-building is carried on, and there is also a large business in roofing-slates, potatoes, ice, hay, steam-boilers, moccasins and machinery.

The granite Custom House and Post Office, the Norombega Hall with seats for 2,000 persons, and the Bangor Theological Seminary, and some of the churches are handsome structures.

The "Pine Tree State," State of Maine, was settled by the English at Bristol, 1624, and admitted, 1820.

Area, 33,040 square miles, extreme length, 300 miles; extreme breadth, 210 miles; shore line, over 2,400 miles, including islands; the Penobscot, Androscoggin, Saco, St. Croix, Aroostook and St. John are the most important rivers.

Temperature at Portland: winter, 23° to 38°; summer, 63° to 69°. Rainfall at Brunswick, 45 inches.

Biddeford, an important manufacturing town, has 12,651 inhabitants, and Lewiston, the principal seat of cotton manufactures, 19,083 population.

Number of farms, 64,309; average value per acre, cleared land, $12.87; woodland, $12.66. Hay the most valuable crop.

Lumbering, one of the chief industries, forests covering over 10,000,000 acres; number of saw-mills, 848. Fisheries give employment to 11,071 persons. Valuable slate-quarries from the Kennebec to the Penobscot; granite is obtained in blocks of immense size. The State has 379 ship-building establishments.

Population, incl. 1,451 Colored, 8 Chinese, and 625 Indians, 648,936.

Number of colleges, 3; system of common, high and normal schools excellent; of 519,969 persons, 10 years old and upward, 3.5 per cent. are unable to read; school age, 4-21.

Returned to New York City, and remaining there about 3 weeks; I started on the Pennsylvania Rail

Road to explore the State of Pennsylvania and traveled direct to Philadelphia.

The city of Philadelphia was founded by William Penn, who came over from England in 1682, accompanied by a colony of Quakers, and purchased the site from the Indians.

The emigration thither was very rapid and in 1684 the population was estimated at 2,500.

Penn presented the city with a charter in 1701. It prospered greatly and was the most important city in the country during the colonial period and for more than a quarter of a century after the Revolution. The first Continental Congress assembled here in 1774, as did also the subsequent Congresses during the war. The Declaration of Independence was made and issued here, July 4, 1776. The Convention which formed the Constitution of the Republic assembled here in May, 1787. Here resided the first President of the United States, and here Congress continued to meet until 1797. Until 1799 it was the capital of the colony and State of Pennsylvania, and from 1790 to 1800 was the seat of the Government of the United States. The city was in possession of the British from September, 1777, to June 1778, a result of the unfortunate battles of Brandywine and Germantown. Since the Revolution the city has grown steadily and rapidly. The population, which in 1800 was 67,811 has increased to 846,984 in 1880. The commerce of Philadelphia is large and increasing, but manufactures are its chief source of wealth. In heavy manufactures Philadelphia is only approached by Pittsburg. The leading industries are the manufacture of locomotives and all kind of iron-ware, ships, carpets, woolen and cotton goods, shoes, umbrellas, and books. In commerce Philadelphia ranks very high among the cities of the United States.

The city contains numberless fine and extensive public and private buildings, among which are of special note, the Merchants Exchange, the U. S. Custom House, the Provident Life and Trust Company's, the Philadelphia Trust Company's, the Farmers and Mechanic's Bank, the Philadelphia Bank, the Pennsylvania Life Insurance Company's, the costly buildings of the Fidelity Safe Deposit Company, the First National Bank and the Guarantee Trust and Safe Deposit Company.

Of extraordinary interest is: Independence Hall. In the Hall, the Continental Congress met, and here on July 4, 1776, the Declaration of Independence was adopted and publicly proclaimed from the steps on the same day. The "Liberty Bell," the first bell rung in the United States after the passage of Declaration, is preserved in the Hall. In Congress Hall, in the second story, Washington delivered his farewell address. Carpenter's Hall, where in 1774 the first Congress of the United Colonies assesmbled, is also of great interest.

Other noteworthy public buildings and educational and charitable institutions are: the Philadelphia Library, founded in 1731 through the influence of Benjamin Franklin, whose grave is in the neighborhood, the Pennsylvania Hospital, the Post Office, Mercantile Library, U. S. Mint, the Academy of Natural Sciences, the Ridgway Library, Academy of Music, Public Buildings (for law-courts and public offices), the Union League Club, Masonic Temple, the Girard College, the University of Pennsylvania, Pennsylvania Hospital for the Insane, the Eastern Penitentiary and the U. S. Naval Asylum, and hundred others.

Among the many churches of Philadelphia, Christ Church, the Cathedral of St. Peter and St. Paul, and the Synagogue Rodef Shalom deserve special mention as does Baptist Beth-Eden Church.

The Academy of Natural Sciences contains a library of 26,000 volumes and extensive collections in zoölogy, ornithology, geology, mineralogy, conchology, ethnology, archæology and botany. The museum contains about 250,000 specimens, and Agassiz pronounced it one of the finest natural science collections in the world.

On Washington Square, a public park in the heart of the city, nearly every variety of tree that will grow in this climate, whether indigenous or not, is contained and not far from here is the Athenæum, with a library of 25,000 volumes. An other famous institution is Jefferson Medical College, and the Academy of Fine Arts has an excellent collection of pictures, statuary, casts, etc.

Fairmount Park is the largest city park in the world, extends along both banks of the Schuylkill river for more than 7 miles and along both banks of the Wissahickon Creek for more than 6 miles and embracing a total area of 2,740 acres. Fairmount Hill is the site of 4 reservoirs of the Schuylkill Water-Works, for the supply of the city, and the Zoölogical Gardens in the Park contain a fine assortment of American and European animals.

Memorial Hall, a splendid edifice of stone, was used as an art gallery during the Exposition in 1876 and is designed for a permanent art and industrial collection. The Horticultural Building, also in the Park, is a conversatory filled with tropical and other plants and around it are 35 acres of ground devoted to horticultural purposes. Laurel Hill, adjoining the upper part of East Fairmount Park is one of the most beautiful cemeteries in the country.

I made Philadelphia my starting-point for the excursions into the interior of this State, and bound en route to Pottsville, I visited Valley Forge, memorable as the headquarters of General Washington and the American army during the dismal winter of 1777.

The building occupied by Washington is still standing near the railroad. 4 miles from the latter place, in Phœnixville, a flourishing town of 7,000 inhabitants, I had occasion to see the Phœnix Iron Works, the largest in America, and several rolling-mills and furnaces.

Beyond Phœnixville the train traverses a tunnel 2,000 ft. long and passes through Pottstown, a pretty village, crossing the Manatawny Creek and runs to

Reading, the third city in Pennsylvania in manufactures and with a population of 43,280 in 1880. It is pleasantly situated on an elevated and ascending plain, backed E. by Penn's Mountain and S. by the Neversink Mountain, from both of which flow streams of pure water, abundantly supplying the city. Of public buildings the following are noteworthy: the Court House, City Hall, the Grand Opera House, Academy of Music, and the County Prison.

Among the 31 churches, the Trinity and the Christ Church are the most imposing. There is a large trade in the city, the same being surrounded by a rich farming country. Most of the inhabitants of this district are of German origin, and a dialect of German, known as Pennsylvania Dutch, still prevails to some extent. The production and working of iron holds the first rank in the manufactures of this place. There are some interesting resorts in the vicinity.

At Reading the route is intersected by the Allentown line, and runs to the city of Allentown, a thriving city of 18,000 inhabitants, built upon an eminence between Jordan Creek and Lehigh River. The County Court House and County Prison are handsome edifices and several of the school-buildings are noteworthy. Muhlenberg College is a fine institute, and Mammoth Rock, 1,000 ft. high, and several mineral springs near the city, are interesting points. In Betlehem, not far from Allentown, is the chief seat of the Moravians, or United Brethren, who settled here under Count Zinzendorf in 1741. The Moravian Female Seminary, founded in 1749, has a high reputation. The Lehigh University founded in 1865 and liberally endowed by Asa Packer, and in which tuition in all branches is free, stands high amongst the educational institutions in the country. It has 10,000 inhabitants and most of the old Moravian buildings are in fair state of preservation.

Returning over the same road, I proceeded on my journey to the famous, world-renown Cornwall Ore Banks, touching Lebanon, on the Swatara River and with 7,000 inhabitants. The Cornwall Ore Banks are three hills formed of masses of iron-ore, and called Grassy, Middle and Big Hill. It has been estimated that Big Hill contains 40 million tons of ore above the surface of the ground, yielding 70 per cent. of pure iron. Veins of copper are found among the iron, and 6 miles from Lebanon, near the Swatara River, are quarries of fine gray marble.

Resuming my journey to the heart of the Pennsylvania coal-region, I reached the little village of Mauch Chunk. It lies in a narrow gorge between and among high mountains, its foot resting on the Lehigh River and its body lying along the hillsides, in the midst of some of the wildest and most picturesque scenery in America.

The village is but one street wide, and the valley is so narrow that the dwelling-houses usually have their gardens and outhouses perched above the roof, and there is barely room for the 2 railroads, river, street and canal, which pass through the gorge side by side.

Some fine views are obtained from the Flagstaff Peak. 2 miles from the village, on Broad Mountain, is a wild and beautiful ravine, 2,700 ft. long and from 120 to 240 ft. wide, presenting a continuous succession of cascades, rapids, and pools. The coal trains passing through the village every day, and the constant procession of canal boats laden with coal are almost numberless. The coal mines which supply this traffic are situated in the Wyoming, Hazelton, Beaver Meadow, Mahanoy, and Lehigh regions, on Sharp and Black Mountains. The "Switch Back," used only as a pleasure road, is run by gravity. The cars are drawn to the top of Mount Pisgah by a powerful engine on the summit, whence they descend 6 miles, by gravity, to the foot of Mount Jefferson, where they are again taken up by means of a plane, which ascends 462 ft. in a length of 2,070 ft. and then run on the Summit Hill. From that point the cars return, all the way, by the "Back Track," or gravity road, to Mauch Chunk, landing the passengers but a short distance from the spot where they commenced the ascent over Mount Pisgah. After a close inspection of these and other coal mines in that region, I returned to Philadelphia for the purpose of assorting my mineral and geological collection, and to rectify my table of statistics, and dispatching specimens to Europe.

This done, I started for Gettysburg, 136 miles from Philadelphia. It is a town of 2,800 inhabitants and is pleasantly situated on a fertile plain, surrounded by hills. The Pennsylvania College and the Lutheran

Theological Seminary are among the institutions of the place. The former has a library of 18,300 volumes and in the library of the latter are 10,100 volumes. Near by are the Gettysburg Springs with Katalysine waters. The chief interest of Gettysburg is historic. A great battle, perhaps the most important of the civil war, was fought here on the 1st, 2d and 3d of July, 1863, between the National forces under General Meade and the Confederate army under General Lee. Cemetery Hill forms the central and most striking feature of Gettysburg. Here were the Union headquarters, and about a mile distant is Seminary Ridge, on which were General Lee's headquarters and the bulk of the Confederate forces. The National Cemetery, containing the remains of the Union soldiers who fell in the battle of Gettysburg, was dedicated with imposing ceremonies, and an impressive address by President Lincoln, on November 19, 1863. A Soldiers' Monument, dedicated July 4, 1868, occupies the crown of the hill, is 60 ft. high, and is surmounted by a colossal marble statue of Liberty. At the base of the pedestal are 4 buttresses bearing colossal marble statues of War, History, Peace, and Plenty. Around the monument are arranged the graves of the dead. The number of bodies interred here is 3,564, of which 944 have not been identified. Near the entrance to the Cemetery is the bronze statue of Major-General Reynolds, who was killed in the battle. Opposite the cemetery is an observatory, 60 ft. high, from which a fine view of the entire battle-field and surrounding country is obtained.

York, situated on the Codorus Creek, and containing 14,000 inhabitants, is on the road to Harrisburg. It was settled in 1741, incorporated in 1787, and the Continental Congress sat here from September 30, 1777, to July 1778. During the Confederate invasion of Pensylvania in 1863, it was occupied by Early, who levied a contribution of $100,000 on the citizens, but left the place unharmed. York contains several large car-shops, some of the most extensive manufactories of agricultural implements in the country, a shoe and a match factory, and the Codorus paper-mills. After traversing York for some distance, the train descends into the rich Codorus valley, and from Bridgeport a long bridge crosses the Susquehanna river to Harrisburg, the capital of the State, beautifully situated on the E. bank of the Susquehanna river. The city is handsomely built and lies in midst a magnificent scenery.

The State House contains in its library 30,000 volumes and cabinets of curiosities, and on the grounds is a beautiful monument, commemorating the soldiers who fell in the Mexican War. The State Arsenal, Court House, and the State Lunatic Asylum are spacious and imposing buildings. The iron manufactures of Harrisburg are extensive, and 6 important railways converge here.

At the head of the Tuckahoe Valley and at the foot of the Alleghanies is Altoona, a pretty city of 20,000 inhabitants, built up since 1850, when it was a primtive forest, by being selected as the site of the large machine-shops of the Pensylvania R. R.

Just beyond Altoona the ascent of the Alleghanies begins, and for the next 10 to 11 miles some of the most brilliant scenery and marvellous engineering on the whole line are to be seen. The road mounts within this distance to the tunnel at the summit by so steep a grade that, while in the ascent double power is required to move the train, the entire distance of descent is run without steam, the speed of the train being regulated by the brakes.

The curves at some points are very short and the road hugs the sides of the mountains. The summit of the mountain is pierced by a tunnel 3,612 ft. long, through which the train passes before commencing to descend the W. slope.

Cresson Springs, $2\frac{1}{2}$ miles beyond the tunnel, are 3,000 ft. above the sea. The waters of the 7 springs are famous for their curative virtues. The climate is excellent and the thermometer rarely reaches 75° during the hottest summer month. In descending the mountains from Cresson Springs the stream, almost continuously in sight, is the Conemaugh Creek, which is crossed by a stone viaduct near Conemaugh Station, the terminus of the mountain division of the road.

3 miles from the station is Johnstown, a busy manufacturing borough at the confluence of the Conemaugh and Stony Creeks. The Cambria Iron-Works near by, are among the most extensive in the United States. 70 miles from here is Pittsburg, the second city of Pennsylvania in population and importance, and one of the chief manufacturing cities in America. Situated

at the confluence of the Alleghany and Monongahela rivers, which here form the Ohio, the city occupies the delta between the two rivers and has about 190,000 inhabitants. 9 bridges span the Alleghany river and 5 the Monongahela. From its situation, Pittsburg enjoys excellent commercial facilities and is the center of an extensive commerce with the Western States and Territories; while its vicinity to the inexhaustible iron and coal mines of the State made it a great manufacturing center. The extent of its steel, glass, and iron manufactures has given it the name of "Iron City," while the heavy pall of smoke that constantly overhangs it has caused it to be styled the "Smoky City." The manufactories of iron, steel, and glass in Pittsburg have immense dimensions. 35,000 hands are employed in the 3 mentioned interests; some of the works employing from 1,000 to 3,000 hands each. In the coal and coke interests of the city over 20,000 people are constantly employed.

Among the public buildings are the Municipal Hall, the Custom House and Post Office, the U. S. Arsenal, and the New Court House, in course of erection, the most prominent.

Of the 170 churches, the most imposing is the Roman Catholic Cathedral of St. Paul, and Trinity Church (Episcopal). The Mercantile library contains 17,000 volumes and in the same building are the collections of the Pittsburg Art Association. The Pittsburg Female College and the Pennsylvania Female College are flourishing institutions. The Western

Pennsylvania Hospital, the City General Hospital, the Homæopathic Hospital, Mercy Hospital, the Episcopal Church Home, the Convent of the Sisters of Mercy, the oldest house of the order in America, and the Roman Catholic Orphan Asylum, are the principal charitable institutions in the city. The new Riverside Penitentiary, the Passionist Monastery of St. Paul, and the Franciscan Convent are at Manchester, 2 miles below Pittsburg, now a part of Allegheny City.

Since the introduction of Natural Gas and its supply to the great iron and glass works of Pittsburg, instead of other costly fuel, the manufacturing and commercial prosperity of that city has entered upon a new era, which places it on a level with some of the largest cities in the United States. The Natural-Gas industry in Western Pennsylvania, especially in Pittsburg, where the gas is also used for domestic purposes, has rapidly developed and promises to become a source of immense value.

The so-called coal-fields of Pittsburg comprise an area of 15,000 square miles and, according to assertions made by famous geologists in the State of Pennsylvania, will not exhaust in a thousand years. The coal trade in Pittsburg can almost be called its speciality, but not only coal, in its crude state, is it, that gives it such importance, the manufacture of coke adds greatly to the interests of this wealthy and unique city in the Universe.

Though coke has been an important product of Western Pennsylvania as far back as 60 years, its present importance has gradually developed itself within the last 20 years.

The chief area of the coke industry is centred in and around Connellsville, 30 to 50 miles from Pittsburg, in Alleghany, Westmoreland, and Fayette Counties, but is directed by Pittsburg firms. During my stay in Pittsburg I had received many favors and valuable services of the Austrian Consul Mr. Schamberg, the well-known State Geologist, Professor Chas. A. Ashburner, and the Attorney, Mr. Josiah Cohen, and I herewith express my heartfelt thanks to them.

Allegheny City, opposite Pittsburg, with which it is connected by 9 bridges, is situated on the W. bank of the Alleghany River. Its manufacturing interests are large. In 1880 the city had a population of 78,681. The finest church in the city is St. Peter's (Catholic), and there are several Theological Seminaries. The Western University formerly in Pittsburg has a valuable geological and natural-history collection. The Allegheny Observatory is a department of this institution. The Allegheny General Hospital is the principal hospital, and the Soldiers Monument, erected to the memory of the 4,000 men of Alleghany County who lost their lives in the civil war, is very graceful.

In the center of the Wyoming Valley, picturesquely situated on the Susquehanna river, is Wilkesbarre, a prosperous city of 23,393 inhabitants, with handsome public and private buildings. There are several fine churches and a good library in the city.

9 miles beyond Wilkesbarre is Pittson, on the Sus-

quehanna, W. of the town are the Lackawannock Mountains filled with rich coal mines which here find an outlet.

From this latter place I traveled to Oil City, the center and headquarters of the Oil Region. It is situated on the Alleghany river at the mouth of Oil Creek. Its population is 8,000 and, though not particularly attractive, is interesting on account of witnessing the various operations of obtaining, refining, barreling, gauging and shipping the precious petroleum. The wells in the vicinity yield 600 barrels daily, and about two million barrels are annually sent thence to market.

The great iron tanks for storing the oil are worth visiting.

18 miles beyond Oil City, on the road to Buffalo, is Titusville, a city of 10,000 inhabitants and the largest place in the Oil Regions. It is situated in a broad and beautiful valley, through which flows Oil Creek. The city is nicely built and owes its rapid growth and prosperity mainly to the oil wells in the vicinity, which are very productive; and here are the capacious refineries of the Standard Oil Company. Besides the oil-works there are extensive iron-works, foundries and machine-shops, and various other manufactories.

Before concluding my six weeks travels through the State, I visited Scranton and Carbondale. Scranton is a flourishing city, occupying the plateau at the confluence of Roaring Brook and the Lackawanna river.

It is handsomely laid out and has 45,850 inhabitants. Its importance is due to its situation in the most northern of the anthracite basins, and to its railroad facilities. The trade in mining supplies is extensive, and the shipments of coal are immense. Its iron manufactures are very important, and there are large blast-furnaces, rolling-mills, foundries, machine-shops, etc.

Carbondale has 8,000 inhabitants and is at the N. end of the anthracite coal region, near several extremely rich coal-mines. The chief object of interest here is the Gravity Railroad, a series of inclined planes on which immense coal-trains are sent over the mountains to and from Honesdale, on the Delaware and Hudson Canal, with no impelling force but gravity, save at one point.

The Keystone State, Pennsylvania, one of the 13 original States, is named in honor of William Penn, the grantee. First permanent settlement made by Swedes at Chester, 1638.

Area, 45,215 square miles; extreme length, 303 miles; greatest breadth, 176 miles.

Largest rivers, Delaware, Susquehanna, Alleghany, Monongahela, Ohio.

Temperature at Philadelphia: winter, 31° to 42°; summer, 70° to 75°; rainfall, 44 inches.

Philadelphia founded 1682; second city in the United States. Philadelphia, Pittsburg and Erie are ports of entry.

Number of farms, 156,357, averaging about 100

acres each; average value per acre, cleared land, $45.-75; woodland, $29.75.

Manufacture of pig iron the greatest industry; number of manufacturing establishments, 10,381; flour and grist-mills, 2,873; iron and steel works, 321; sawed lumber, 2,826; paper-mills, 78; woolen-goods, 324.

Anthracite coal field in central division; bituminous in west and southwest. Produces all the anthracite and more than half the bituminous coal of the United States. Ranks first in rye, iron and steel, petroleum and coal; second in buckwheat, potatoes and printing and publishing.

Population of 4,282,891 includes 85,535 Colored, 148 Chinese, 8 Japanese and 184 Indians.

Non-tax payers and political bribers excluded from voting.

Number of colleges, 26; enrolled in public schools, 945,345; school age, 6–21.

On the route from Philadelphia to Baltimore, Maryland, the city of Chester, the seat of the famous ship-building establishment of the late John Roach, is passed. Chester has 14,996 inhabitants and is interesting as the spot where in September, 1777, the battle on the banks of the Brandywine was fought. 14 miles from Chester is the city of Wilmington, Delaware, the most important in that State, with a population of 42,-500, and various and extensive manufactures, embracing ship-building, car-factories, cotton and woolen manufacturies, flour-mills, powder-mills, and shoe and leather factories. The city is nicely laid out and contains several fine public and private buildings and handsome churches.

At Havre de Grace, the Susquehanna river is crossed on a lofty iron bridge nearly a mile long, and Baltimore is entered into. Baltimore is the chief city of Maryland and in population and commerce one of the most important in the Union. It is picturesquely situated on the N. branch of the Patapsco river, 14 miles from its entrance into Chesapeake Bay, and about 200 miles from the ocean. Jones's Falls, a small stream running N. and S., spanned by several bridges, divides the city into two nearly equal parts known as East and West Baltimore.

The harbor is capacious and safe, consisting of an inner basin and an outer harbor accessible to the largest ships. The entrance is defended by Fort McHenry, which was unsuccessfully bombarded by the British fleet in the war of 1812.

The present site of Baltimore was chosen in 1729 and its name was given it in 1745, in honor of Lord Baltimore, the proprietary of Maryland. The charter of the city dates from 1797. The population which at that time was 26,000, had increased by 1860 to 212,418, and in 1880 it had reached 332,190. The commerce of the city is very large, and through the two rail roads of the Baltimore and Ohio and the Northern Central, the city is successfully competing for the trade of the north and northwest. Large shipments of grain are made to Europe, and tobacco, cotton, petroleum, bacon, butter, cheese and lard, are also exported.

Baltimore is the chief point for working the rich copper-ores of Lake Superior, and produces nearly 4,000 tons of refined copper yearly; the smelting-works are in Canton, and employ 1,000 men. There are also iron-works, rolling-mills, nail-factories, locomotive-works, cotton-factories, and other industrial establishments, 2,261 in all. The canning of oysters, vegetables and fruits, is estimated to reach the annual value of $10,000,000; and half a million hides are annually made into leather and sent to New England.

Baltimore is called the "Monumental City," from the number of its monuments; its chief monument is the Washington Monument, and Battle Monument was erected 1815, to the memory of those who fell defending the city from the British in September, 1814.

There are a great many churches in this city, among which the following are the finest: the Cathedral, Mount Vernon Church, First Presbyterian, and Unitarian Church. The Hebrew Synagogue is a large and handsome edifice.

Of educational institutions, of which there are also a great number, the first of all, and the greatest in Maryland is the Johns Hopkins University.

The Peabody Institute, containing 75,000 volumes in its library; the Athenæum, with the Baltimore Library (15,000 volumes), and the collections of the Maryland Historical Society, comprising a library of 10,000 volumes, numerous historical relics and pictures and statuary; the Maryland Institute, designed for the promotion of the mechanic arts, containing a library of 14,000 volumes; the Academy of Science with a fine museum of natural history, including rich collections of birds and minerals, and a complete representation of the flora and fauna of Maryland; the State Normal School; the City college; and the Enoch Pratt Free Libray, containing 25,000 volumes, are of high standing.

Prominent charitable institutions are the Johns Hopkins Hospital, connected with the Medical Department of the Johns Hopkins University; the Maryland Hospital for the Insane; the Mount Hope Hospital; the State Institution for the Instruction of the Blind; the Episcopal Church Home; State Insane Asylum; Bay View Asylum; the Sheppard Asylum for the Insane; and the Mount Hope Retreat for the Insane and Sick, 4 miles from the city.

The City Hall, the Exchange and the Masonic Temple are exceedingly elegant structures, and there are numerous fine business buildings. Druid Hill Park, 680 acres in area, is a beautiful pleasure ground, and from the tower at the head of Druid Hill Lake, a superb view of the city and the harbor is obtained. On Federal Hill, a commanding eminence on the S. side of the inner basin, is the U. S. Signal Station. The Baltimore and Potomac Tunnel, next to the Hoosac Tunnel the largest in America, (6,969 ft.) and the Union Tunnel, (3,410 ft.) are among the wonders of Baltimore.

At an excursion to Cumberland in the mountain region, and which in point of population and commerce is the second city, I was greatly surprised to find such an enormous activity in it. It has 11,000 inhabitants and is the site of the great rolling-mills of the R. R. Company, for the manufacture of steel rails. A few miles W. of Cumberland upon the summit of the Alleghanies, begins the district known as the Cumberland Coal Regions, which extends W. to the Ohio River. On that pretty long journey I had occasion to study the country profoundly, and started for the capital of the State, Annapolis. The capital contains the U. S. Naval Academy, some excellent State Institutions, and 5,744 inhabitants. The situation of Annapolis is of great beauty, on Chesapeake Bay.

The State of Maryland, named in honor of Maria, wife of Charles II, King of England, is one of the 13 original States; first settlement made by English Roman Catholics at St. Mary's, 1634.

Area, 12,210 square miles; greatest length, east and west, 196 miles; sea coast, 33 miles; or, including the tidewater region of the Chesapeake Bay, 411 miles; and, with shores of islands, 509 miles.

Temperature at Baltimore: winter, 33° to 41°; summer, 73° to 79°. Rainfall, 41 inches.

Number of farms, 40,517; average value per acre, cleared land, $35.50; woodland, $24.65. Number of manufacturing establishments, 6,787; hands employed, 74,945; flour and grist mills, 546.

Copper is found in Frederick and Carroll counties; iron ore in Alleghany, Anne Arundel, Carroll, Baltimore, Frederick and Prince George's counties.

Population, 934,943, incl. 210,230 colored, 5 Chinese and 15 Indians. Slaves in 1860, 87,189. Bribers excluded from voting. Number of colleges, 11; school population, 319,201; school age, 5-20.

40 miles from Baltimore lies Washington City, the capital of the Republic. Owing to its number and magnificence of its public buildings, Washington is one of the most interesting cities in America. It is situated on the N. bank of the Potomac river, at its confluence with the Eastern Branch.

The site of Washington City was selected through the agency of Washington, who himself laid the corner stone of the Capitol, on September 18, 1793, seven years before the seat of government was removed thither from Philadelphia. Under Washington's direction the city was planned and laid out by Andrew Ellicott. It appears to have been Washington's desire that it should be called the "Federal City," but the name of "the city of Washington" was conferred upon it on September 9, 1791. Its ancient name was Conococheague, derived from a rapid stream of that name which ran near the city, and which, in the Indian tongue, means the Roaring Brook. The city was incorporated May 3, 1802. Its population in 1860 was 60,000, and 1880, 147,307.

The commerce and manufactures of Washington are unimportant. The public buildings are the chief attraction of Washington, and the Capitol is probably the most magnificent public edifice in the world. It is almost impossible to give a true description of all the curiosities and brilliant ornamentations of this unique marvel of monumental architecture.

The Library of Congress is the largest collection in the United States, and numbers now nearly 450,000 volumes, exclusive of pamphlets, and is increasing at the rate of 10,000 to 15,000 volumes a year. The total cost of the Capitol was $13,000,000.

The Executive Mansion, usually called the "White House," whose corner-stone was laid in 1792, was first occupied by President Adams in 1800. The building stands on an area comprising 75 acres, handsomely laid out, and contains in the inclosed 20 acres of ground for the President's private use, extensive conservatories and a beautiful fountain.

The U. S. Treasury, State, War, and Navy Departments, Patent Office, Department of Agriculture, Post Office Department, and the Pension Building are extensive and brilliant structures.

Smithsonian Institution, founded by James Smithson, an Englishman, " for the increase and diffusion of knowledge among men," contains a museum of natural history, with numerous specimens, and metallurgical, mineralogical and ethnological collections, with many curiosities.

In the "Annex" of the Institution is the National Museum, which contains the Centennial exhibits of the United States, and donations of foreign Governments to America. Botanical Gardens consist chiefly of a series of large conservatories filled with rare and curious plants, flowers and fruits, and N. of it stands the

Bartholdi Fountain, so much admired at the Centennial Exhibition.

The U. S. Naval Observatory occupies a commanding site on the bank of the Potomac. It was founded in 1842, and is now one of the foremost institutions in the world. It possesses many fine instruments, including a 26-inch equatorial telescope and a good library of astronomical works. The Army Medical Museum contains 16,000 specimens, illustrating every species of wound and disease.

The Navy-Yard, containing the Naval Museum, the Experimental Battery and the fleet, has an area of 27 acres.

There are a number of very fine churches in Washington.

The Corcoran-Art Gallery, founded by the banker W. W. Corcoran, contains numerous paintings, most of them masterpieces, and the finest collection of casts in America; marble statuary; the richest bronzes in the U. S.; porcelain; and specimens of majolica-ware, bric-à-brac, etc.

The Washington Monument, considered to be the loftiest in the world, was dedicated on Washington's Birthday, 1885, and the Statues of Washington, General Scott, Lincoln, General Rawlins, General Thomas, General McPherson, and the Naval Monument are of large proportions and beauty. A second statue of Lincoln was erected by contributions of colored people.

The Soldiers Home consists of several spacious

marble buildings surrounded by a beautiful park of 500 acres. President Lincoln passed some of the last hours of his eventful term in the Home, and near by is the National Cemetery.

The Government Asylum for the Insane is an extensive and noble building. Howard University, founded in 1864, for the education of youth "without regard to sex or color," is a vast structure.

Georgetown, now called West Washington, is connected by 4 bridges with Washington and is beautifully situated on a range of hills which command a view unsurpassed in the Potomac Valley. Georgetown College, the most famous institution of learning of the Roman Catholic Church in the United States, is under the control of the Jesuits, and contains a library of 30,000 volumes, some beautifully illuminated missals, some rare old manuscripts, an astronomical observatory, and a museum of natural history.

The Aqueduct, by which the waters of the Chesapeake and Ohio Canal are carried across the Potomac, is worth inspecting. 15 miles below Washington is Mount Vernon on the Virginia side of the Potomac, then known as the "Hunting Creek estate," was bequeathed by Augustine Washington, who died in 1743, to Lawrence Washington. The latter named it after Admiral Vernon, under whom he had served in the Spanish wars. George Washington inherited the estate in 1752. The central part of the mansion, which is of wood, was built by Lawrence, and the wings by George Washington. It contains many interesting historical relics, among which are the key of the Bastile, presented by Lafayette, portions of the military and personal furniture of Washington, portraits, etc. The Tomb of Washington stands in a retired situation near the mansion. It is a plain but solid brick structure, with an iron gate, through the bars of which may be seen the marble sarcophagi containing the remains of George and Martha Washington. The Mount Vernon domain, including the mansion and 6 acres, which had remained since the death of Washington in the possession of his descendants, was purchased in 1856 for the sum of $200,000, raised by subscription, under the auspices of the "Ladies' Mount Vernon Association" aided by the efforts of Edward Everett. It is, therefore, and will continue to be, the property of the nation.

Leaving the beautiful city of Washington I traveled to Harper's Ferry, delightfully situated at the confluence of the Potomac and Shenandoah Rivers. The town is irregularly built around the base of a hill. The scenery around Harper's Ferry is wonderfully picturesque. The Maryland Heights, across the Potomac, and Bolivar Heights, above the town, are worth to be climbed. The chief interest pertaining to Harper's Ferry, now a village of about 800 inhabitants, is historical.

It was the scene of the exploits which in October 1859, rendered the name of John Brown, of Ossawattomie, Kansas, notorious; and Charlestown, the county-seat where Brown and his followers were tried and executed, is only 7 miles distant on the road to Winchester. During the civil war Harper's Ferry was alternately in the hands of the Federals and Confederates.

During my stay in Washington I had the honor to be introduced to President Cleveland, by the well-known Mr. Simon Wolf, and to the President of the United States Senate, Mr. Sherman. The latter had the kindness to detach his Secretary, Mr. Babcock, to act as my companion and guide.

In all the Governmental Departments I was cordially received, and of some of the professional Scientists of the different scientific institutes in the city, f. i. Professor Baird, the famous Ichthyologist, the well-known Archaeologist, Professor Rau, the successful Ethnologist, Professor Otis, and above all, my worthy friend, the indefatigable Ethno-Geologist, Major Powell, as well as of the Secretary for foreign exchange at the Smithsonian Institute, Mr. Boehme, I received valuable informations and favors which will never be forgotten by me and for which I herewith thank them heartily.

The District of Columbia in which Washington is situated, comprises an area of 75 square miles, and lies on the Potomac. Georgetown, too, is in it.

By approbation of an act of Congress on February 21, 1871, a Territorial Government was instituted, but in 1874, the territorial system was abandoned and all public affairs entrusted to 3 Commissioners.

In 1860, the population numbered 75,080; the Slaves, 3,185. In 1880 there were 177,624 inhabitants in the District, among these, 59,402 negroes.

After my return to Philadelphia, I visited Camden, a flourishing city of 25,000 inhabitants, on the Deleware opposite Philadelphia, with which it is connected by ferries.

There are extensive ship-yards and manufactures of iron, glass and chemicals.

Cape May, the Long Branch of Philadelphia, is the extreme southern point of New Jersey, fronting the Atlantic at the entrance of Delaware Bay. Cape May is a favorite resort of Southern and Western people and there are some nice places of amusements in the vicinity.

Like Cape May, Atlantic City is a favorite resort of Philadelphians, and during the season a great many people visit the place. A short distance N. of Atlantic City, is the beautiful but ill-omened Brigantine Beach, called by the sailors "the Graveyard," on account of the number of fatal wrecks that have occurred there. Continuing my travels through the State New Jersey, Long Branch was begun with. This is a great summer resort in the vicinity of New York, situated on the Jersey shore of the Atlantic, where a long beach affords admirable facilities for bathing. The Monmouth Park Race-Course and the Iron Pier are worth attention.

Jersey City is situated on the Hudson river, opposite New York, of which it is practically a portion. It is a place of much commercial and industrial activity, and had in 1880 a population of 120,728. It contains the depots of several of the most important railways leading South and West from New York, and the docks of leading transatlantic steamers, but nothing else of special interest, except a few nice churches and several good educational institutions.

Newark, on the route to the capital of the State of New Jersey, is a large manufacturing city with 136,400 inhabitants.

The city is built on an elevated plain upon the right bank of the Passaic river, 4 miles from Newark Bay, and is regularly laid out.

Of the literary institutions, the most noteworthy are the State Historical Society, the Library Association, containing 20,000 volumes, and the Newark Academy. Newark is distinguished for its manufactures of jewelry, carriages, paper, leather, and hats, and some of the public buildings are very fine. Newark Lager-bier has great fame in the U. S.

6 miles beyond Newark is Elizabeth, the nicest city in New Jersey, with 28,229 inhabitants, and many fine residences; but little industry.

New Brunswick, on Raritan river, has 18,000 inhabitants and immense manufactures of India-rubber, harness and hosiery. Rutger's College in the city, is an old richly-endowed and flourishing establishment, and 16 miles distant from here is Princeton-Junction, and 2½ miles from the latter Princeton College, one of the most famous institutions of learning in America.

A detour to Patterson, a busy manufacturing city of 50,887 inhabitants was well worth undertaking. Patterson is situated on the right bank of the Passaic river, immediately below the falls. It was founded in

1791 by Alexander Hamilton, in the cotton interest, and its cotton factories are now very extensive. Its most important interest, however, is silk manufacturing, for which it has 30 factories, employing about 8,000 persons, and turning out a product of $4,000,-000. It has also extensive manufacturing interests in velvet, woolen, linen, locomotives, and heavy machinery.

Next to Newark it is the largest manufacturing city of New Jersey. The Passaic Falls have a perpendicular descent of 50 ft., and the scenery in the vicinity is very picturesque. Ramapo, 17 miles distant, has the Torn Mountain in its neighborhood, from the summit of which there is a wide-extended view. During the campaign of 1777, Washington often ascended this mountain to watch the movements of the British army and fleet around New York.

Trenton, the capital of New Jersey, is beautifully situated on the Delaware. Its manufacturing interests are important, and among these, the Potteries are chief. The population in 1880, was 29,910, and the city is remarkably well built, and clean.

The leading event in the past history of Trenton is the famous victory over the Hessians won by Washington, December 26, 1776; and its chief present attractions are the public buildings. It contains the State House, State Penitentiary, State Arsenal and the State Lunatic Asylum.

The State of New Jersey, "Jersey Blue," was named in honor of a grantee, Sir George Carteret, at one time Governor of the Island of Jersey. It is one of the 13 original States. Settled by Dutch, at Bergen, 1620.

Area, 7,815 square miles; extreme length, 157 miles; breadth, 37 to 70 miles; frontage on Atlantic and Delaware Bay, about 120 miles each.

Temperature at Atlantic City: winter, 32° to 42°; summer, 66° to 73°. Rainfall at Newark, 45 inches.

Newark, Perth Amboy, Great Egg Harbor, Tuckerton, Bridgeton and Lumberton are ports of entry. Extensive zinc works at Newark and Jersey City. Hoboken has a population of 37,721, and is practically a part of New York; many business men residing there, and except the large docks of European Steamship companies has little to offer.

Hay is the most valuable crop. Cranberry growing a specialty, Burlington, Ocean and Atlantic counties being especially adopted to this industry. Central region, a vast market garden. Latest reports give 108 factories for silk and silk goods, and number of hands employed in them 12,549; 2,234 hands employed in jewelry factories; number of flour and grist mills, 481; brick and tile factories, 107. Ranks first in fertilizing marl, zinc and silk goods.

Population, 1,131,116, incl. 38,853 Negroes, 172 Chinese, and 74 Indians.

Number of colleges, 4; number enrolled in public schools, 209,526; school age, 5–18.

The next exploration tour was intended for Nebraska and other Western States and Territories, and starting from Chicago, by the Chicago, Rock Island

and Pacific R. R., I passed many already described places, and visited first, the important stone quarries around Lockport, near Joliet, Illinois. Joliet is situated on both banks of the Des Plaines river and on the Illinois and Michigan canal of which it receives its water-power. The city is beautifully built, and here is located one of the finest prisons in America, the State Penitentiary.

The vicinity is very productive and the city is the chief point of shipping. Besides flour-mills, there are also manufactories of agricultural implements, and Joliet contains 16,145 inhabitants.

23 miles beyond Joliet is the flourishing town of Ottawa, on Illinois river, close below the entrance of Fox river, which has here a fall of 29 ft., affording an immense water power which is extensively used in manufactures. The population is 8,000. There are several grain-elevators, and large quantities of wheat are shipped from this point.

La Salle, 36 miles distant, with 8,000 inhabitants, on the Illinois river, is a busy manufacturing city. Here terminates the Illinois and Michigan Canal, 100 miles long, which connects it with Chicago. It is the center of extensive mines of bituminous coal, of which large quantities are shipped.

Moline, on the E. bank of the Mississippi, with 9,000 inhabitants, and various factories, which obtain an immense water-power by means of a dam, is picturesquely situated and the surrounding country is rich in coal.

Below Moline is the flourishing city of Rock Island, on the E. bank of the Mississippi, with a population of about 16,000.

The river is here divided by the island of Rock Island, which is 3 miles long; and from 16 miles above Moline to 3 miles below are the Upper Rapids. The city of Rock Island is at the foot of the rapids and at the confluence of Rock River with the Mississippi.

It is an important railroad center, is the shipping point for the productive country adjacent, and has many varied manufactures.

The Augustana College and Theological Institute are located here. The island of Rock Island (960 acres) is Government property and the site of the Great Arsenal and Armory, intended to be the central United States Armory.

Opposite Rock Island, on the Iowa side of the river, is the city of Davenport and the train crosses the river between them on the magnificent railroad and wagon bridge, built by the Government. Davenport is the second city of Iowa in size, has 22,000 inhabitants, and is the great grain depot of the Upper Mississippi. It is also an important manufacturing center, and is situated in the heart of extensive bituminous coal-fields. The city is nicely laid out, and handsomely built. Griswold College, the Academy of the Immaculate Conception, and the Academy of Natural Sciences are located here, and there are some fine churches and several nice buildings.

Continuing my travels in Iowa, I next visited Iowa

City, formerly the State Capital, and now the seat of the State University. The State Historical Society has a library of about 4,000 volumes, and there are some factories for which the Iowa River furnishes the water power. The population is about 8,000. Iowa College, removed from Davenport, is now in Grinnell, 75 miles from Iowa City.

Des Moines, the present capital of Iowa, is situated on the Des Moines river, at its confluence with the Raccoon. The city is intersected by both rivers, which are spanned by 8 bridges, and has 35,000 inhabitants. The new Capitol is a splendid building, and cost $3,000,000. The Post Office contains also the U. S. Courts, etc., and the two medical colleges, the Drake University, and the Calinan College are famous schools of learning. The State Library contains 15,000 volumes, and there is also a Public Library and 15 churches, and a Baptist college in the city. Twelve railroads pass through the city, making it a railroad center.

Beyond Des Moines the road passes through the flourishing cities of Avoca and Atlantic, descends the bluffs into the Missouri Bottom and soon reaches Council Bluffs, with a population of 22,000. It is the converging-point of all the railroads from the East which connect with the Union Pacific, and communicates by steam-railroad with Omaha, on the opposite river bank. The great Missouri River Bridge which connects the two cities, is 2,750 ft. long. Council Bluffs is well laid out, and near here is the State Institute for the Deaf and Dumb. The views from the bluffs above the city are very fine.

By a decision of the U. S. Supreme Court, Council Bluffs is the E. terminus of the Union Pacific R. R.

The "Hawkeye State," Iowa, whose name is of Indian origin, and means "The Beautiful Land," is part of the Louisiana purchase, merged into Missouri Territory, 1812; into Michigan, 1834; into Wisconsin, 1836. First white settlement at Dubuque, 1788. Admitted as a State, 1846.

Area, 56,025 square miles; extent, north and south, 208 miles; east and west, about 300 miles. Principal rivers within the State: Des Moines, Iowa and Little Sioux.

Temperature at Davenport; winter, 21° to 37°; summer, 70° to 76°. Rainfall at Muscatine, 43 inches.

Burlington, Keokuk and Dubuque are U. S. ports of delivery.

Number of farms, 185,351; average value per acre, cleared land, $39.36; woodland, $27.36. Dairy interest growing in importance, creamery and factory products bringing high prices. Manufacturing establishments are numerous, including canning factories, stove and other foundries, engine-building, paper and woolen mills, lumber and saw-mills, etc. Ranks first in hogs; second in milk cows, oxen and other cattle, corn, hay and oats.

Population, 1,753,980, incl. 9,310 colored, 33 Chinese and 466 Indians.

Number of Colleges, 19; school population, 604,739; school age, 5-21.

Opposite Council Bluffs, as already stated, lies the city of Omaha, the largest city of Nebraska and of the Missouri Valley. It occupies a beautiful plateau, rising gradually into bluffs and toward the end of 1884 had 60,000 inhabitants. On the bluffs stand the handsome residences of the wealthier citizens. The U. S. Post-Office and Court House, the High-School Building, the Union Pacific Headquarters Building, the Union Pacific R. R. Depot, the Douglas County Court House and Boyd's Opera House are magnificent structures and several of the churches are costly and elegant edifices. Its prosperity is due chiefly to its having been for a long period the real E. terminus of the Union Pacific R. R.

It has an immense trade and many important manufactories, the principal of which latter are the Omaha Smelting-Works, considered to be the largest in America, several large breweries and distilleries, extensive linseed-oil works, steam-engine works, brick yards, stock yards and pork-packing establishments, and the extensive machine-shops, car-works and foundry of the Union Pacific R. R. The system of water-works in the city is unsurpassed. Fort Omaha is 4 miles from Omaha city and has a large post, but the headquarters of the Department of the Platte are in the city.

The Burlington and Missouri River R. R. extends to Denver, Colorado, whence I intended to go after visiting the capital of Nebraska, Lincoln, and procuring passage on that line, I started for Lincoln.

This is a city of 20,000 population, and is the seat of the State University and several other educational and charitable institutions. It is romantically situated and has a lively commerce.

My explorations in the State of Nebraska were not of an extensive character and I was compelled to get furnished with the details of this country from the most reliable sources, and reproduce the same as given to me.

The State of Nebraska, whose name is taken from the Indian, signifying "Shallow water" and applied first to the river, was organized as a Territory in 1854; admitted 1867.

Area 76,855 square miles; width, north and south, about 210 miles; greatest length in center, about 420 miles. Platte the principal river, extending through the State east and west.

Temperature at Omaha; winter, 20° to 34°; summer, 72° to 78°. Rainfall at Fort Kearney, 25 inches.

Population of Plattsmouth, 5,796; of Nebraska City, 5,597. Rye, buckwheat, barley, flax and hemp yield abundant crops. Apples, pears, plums, grapes, and berries are plentiful. Herd law excellent, and grazing land good. Cattle raising the great industry of the State, next to agriculture. Manufacturing establishments show a wonderful increase of from 670 in 1870 to 1,403 in 1880. Homesteads obtained under timber claims, or by pre-emptions; cash expense of first, $18 to $26; of second, $14.

Population, 452,402, incl. 2,385 Colored, 18 Chinese and 235 Indians. U. S. Army excluded from voting.

Number of colleges, 9; school population, 135,511; school age, 5–21.

On the route from Omaha to Denver by the Union Pacific R. R., numerous small cities, etc., are passed, offering nothing noteworthy, though the distance is 565 miles.

The peculiar position of the Pacific Rail Roads induce me to describe their history in a brief extract.

As early as 1846, the project of a railway across the continent was advocated by Asa Whitney, and in 1853 Congress passed an act providing for surveys by the corps of topographical engineers. In 1862 and 1864 further acts were passed providing for a subsidy in U. S. 6 per cent. gold bonds at specified rates per mile. By these acts, the companies undertaking the work, received 12,800 acres of land for each mile of railroad built, or 25,000,000 acres in all. The Union Pacific Company built the railroad from Omaha to Ogden, a distance of 1,033 miles, and the Central Pacific Company that from San Francisco to Ogden, 883 miles. Work began in 1863; the first 40 miles from Omaha to Fremont were completed in 1865, and on the 12th of May, 1869, the railroad communication from the Atlantic to the Pacific Ocean was opened. Nine Mountain ranges this route crosses, the highest of which are the Black Hills, at an elevation of 8,242 ft. above the sea, and the lowest Promontory Mountains, W. of Great Salt Lake, 4,889 ft. The aggregate length of the tunnels, of which there are 15, all situated in the Sierra Nevada or its spurs, is 6,000 ft. The gradients do not often exceed 80 ft. to the mile.

The cost of the Union Pacific Road was reported to the Secretary of the Interior at $112,259,360; but the liabilities of the company at the date of the completion of the road were $116,730,052. In 1868 Jesse L. Williams, a civil engineer and one of the Government directors, reported the approximate cost of the Union Pacific Road in cash at $38,824,821. The cost of the Central Pacific Road and branches (1,222 miles) in liabilities of every sort was reported in 1874 at $139,746,311.

During my repeated stays in the city of Denver I had formed many valuable acquaintances, and enjoyed the hospitality of Ex-Governor Eaton, Lieutenant-Governor Breen, Doctor Elsner and Mr. Rose. Doctor Elsner, a celebrated Physician in Denver, and his amiable family were indefatigable in their efforts to make my sojourn as pleasant and agreeable as possible. Doctor Elsner's mineralogic-geological collection is the second largest in the United States, and as a specific American (from the Rocky Mountains), the first in the world.

Of Mr. Addy, General Passenger Agent of the Union Pacific R. R. Company; Major K. Hooper of the Rio Grande R. R. Company—the latter well-known in the country as the author of descriptions of travels and other journalistics—; of the Administration of the Atchison, Topeka and Santa Fé R. R. Company, and

Commissioner Rich, I received many favors and important informations, and to all of them I am under deep obligations; thanking them with all my heart.

By the Denver and Silverton Division of the Denver and Rio Grande R. R., I crossed the Sangre di Christo range by the wonderful La Veta Pass, at an altitude of 9,486 ft. amid scenery of a remarkable beauty and grandeur. The view of Sierra Blanca 14,464 ft. high, flanked by the serrated peaks of the Sangre di Christo range, as seen from Alamosa, is nowhere surpassed. W. of Antonita, 29 miles distant, are the Los Pinos Cañon and the Toltec Gorge, the most wonderful scenic attractions of Colorado. For a distance of 8 miles the railway runs just below the brow of a precipitous mountain-range at the terror-inspiring height of 1,200 ft. above the stream, following the irregular contour of the mountains, through deep cuts and over high hills, (Phantom Curve), till it comes to the end of a mountain-wall that juts into the cañon, narrowing it to a mere gorge, 1,400 ft. in depth. Not far from the gorge, the railway suddenly enters a tunnel in the solid granite cliff, and 600 ft. further on emerges upon a trestle-bridge and reaches Durango, which is the supply depot for the famous San Juan mining district, and the road continues to Silverton, 495 miles from Denver. At a distance of 30 miles from Durango are the prehistoric cliff dwellings on the Rio Mancos, among the most wonderful in America. At Antonita the New Mexico Division of the R. R. branches off to the S. and runs in 91 miles to Española, near which place are 8 ancient pueblos, inhabited by Pueblo Indians whom the Spaniards found there only 48 years after the discovery of America, and in the neighboring cliffs are numerous cave-dwellings prehistoric in their origin.

Boulder was next visited. This is a mining town and contains the State University, and in its proximity, the famous Boulder Cañon, a stupendous mountain-gorge, 17 miles long, with walls of solid rock that rise precipitously to a height of 3,000 ft. in many places.

About 8 miles from Boulder are the Falls of Boulder Creek and at Longmont, 13 miles beyond Boulder, is the starting point for an excursion through the picturesque Estes Park, to the summit of Longs Peak, 14,088 ft. high, affording one of the grandest views to be obtained in Colorado. Beyond Longmont the railway gradually nears the mountains, crosses the beautiful and productive Cache la Poudre Valley at Fort Collins, and for the last 50 miles runs at the base of the Rocky Mountains.

In that region Tellurium mines are to be found, this rare metal appearing in different admixtures, and according to assurances made to me by the well-known Geologist Professor Smith, yield exceedingly well. To this Scientist also I am indebted for his kindness, which induced me to prolong my stay in that region.

Fort Collins is a military post and contains the Agricultural Institute and several handsome buildings.

Concluding thus my travels through the State of Colorado, I proceeded to Wyoming Territory.

The "Centennial State," Colorado, is part of Louisiana purchase of 1803. First explored by Vasquez Coronado under the Spanish, 1540.

First expedition sent out by U. S. Government, under Major Pike, 1806, a second under command of Col. S. H. Long, 1820, and in 1842-44, Gen. John C. Fremont made his celebrated trip across the Rocky Mountains. First settlements made by miners, 1858-1859; formed from parts of Kansas, Nebraska, Utah and New Mexico; organized as a Territory, February, 1861; admitted, August 1, 1876.

Area, 103,925 square miles; length, 380 miles; breadth, 280 miles; principal rivers, North and South Platte, Arkansas, Snake, White and Green.

Temperature at Denver: winter, 25° to 37°; summer, 72° to 74°. Rainfall of the State, from 15 to 20 inches, falling mostly between May and July. The School of Mines is at Golden City. Colorado is the richest State in the Union in mineral productions, ranking first in silver, and fourth in gold. Cattle raising a safe and profitable business; sheep husbandry still more profitable.

Population, 243,910, incl. 3,262 colored, 861 Chinese and 202 Indians.

Number of colleges, 3; school population, 40,208; school age, 6-21.

Though I had formerly been in the Territory of Wyoming, but only en route to the far West, I boarded a train of the Union Pacific R. R. for Cheyenne, the capital of Wyoming. Cheyenne has a population of

6,000, representing chiefly the stock and mining interests. The city is substantially built and contains a fine Court House and Jail, a pretty City Hall and an extensive round-house and shops.

The military post of Fort D. A. Russell is located here.

A few miles beyond Cheyenne the ascent of the Rocky Mountains begins, and at a distance of about 33 miles the train passes Sherman, one of the highest R. R. stations in the world, 8,235 ft. high. Here commences the descent to the Laramie Plains, which are about 40 miles wide on the average and 100 miles long, bounded by the Black Hills and the Medicine Bow Mountains. Enormous flocks of sheep graze on the plains, said to be the best grazing in the United States. There is an abundance of game, such as antelopes, mountain-sheep and bears, in the neighboring hills.

Laramie City is 56 miles from Cheyenne and is situated on Laramie river, in the midst of the Laramie Plains. Its population is 3,000, but is rapidly increasing. It is the end of a division of the R. R., and has large machine and repair shops, and the rolling-mills of the company. The city is regularly laid out and contains several handsome buildings. Within 30 miles of Laramie there are deposits of antimony, cinnabar, gold, silver, lead, plumbago, and several other minerals. Beyond Laramie the road traverses the Plains for many miles, crosses a region of rugged hills, and descends once more into the valley of the North Platte. Near Miser, 44 miles from Laramie City, are fine views of

Laramie Peak on the right and Elk Mountain on the left. The North Platte is reached at Fort Fred Steele, and then another steep ascent is begun. Creston is upon the dividing ridge of the continent, from which water flows each way; E. to the Atlantic and W. to the Pacific.

At Green River Station, the train emerges from the desolate plains and enters a mountain region, which affords some fine views and in a distance of 121 miles enters Utah Territory.

Wyoming Territory was organized 1869. First settlements, trading posts of Forts Laramie and Bridges.

Area, 97,890 square miles; length, 350 miles; breadth, 275 miles. Largest rivers, Green, Snake, Big Horn, Powder, Big Cheyenne and North Platte.

Temperature at Cheyenne: winter, 23° to 33°; summer, 63° to 69°. Rainfall at Fort Laramie, 15 inches. Union Pacific runs through extreme south from east to west, and connects Cheyenne with Denver.

Wheat, rye, oats and barley flourish, but frosts too frequent for corn. Big Horn Country, in northwest, has an area of 15,000 square miles; fine agricultural country; water plentiful; game and fur-bearing animals numerous, rendering it one of the most desirable hunting grounds of America. Grazing interest important, and increasing rapidly, more than half the area being rich grazing land. Mountains covered with forests of coniferes, which will prove very useful for lumber.

Mineral resources extensive; iron ore abundant; copper, lead, plumbago and petroleum found; gold in the Sweetwater country and near Laramie City; valuable deposits of soda in the valley of the Sweetwater. Coal abundant and of good quality at Evanston, Carbon, Rock Springs and other points; these deposits extensively worked, and furnish nearly all the coal used by the railroads and by settlements hundreds of miles east and west. But little attention has as yet been given to mechanical and manufacturing industries.

Population, incl. 298 Colored, 914 Chinese and 140 Indians· 20,789. Good school system started; school population, 4,112; school age, 7-21.

Returned over the same road to Denver, and staying there a short time, I left that lovely city and its generous and warm-hearted citizens, starting on the trip to Kansas, via Kansas Division of the Union Pacific R. R. The first noteworthy station is Kit Carson, named after the great "Pathfinder," and situated on Sand Creek, about 20 miles above the spot where Colonel Chivington's Indian massacre took place.

Fort Wallace, an important military post on the boundary-line of Kansas, and Fort Hays, situated on a commanding elevation, overlooking the plains, one of the handsomest military posts in the West are passed. Opposite the latter, upon Big Creek, is Hays City, once the center of the Buffalo range. 65 miles beyond is Ellsworth, situated on the Smoky Hill River, in a fine stock-raising country. Numerous thriving villages in a highly productive agricultural region are on the route to Manhattan, a busy and rapidly growing town, containing an Agricultural High School.

Topeka, the capital of Kansas, is situated on both sides of the Kansas River, which is here spanned by a fine iron bridge. It contains one of the finest State Houses in the West, and has 23,000 inhabitants. The river affords excellent water-power, and there are several important educational institutions. In the vicinity, which is very fertile, are deposits of coal.

The U. S. Government Building and State Lunatic Asylum are in course of erection.

At a distance of 30 miles from Topeka, situated on both sides of the Kansas River, and built on a rolling slope, is the beautiful city of Lawrence, with 10,000 inhabitants. The trade of Lawrence is very large, and a dam across the river furnishes water-power for numerous mills. The State University is located here. The terminus of the above mentioned R. R. Division is Kansas City, in the State of Missouri.

Kansas City is the second city of Missouri in importance, contains a population of 115,000, and is situated on the S. bank of the Missouri river, below the mouth of the Kansas river, and near the Kansas border. Its trade is immensely increasing, and due to the 12 important railroads, (which converge here), and the steamboat traffic on the river. Its manufacturing interests are of no importance whatsoever. The first bridge ever constructed across the Missouri, is in Kansas City, and is 1,387 ft. long. The Union R. R. Depot is one of the finest in the West.

There are some handsome public and private buildings in the city.

From Kansas City I traveled again to the neighboring State of Kansas, and visited Leavenworth. There is an important trade in agricultural products in that city, and its population is 29,000. Fort Leavenworth and the Soldiers' Home are of great interest to the traveler.

Atchison, a lively city of 18,000 inhabitants, is pleasantly situated on the right bank of the Missouri river. Nine railroads meet here and about 90 trains arrive and depart every day, making it a railroad center. The industry in manufacturing is very large and incloses flour-mills, machine-shops, breweries, engine-works, furniture, and carriage-factories.

It has several nice churches and a fine iron bridge across the river.

After exploring different rural regions in this State I proceeded to St. Joseph, Missouri.

The "Garden of the West," the State of Kansas, takes its name from the Indian, signifying "Smoky Water." Visited first by Spaniards, 1541, and by French, 1719. Part of Louisiana purchase, and afterward of Indian Territory. Organized as a Territory, 1854, admitted as a State, 1861.

Area, 82,080 square miles; length, 400 miles; breadth, 200 miles. Geographical center of the United States, exclusive of Alaska. Missouri River frontage, 150 miles; largest rivers, Solomon, Neosho, Saline, Arkansas, Republican and Kansas.

Temperature at Leavenworth: summer, 74° to 79°; winter, 25° to 35°; rainfall, 31 inches.

Institution for the Feeble-Minded at Osawatomie, and for the education of the Blind, at Wyandotte; for Deaf-Mutes, Olathe.

Number of farms, 1860, 10,400; 1880, 138,561.

Average value per acre, cleared land, $19.12; wooodland, $11.82. Peculiarly adapted for stock raising.

Number of hands employed in manufactories, 12,064.

Population, 996,096, incl. 43,107 Colored, 19 Chinese and 815 Indians.

Number of colleges, 8; number of school houses, over 5,000; school attendance, 69 per cent. of school population; school age, 5-21.

St. Joseph, Missouri, has 32,431 inhabitants, several educational institutions and an important trade. The city is very wealthy and some of the public and private buildings are very handsome. The river is the demarkation line, and is quite shallow here.

I also visited Jefferson City, the capital of Missouri, which is beautifully situated on high bluffs, overlooking the Missouri River for many miles. It has 6,000 inhabitants and is nicely built. The State House is an extensive building, and the State Library contains 12,000 volumes. There are numerous flourmills and factories in Jefferson City.

The "Pennsylvania of the West," the State of Missouri, whose name is taken from that of the river Missouri, signifying in Indian, "Mud River," was first settled at St. Genevieve by the French, 1755; organized as a Territory, 1812; admitted 1821.

Area, 69,415 square miles; length, north and south, 275 miles; average breadth, 245 miles; Mississippi River frontage, nearly 500 miles.

Temperature at St. Louis: winter, 30° to 43°; summer, 75° to 80°; rainfall, 42 inches.

Number of farms, 215,575; average value per acre, cleared land, $14.52; woodland, $8.25.

Lead is found in southwest, center and southeast, having area of over 5,000 square miles.

Ranks first in mules; third in oxen, hogs, corn and copper.

Population, 2,168,380, incl. 145,350 Colored, 91 Chinese and 113 Indians.

U. S. Army excluded from voting.

Number of Colleges, 17; school population, 741,-632; school age, 6–20.

Per St. Louis and San Francisco R. R. and its branches I continued my voyage, intending to visit a few important places in the State of Arkansas and afterward to explore the Indian Territory.

Passing Eureka Springs and Avoca with nothing noteworthy, I arrived at Little Rock, Arkansas. The capital of Arkansas and chief city of the State has 25,-000 inhabitants, and is built upon the first bed of rocks that is met with in ascending the Arkansas River. The city is regularly laid out, and the residences are surrounded by gardens adorned with shade-trees, presenting a lovely appearance,

Of the public buildings are worth to be mentioned, the State House, New Custom House, Northern Medical College, the Lunatic Asylum, the Military Institute of St. John's College, and some of the churches are also very pretty. The U. S. Arsenal and Land Office, the State Institutions for Deaf-Mutes and the Blind, and the State Penitentiary are located here. The State Library contains 12,500 volumes.

From Malvern, 42 miles S. of Little Rock, the Hot Springs R. R. diverges and runs in 25 miles to the famous Hot Springs.

The town is only an appendage of the Sanitarium and contains 3,000 inhabitants.

The 66 springs issue from the W. slope of Hot Springs Mountain, vary in temperature from 93° to 160° F., and discharge into the Creek about half a million of gallons a day.

The waters are taken both internally and, in the the form of baths, externally, and are remedial in rheumatism, scrofula and diseases of the skin.

Not extending my travels in this State any farther, I was busy in collecting statistic data about Arkansas, and having been successful in obtaining them from official sources, I reproduce the same as follows.

The "Bear State," State of Arkansas, the name of which is of Indian origin, signifying "Smoky Water," with prefix from French meaning "Bow," was settled at Arkansas Post by French, 1685; became a Territory, 1819; admitted as a State, 1836, seceded March 4, 1861; re-admitted 1868.

Area, 53,850 square miles; length, north and south, 240 miles; breadth, from 170 to 250 miles; Mississippi River frontage, about 400 miles.

Temperature at Little Rock: winter, 42° to 51°; summer, 79° to 82°. Rainfall at Fort Smith, 40 inches; and at Washington, 55 inches.

Number of farms, 94,433. Average value per acre, cleared land $11.78; woodland, $3.48.

Number of different industries, 2,070; for tar and turpentine, 26; sawing lumber, 354; flour and grist, 807.

Coal along Arkansas River; iron ores in Ozark Mountains; salt springs near Ouachita; oilstone near Hot Springs; kaolin in Pulaski County.

Population, 802,525, incl. 210,666 Colored, 133 Chinese and 195 Indians. Slaves, 1860, 111,115.

Number of colleges, 5; school population, 289,617; school age, 6–21.

Having procured the necessary permit, etc., I started first per Missouri Pacific, and afterwards per Missouri, Kansas and Texas Division R. R., and passed Fort Scott, established as a military post in 1842, in whose vicinity there is an abundance of bituminous coal; and Parsons, a flourishing city, built on a high rolling prairie between and near the confluence of the Big and Little Labette Rivers, and then reached Vinita, the first station in the Indian Territory.

The railroad traverses the country for 201 miles to Durant, near the Texas border.

The towns, villages, etc., along the road are inhabited by several Indian tribes, and their reservations are inaccessible to white persons, that is, white people are prohibited from settling there. I mention only a few of them: Caddo, Caney, Atoka, Gap, Frink, Checotah, Oaklaha, Muscogee, Leliaetta with the capital of the Cherokee Indians, Tahlequa, the most important town, and near by Adair and Catala, either close to the road or sideways from it.

The Indian Territory, portion of great Louisiana purchase was set apart for home of peaceable Indian tribes; organized 1834. Cut down to form States and Territories, leaving but 64,690 square miles, or 41,401,600 acres; nearly 26,000,000 acres being Indian reservations.

Length east and west on the north, 470 miles, breadth west of 100th meridian, 35 miles, and east of that line, about 210 miles.

Reservations of Cherokees, 5,000,000 acres in north and northeast; Seminoles, 2,000,000 in east central, Creeks, 3,215,495 in east; Chickasaws, 4,377,600 in south; the Oklahoma country near centre. Principal rivers, Arkansas and Red. Number of nations, agencies and reservations, 22.

Temperature at Fort Gibson: winter, 35° to 48°; summer, 77° to 82°. Rainfall in extreme northwest, 20 inches, and at Fort Gibson, 36 inches. Railroad mileage, 372.

Capital of Chickasaws, Tishomingo; of Chocktaws, Tushkahoma; of Creeks, Muscogee; of Osages, Pawhuska; of Seminoles, Seminole Agency; of Pawnees, Pawnee Agency; of Kiowas and Comanches, Kiowa and Commanche Agency.

Corn, wheat, tobacco, cotton and potatoes yield luxuriantly.

Stringent laws to protect from encroachments by whites. They can hold land only by marrying into one of the tribes.

Recent official reports give Indian population about 80,000: Cherokees, 20,000; Chocktaws, 16,500; Creeks, 14,500; Chickasaws, 7,000; Seminoles, 2,500; Osages, 2,390; Cheyennes, 3,298; Arapahoes, 2,676; Kiowas, 1,120; Pawnees, 1,438; Comanches, 1,475.

No Territorial Government has as yet been organized, owing to differences in the views of Congress and the tribes. For each agency a deputy is appointed by the President to represent the United States, but each tribe manages its own internal affairs. Most of the tribes governed by chiefs.

Of first five tribes, 33,650 can read and have 16,200 houses, 195 schools and 6,250 pupils. Expended from tribal funds for educational purposes, $156,856; from government appropriation for freedmen, $3,500.

From the trip to the Indian Territory, en route for Chicago, I took a rest in the latter and again explored the State of Illinois, in order to complete my Statistics of the State.

Kankakee was begun with. It is situated upon the river of the same name, which is one of the principal tributaries of the Illinois, and has 6,000 inhabitants. Its manufactures, including iron-foundries, machine-shops, woolen-mills, tool-works, planing-mills, etc., are very important. In the nearest neighborhood of Kankakee are quarries of a superior kind of lime-stone.

Bloomington was the next city visited. It is an important railroad center, and the seat of large manufacturing and shipping interests, and has 22,000 inhabitants. The Illinois Wesleyan University has 15,000 volumes in its library and is a famous high-school, and there are other important educational institutions in the city. The Major Female College and the Female Seminary are of high standing. Some of the public buildings are handsome, and the construction and repair shops of the Chicago and Alton R. R. cover 13 acres of ground.

Peoria, a city of 30,000 inhabitants, situated on the W. bank of the Illinois river, and at the lower end of Peoria Lake, is an important railway center. The Courthouse, the Normal School, the City Hall and the Library, with 10,000 volumes, and several of the 28 churches are very handsome edifices. The main business is manufacturing, consisting of distilleries, breweries, iron-foundries, machine shops, carriage and furniture factories, engine and locomotive shops, etc. The city is surrounded by a fertile prairie, and in its vicinity very rich mines of bituminous coal are worked.

Quincy, picturesquely situated on a lime-stone bluff

125 ft. above the Mississsippi and with a population of 27,275, is a railroad center. The city is well built, and the trade extensive. The Hanibal and St. Joseph R. R. crosses the river here on a fine bridge.

Extending my journey to Springfield, the capital of Illinois, I remained in that beautiful city several days. It contains 30,000 inhabitants and is built on a beautiful prairie, 5 miles S. of the Sangamon river. The streets are broad and tastefully adorned with shade trees. From the beauty of the place and its surroundings, Springfield is called the "Flower City." One of the finest Capitols in the United States is the Springfield Capitol, and there are numerous noteworthy public and private buildings in the city, among which the U. S. Building, the County Court House, the High School, State Arsenal, St. John's Hospital and the Opera House deserve special mention. In Oak Ridge Cemetery, 2 miles N. of the city, lie the remains of President Lincoln, to whose memory a noble monument was erected. The trade of the city is extensive, the surrounding country very productive, and vast coal-mines in the vicinity. The chief manufacturing establishments are foundries and machine shops, flouring-mills, woolen-mills, rolling-mills, breweries and a watch-factory. The extensive shops of the Wabash R. R. are worth paying a visit.

With this latter city, I concluded my explorations in Illinois.

The "Prairie or Sucker State," the State of Illinois, has its name from a tribe of Indians, signifying, "A superior class of men." First permanent settlement by French at Kaskaskia, 1682; organized as a Territory, 1809; admitted as a State, 1818.

Area, 56,650 square miles; greatest length, 385 miles; greatest breadth, 218 miles; highest land, 1,150 feet. Has 4,000 miles navigable streams.

Temperature at Chicago: winter, 25° to 37°; summer, 68° to 73°. At Cairo: winter, 35° to 54°; summer, 76° to 80°. Rainfall at Peoria, 35 inches.

Kaskaskia, first capital, which was removed to Vandalia, 1818, and to Springfield, 1836.

Number of farms, 255,741, of which 175,497 are occupied by owners. Value per acre, cleared land, $33.03; woodland, $23.68.

First recorded coal mine in America located near Ottawa, 1669. Coal area, cover three fourths of entire State; estimated to contain one-seventh of all known coal in North America. Superior quality lime-stone on Fox and Desplaines rivers; lead, most important mineral; galena in center of richest diggings of the Northwest. Rich salt wells in Salin and Gallatin counties, 75 gallons brine making 50 pounds salt.

Ranks first in corn, wheat, oats, meat-packing, lumber traffic, malt and distilled liquors and miles railway; second in rye, coal, agricultural implements, soap and hogs.

Population, 3,077,871, incl. 46,368 Colored, 209 Chinese, 3 Japanese and 140 Indians. School system excellent; number of colleges, 28; school age, 6-21.

My next aim was the State of Indiana, and the

first place visited, Terre Haute, a long distance from Chicago. On the route to Terre Haute numerous flourishing towns and villages are passed, and a productive agricultural region is traversed. The city contains 33,000 inhabitants and is situated on the E. bank of the Wabash river, which is here spanned by 3 bridges. It contains 2 Orphan Asylums, a number of fine public buildings, Coate's Female College, a Public Library, the Rose Polytechnic School, the State Normal School, St. Anthony's Hospital and several nice churches. Its manufactures are extensive, and consist of carriage and wagon works, machine-shops, nail-works, blast furnaces, car-works, rolling-mills, woolen-mills, and 7 flour mills, with a daily capacity of 3,300 barrels. The Artesian well, 2,000 ft. deep, is celebrated for its medicinal virtue.

Terre Haute is the point of intersection of 9 railroaad lines, and is the center of trade for a populous region.

From here I traveled to Indianapolis, the capital of Indiana.

Indianapolis is the largest city in the State, and situated on the W. fork of White river, near the center of the State. The city is built in a fertile plain and has beautiful and wide streets. Its population is 75,074, and the trade and manufactures very extensive. The principal industry is pork-packing, and manufactures of machinery, agricultural implements, cars, carriages, furniture and flour. It is one of the great railway centers of the West, no less than 14 railways converge here.

Of public buildings are noteworthy: the State House, Court House, the State Lunatic Asylum, State Institute for the Deaf and Dumb, the U. S. Arsenal, the Post-Office, City Hall, County Jail and City Prison. The Butler University admits both sexes, and is 4 miles E. of the city. The principal charitable institutions are: 3 Orphan Asylums, the State Female Reformatory and Asylum, the Catholic Infirmary and a City Hospital. Of churches there are many elegant and costly in Indianapolis.

The Union Passenger Depot is one of the most spacious structures of the kind in the United States. The State Library contains 15,000 volumes and the Free City Library 35,000 volumes.

Among the principal manufacturing industries are the Atlas Engine-Works, Indianapolis Rolling-Mills and Car-Shops, Haugh Iron-Works, Malleable Iron-Works, Kingan Pork-Packing Houses, and the Tile-Works, etc.

Lafayette, one of the principal cities of Indiana, with 14,860 inhabitants, has a flourishing trade with the surrounding country, and a number of important factories, embracing machine-shops and foundries, flour-mills, marble-works, breweries, woolen-mills, etc. It is situated on the Wabash river, built on a rising ground and inclosed in the rear by hills. The University with which is associated the State College of Agriculture and the Mechanic Arts, is a richly endowed institution. Lafayette is the point of intersection of 5 railway lines, and there are several handsome buildings, among them the County Jail, St. Mary's Academy, Ford's School House, and the Opera House. From an Artesian well, 230 ft. deep, near the center of the city, sulphur-water issues freely. S. of the city limits are the County Agricultural Fair Grounds, and 7 miles N. of Lafayette is the battle-ground where General Harrison defeated the Indians, November 7, 1811.

Fort Wayne is known as the "Summit City," from the fact that it is on the water-shed from which the streams run E. and W. It is situated at the point where the Maumee river is formed by the confluence of the St. Joseph and St. Mary's, and takes its name from an old frontier fort which was built here in 1794, and which was retained as a military station until 1819. It is one of the chief cities of Indiana, with a population of 26,880, and extensive manufactures. The vast machine-shops of the Pittsburg, Fort Wayne and Chicago R. R., and of the Wabash, St. Louis and Pacific R. R. are located here.

Among the public buildings are the Court House and County Jail, and the Concordia College and the Fort Wayne College are prominent educational institutions.

The "Hoosier State," the State of Indiana, was first settled by Canadian voyagers at Vincennes, 1702; organized as a Territory, 1800, admitted as a State, 1816.

Area, 36,350 square miles; extreme length, 276 miles; average breadth, 140 miles; shore line on Lake Michigan, 40.

Michigan City the lake port.

Temperature at Indianapolis: winter, 29° to 41°; summer, 73° to 78°. Rainfall at Richmond, 43 inches.

Evansville, commercial center of the southwest; population, 29,280.

Number of farms, 194,013; average value per acre, clear land, $30.46; woodland, $26.90. Corn the most valuable crop. Coal fields about 6,500 square miles, extending from Warren County south to the Ohio; varieties are coking coal, Indiana block and cannel.

Ranks second in wheat.

Population, 1,978,301, incl. 39,228 Negroes, 29 Chinese and 246 Indians.

Number of colleges, 15; State University at Bloomington; Medical School at Indianapolis; University at Notre Dame; flourishing common-school system; school population, 708,596; school age, 6-21.

The neighboring State of Michigan was explored from the starting-point, Fort Wayne, and the first place visited was Adrian, the largest city in South Michigan, with about 10,000 inhabitants and flourishing varied manufactures.

The monument, erected in honor of the 77 inhabitants of the city who lost their lives in the last civil war, is exceedingly pretty. The city is regularly laid out and has many fine structures.

Ann Arbor, a city of 8,000 inhabitants, situated on both sides of the Huron river, is well known in the Union as the seat of the University of Michigan, one of the leading institutions of learning in the West, containing departments of law, medicine, dentistry, etc., and is open to both sexes.

The Observatory of the University is a mile from the other buildings. The Library of the same, contains 45,000 volumes, and the Museums are large and valuable.

The Union School at Ann Arbor is also famous, and there are 5 mineral springs in the city, and several fine churches.

Not far from here is the thriving city of Ypsilanti, with 5,000 inhabitants, situated on the Huron river, which furnishes water-power for several flour-mills, paper-mills and other factories. The State Normal School is located here.

Per Michigan Centeral R. R., traversing a fine agricultural country, the City of Detroit is reached. The chief city of Michigan, Detroit, is situated on the N. bank of the Detroit river, 20 miles long, and connecting Lakes Erie and St. Clair.

For at least 6 miles the river front is lined with mills, dry-docks, foundries, ship-yards, railroad-depots, grain-elevators, lumber-yards, rolling-mills, and warehouses.

In 1783 Detroit was ceded to the United States, but the Americans did not take possession of it till 1796. During the war of 1812 it fell into the hands of the British, but was recaptured in 1813. It was incorporated as a city in 1824, when its population was less than 2,000, and now, in 1884, it has more than

150,000 inhabitants. The manufactures of the city are numerous and important, including extensive machine-shops and iron-works, railroad-car factories, tanneries, boot and shoe factories, chemicals, potteries, manufactories of railway and vessel supplies, etc. Pork and fish-packing employ numerous hands, and the shipping interests are also large.

The Campus Martius on which the City Hall and the Soldiers' Monument stand, is a charming open space, 600 ft. long and 250 ft. wide.

Of the churches in the city, special mention deserve: the Cathedral of St. Peter and St. Paul (Catholic), St. Paul's (Episcopal), Fort St. Presbyterian and Central Church (Methodist).

Whitney's Opera House is one of the finest in America. The Police Headquarters Building and the Freight Depot of the Michigan Central R. R. are the most spacious and noteworthy structures in the city. There are several educational and charitable institutions in this beautiful city, and the parks and suburbs marvellously pretty. About 3 miles below the Michigan Central Depot, in whose neighborhood are the great Wheat Elevators, is Fort Wayne, a bastioned redoubt, standing upon the bank of the river and completely commanding the channel.

In Detroit live relatives of my family, and they, as well as the famous musical composer, Mr. Anton Streletzki, a resident of that city, received me most cordially, for which I here express my heartfelt thanks to them.

Before starting for the Dominion of Canada, I

visited Lansing, the capital of the State, with 9,776 inhabitants, magnificent State Buildings, and several famous institutions. The city is beautifully situated, and the trade and few manufactures are important.

The "Wolverine or Lake State," the State of Michigan, whose name is of Indian origin, signifying "Lake Country," had first white settlements within limits of State, Sault Ste. Marie, 1668; organized as a Teritory, 1805; admitted, 1837.

Area, 58,915 square miles; length of lower peninsula, from north to south, 277 miles; greatest breadth, 259 miles. Length of upper peninsula, east to west, 318 miles; width, 30 to 164 miles. Length, lake shore line, 1,620 miles.

Temperature at Detroit: winter, 24° to 36°; summer, 67° to 72°; rainfall, 30 inches.

Grand Rapids, manufacturing city; population, 41,934; Bay City, 29,413 inhabitants; East Saginaw 29,100; Jackson, 19,136; Muskegon, 17,845; Saginaw, 13,767.

Detroit, Marquette, Port Huron and Grand Haven are ports of entry.

Number of farms, 154,008. Value per acre, cleared land, $34.39; woodland, $20.27.

Fruit raising an important industry. Copper mines in Houghton, Ontonagon, and Keweenaw counties; valuable iron ores in Marquette and Delta counties; coal in Shiawassee, Eaton, Ingham and Jackson counties.

Salt manufactured in year ending November 30, 1884, 3,252,175 barrels.

Ranks first in copper, lumber and salt; second in iron ore.

Grand Haven, Au Sable and Detroit are centers of valuable fishing interests.

Population, incl. 17,548 Colored and 8,259 Indians: 1,843,369.

Duelists are excluded from voting.

Number of colleges, 9; efficient public schools; school age, 5–20.

Opposite Detroit, on Canadian soil, is the village of Windsor, connected with Detroit by a steam-ferry, on which the railroad train is carried across, and in 15 miles reaches Hamilton, a middle-sized, busy place, and from here the Grand Trunk R. R. runs to Toronto, the capital of the Province of Ontario. Situated on a beautiful circular bay on the N. W. shore of Lake Ontario, between the rivers Don and Humber, the city is gently rising from its low site.

Toronto was founded in 1794 by Governor Simcoe, who gave it the name of York, changed, when it was incorporated as a city, in 1834, to Toronto—meaning, in the Indian tongue—"The Place of Meeting."

In 1813 it was twice captured by the Americans, who destroyed the fortifications and burned the public buildings. In 1817 the population was 1,200, and now it is over 110,000.

Among the manufactures are iron and other foundries, distilleries, flour-mills, breweries, paper, furniture, etc. The finest buildings in the city and among the finest of the kind in America are those of the University of Toronto. The University Library contains 20,000 volumes, and there is a fine Museum of Natural History. Knox College, the College of Technology, the Normal School, Model Schools, the Educational Museum, Trinity College, the Upper Canada College, and the Public Library are eminent schools of learning and beautiful structures.

Among the churches, the Episcopal Cathedral of St. James, the Wesleyan Methodist Church, and the Cathedral of St. Michael (Catholic), are richly decorated, massive edifices. Osgoode Hall, containing the Provincial Law Courts, the Provincial Lunatic Asylum, the General Hospital, Crystal Palace, Masonic Hall, Grand Opera House and the Horticultural Garden-Pavilion and St. Lawrence Hall are noteworthy, imposing buildings.

The Loretto Abbey is the principal nunnery in the city, and the City Hall, Post Office, Custom House, Court House and the Lawrence Market, unpretentious, fine and spacious architectures. In the Queens Park is the colossal marble statue of Britania, to the memory of the Canadians who fell in repelling the Fenian invasion of 1866.

The trip down the St. Lawrence usually begins at Kingston, which place I had reached from Toronto. Kingston has 13,000 inhabitants, and is situated at the foot of Lake Ontario. After leaving Kingston the steamer enters the Lake of the Thousand Islands (in the St. Lawrence).

These islands are 1,692 in number and they extend for 40 miles below Lake Ontario.

They are of every imaginable size, shape and appearance, some scarcely visible, and others covering many acres, some consisting of bare masses of rock, others thickly wooded. The numerous light-houses, marking out the navigable channel are fragile wooden structures of rather dreary appearance. The chief summer resort of the Thousand Islands is Alexandria Bay. On the islets near the bay are many elegant villas, among which one is owned by Mr. Pullman, of palace-car fame. About 8 miles S. E. of Alexandria Bay are the romantic Lakes of Theresa, (Clear, Crystal, Mud, Butterfield, and Lake of the North). Brockville, on the Canadian shore, is an important town of nearly 6,000 inhabitants, and at this point in the river the Lake of the Thousand Islands ends. Thirteen miles from Brockville, on the Canadian side, lies Prescott, and opposite the flourishing American city of Ogdensburg. A few miles below Ogdensburg the descent of the first rapids (Gallopes Rapids) is made, and immediately afterward of the Rapide de Plat. Dickinson's Landing is at the head of the famous Long Sault Rapids, which are 9 miles in length. Here the celebrated sensation, known as "Shooting the Rapids" is experienced. Until 1840 this passage was considered impossible; but by watching the course of rafts down the river, a channel was discovered and steamboats then attempted it, for the first time, under the guidance of the Indian pilot Teronhiahéré. The Cornwall

Canal, 11 miles long, enables vessels to go round the Rapids in ascending the river.

Cornwall is a thriving town at the foot of the Rapids, opposite which is the large Indian village of St. Regis. Just below this place the St. Lawrence, now entirely in Canada, expands into Lake St. Francis, 25 miles long and 5 miles wide. Coteau du Lac, 30 miles below Cornwall, is at the head of the Coteau Rapids, which, 9 miles below, take the name of the Cedars, and, still further on, of the Cascades. At the foot of the Cascades is Beauharnois, at the lower end of a canal 11¼ miles long, around the Rapids. From this point to the head of the Lachine Rapids the expanse of the river is called Lake St. Louis, which is 12 miles long and 5 miles wide. One of the most noticeable features of this lake is Nun's Island, formerly an Indian burying-ground, but now the property of the Grey Nunnery at Montreal. Lachine is at the head of the Lachine Rapids which, though the shortest, are the most turbulent and dangerous on the river. In calm water again, the spires, domes and towers of Montreal are visible and soon afterward the city is reached.

Montreal, the largest city and commercial metropolis of British North America, is situated on an island of the same name, at the confluence of the Ottawa and St. Lawrence Rivers, in lat. 45° 31′ N. and lon. 73° 35′ W. I derives its name from Mont Réal, or Mount Royal, which rises 700 ft. above the river, and closes the city in on that side. The quays of Montreal are built of solid limestone, and uniting with the locks and cutstone wharves of the Lachine Canal, they present for about 2 miles a display of continuous masonry which has few parallels. The first visit to Montreal dates from 1535, when Jacques Cartier arrived, who named its mountain.

In 1642 arrived the first installment of European settlers, and the original Indian name "Hochelaga" gave place to the French one of "Ville Marie." This name was afterward replaced by the present one. In November 1775, Montreal was captured by the Americans under General Montgomery and held until the following summer. In 1779 it contained about 7,000 inhabitants. In 1861 the population had increased to 90,323, and in 1880 to 140,747. The commerce of Montreal is very large, it being the chief shipping-port of the Dominion of Canada. Its manufactures are varied and important, the principal are axes and saws, steam-engines, printing-types, India-rubber shoes, paper, furniture, woolens, cordage, and flour.

The Court House contains a library of 15,000 volumes, and back of it is the Champ de Mars, a fine military parade-ground.

The City Hall, the Bank of Montreal, Molson's Bank, the huge Victoria Skating-Rink, used in summer for horticultural shows, and the Mechanics' Institute are elaborately decorated structures.

Few American cities equal Montreal in the size and magnificence of its church edifices. The Roman Catholic Parish Church of Notre-Dame is next to the Cathedral of Mexico the largest on the continent, capable of seating from 10,000 to 12,000 people. In one of the six towers is a fine chime of bells, the largest of which, the "Gros Bourdon," weighs 24,900 pounds. The Cathedral of St. Peter, now in the course of erection, (after the plan of St. Peter's at Rome), will surpass this huge structure in size. Christ Church Cathedral (Episcopal), the Church of the Gesù (Jesuit), and St. Andrew's Church (Presbyterian), are the most eminent of the numerous churches in this city.

First among the educational institutions is the University of McGill College, with one of the finest museums in the country.

The museum of the Natural History Society has also a valuable collection, and the Seminary of St. Sulpice, for the education of Catholic Priests, is very famous. The Grey Nunnery, the Black or Congregational Nunnery, and the great Convent of the Holy Names of Jesus and Mary are devoted to the education of young persons of the female sex.

The Hotel Dieu, founded in 1644 for the cure of the sick is an imposing structure, and the Montreal General Hospital, and the Deaf and Dumb Asylums are noble charities. The old Government House, the Nelson Monument, the Water Works and the Bonsecours Market are of special interest and worth visiting.

The eighth wonder of the world, as it has been called, is the Victoria Bridge in Montreal, which spans the St. Lawrence, connecting the city on the island with the mainland to the S. The total cost of the bridge, formally opened by the Prince of Wales, during his visit to America in the summer of 1860, was $6,300,000.

After seeing the Lachine Rapids most advantageously, I proceeded to the White Mountains, via Grand Trunk R. R. to Gorham.

The aboriginal name of the White Mountains, the "Switzerland" of America, was Agiochook or Agiocochook, signifying "Mountain of the Snowy Forehead and Home of the Great Spirit." The first white man to visit them, according to Belknap, the State Historian, was Walter Neal, in 1632.

The White Mountains rise from a plateau in Grafton and Coös Counties, New Hampshire, about 45 miles long by 30 broad, and 1,600 ft. above the sea. Some 20 peaks of various elevations rise from the plateau, which is traversed by several deep, narrow valleys. The peaks cluster in two groups, of which the eastern is known locally as the White Mountains, and the western as the Franconia Group. They are separated by a table-land varying from 10 to 20 miles in breadth. The principal summits of the eastern group are Mounts Washington, 6,293 ft. high, Adams, 5,759 ft., Jefferson, 5,657 ft., Madison, 5,361 ft., Monroe, 5,349 ft., Franklin, 4,850 ft., Pleasant, 4,712 ft., Webster, Clinton, and Clay. The principal summits of the Franconia Group are Mounts Pleasant, Lafayette, 5,280 ft. high, Liberty, Cherry Mountain, and Moosilaukee. Near the S. border of the plateau rise Whiteface Mountain, Chocorua Peak, Red Hill, and Mount

Ossipee; and in the S. E., Mount Kearsarge. With the exceptions of the Black Mountains of North Carolina, several of these peaks are the highest elevations in the United States E. of the Rocky Mountains.

Multitudes of little streams force their way down steep glens from springs far up the mountain-sides, and flow through narrow valleys among the hills. The courses of these rivulets furnish irregular but certain pathways for the rough roads that have been cut beside them, and by which the traveler gains access to these wild mountain-retreats.

Gorham is the N. E. gateway to the mountain-region. It is a thriving village, situated in a broad and beautiful valley at the confluence of the Androscoggin and Peabody Rivers, 800 ft. above the sea. The scenery in the vicinity of the village is remarkably striking, both in the views of the mountain-ranges and isolated mountains, and of rivers and waterfalls. The range of Mounts Moriah, Carter, and The Imp, in particular is seen to great advantage.

Mount Carter is one of the highest and Mount Moriah the most graceful of the larger New Hampshire hills. The noble chain of hills to the N. W. of Gorham is known as the Pilot Range; while on the E. and S. E. the valley is walled in by the stalwart and brawny Androscoggin Hills. Mount Hays, the highest of these latter, 2,500 ft., is directly N. E. of the village and is ascended in about 2 hours.

Though I had stayed a considerably long time in that mountain-region, it is, nevertheless, impossible to describe all the visited spots, and concluding my graphics on the White Mountains, I board a train of the Grand Trunk R. R , bound for Quebec.

Quebec, the oldest, and after Montreal the most important city in British North America, is situated on the N. W. bank of the St. Lawrence River, at its confluence with the St. Charles, nearly 300 miles from the Gulf of St. Lawrence. It is built on the N. extremity of an elevated tongue of land which forms the left bank of the St. Lawrence for several miles. Cape Diamond, so called from the numerous quartz-crystals formerly found there, is the loftiest part of the headland, 333 ft. above the river, on which the vast fortifications of the Citadel are located. They occupy about 40 acres, and were once considered so impregnable, that they obtained for Quebec the name of the "Gibraltar of America." The city is divided into the Upper and Lower Town, the ascent from the latter is very steep and winding and called Mountain Street, or Côte de la Montagne.

The site of Quebec was visited by Cartier in 1534, and the city was founded by Champlain in 1608. It was taken by the English in 1629, and restored to France by the treaty of 1632. In 1690 the neighboring English colonies made an unsuccessful maritime expedition against it, and in 1711 the attempt was renewed, with no better success. In 1759, during the Seven Years' War, the English under General Wolfe attacked the city and bombarded it. On September 13, the first battle of the plains of Abraham took place, in which both Wolfe and Montcalm, the French Commander, fell, and England gained at one blow an American Empire. The French recaptured the city the next spring, but at the treaty of peace in 1763 Louis XV ceded the whole of New France to the English. In December 1775, a small American force, under General Montgomery, attempted its capture, but failed, after losing 700 men and their commander. The population of the city at that time was only 5,000. In 1861 it was 59,900, and in 1881, 62,500. Quebec has a large maritime commerce and is one of the greatest lumber and timber markets on the American Continent. The chief articles of manufactures are ships, saw-mill products, boots and shoes, confectionery, bakery-products, furniture, foundry-products, machinery, paper, leather, cutlery, musical instruments, and India-rubber goods.

The five original gates in the city wall were removed some years ago, but new ones of a more ornamental character have since been built, viz.: Kent Gate, named in honor of the father of Queen Victoria, the Duke of Kent; St. Louis Gate, and St. John's Gate. Dufferin Terrace, lies along the edge of the cliff, towering 200 ft. above the river, and overlooking the Lower Town. Part of it occupies the site of the old Chateau St. Louis, built by Champlain in 1620, and destroyed by fire in 1834. Dufferin Terrace, opened to the public in June, 1879, by the Marquis of Lorne and Princess Louise, is an unequalled promenade over ¼ mile long.

The outlook from the Terrace is one of the finest in the world. The Esplanade is another attractive promenade. The view from the Grand Battery is considered by some finer even than that from the Terrace.

Laval University contains a spacious chemical laboratory, with complete apparatus; the geological, mineralogical, and botanical collections; the museum of zoölogy, containing upward of 1,300 different birds and 7,000 insects; and the especially complete museum of the medical department. The Library numbers nearly 90,000 volumes, and the Picture Gallery is one of the finest. The Quebec Literary and Historical Society has rich collections of manuscripts. The Seminary of Quebec, founded 1663 by M. de Laval, first bishop of Quebec, contains in its Chapel some fine paintings. Morrin College has in its buildings the museums of the Historical Society and the library, containing 12,000 volumes.

The former Cathedral of Quebec, now the Basilica, is a spacious cut-stone building, seating 4,000 persons and contains in its richly decorated interior several original paintings of Vandyke, Caracci, Hallé and others. In this Basilica lie the remains of Champlain, the founder and first Governor of the city. There are numerous churches and chapels in Quebec, some of them handsome edifices.

Other noteworthy buildings are the Ursuline Convent, founded in 1639; in the Chapel of the Convent are some original paintings by Vandyke, Champagne, and others, and here are buried the remains of the Marquis de Montcalm; the Grey Nunnery, which has a richly ornamented Chapel; the Hôtel Dieu, with its convent and chapel, founded in 1639, by the Duchess d'Aiguillon, and in whose convent chapel are some valuable paintings; the Black Nunnery; the Post-Office; Custom House; Marine Hospital; General Hospital; and the Parliament and Departmental Buildings (not completed), and numerous others. The historic Plains of Abraham are in the suburbs, and on the spot where General Wolfe fell in the memorable battle of September 13, 1759, stands Wolfe's Monument. On the plains stands the Monument commemorating the victory won by the Chevalier de Lévis over General Murray in 1760.

Within excursion distance of Quebec are several points of interest and fine drives. Lorette, an ancient village of the Huron Indians, is 9 miles distant, and the Falls of the Little River, near the village, are very picturesque. Eight miles below Quebec are the Falls of Montmorenci, wonderfully beautiful, and the Falls of Chaudière, ten miles from the city. The rapid river plunges, in a sheet 350 ft. wide, over a precipice 150 ft. high, presenting very much the look of boiling water.

The Quarantine for Quebec is at Grosse Isle, 30 miles down, and a little beyond Chateau Richer is St. Anne de Beaupré, famous for its church of St. Anne, in which miraculous cures are said to be effected by the relics of the Saint, which are exhibited at morning mass. The celebrated Falls of St. Anne are very beautiful. The lower fall is 130 ft. high, and below it the water rushes down through a somber, and picturesque ravine.

Eight miles below St. Anne is Cape Tourment, a bold promontory, and a little beyond are the frowning peaks of Cape Rouge and Cape Gribaune.

From Goose Island to the Saguenay River, the St. Lawrence is about 20 miles wide, and black whales are often seen in its waters. Rivière du Loup, and Cacouna, 6 miles below, the favorite summer resort of the Canadians, are miraculously pretty places, and opposite the latter is the mouth of the Saguenay River. Tadousac was the first place visited, en route the Saguenay River. It is a small village, situated a short distance above the mouth of the river, and apart from its attractions as a watering-place, is interesting as the spot on which stood the first stone-and-mortar building ever erected by Europeans on the Continent of America. The scenery here is wild and romantic in the extreme. St. John's Bay, Eternity Bay, the latter offering the most striking feature of the river scenery, are unequalled, and farther on is Statue Point, a grand bowlder, 1,000 ft. high, noticeable for a cave half way up its face, utterly inaccessible from above or below, and still farther above is Le Tableau, a lofty plateau. A few miles beyond is the entrance to Ha! Ha! Bay, which runs 7 miles S. W. from the Saguenay River. It was so named on account of the delightful contrast which the first French Voyagers there beheld after the awful solitude of the lower river. Chicoutimi, about 20 miles above Ha! Ha! Bay, is the head of navigation on the river, and has considerable trade. Before entering the Saguenay, the Chicoutimi River plunges over a granite ledge 50 ft. high. Nine miles above Chicoutimi begin the Rapids of the Saguenay, said to be little inferior in grandeur to those of the Niagara and a great deal longer.

The Saguenay. is the largest tributary of the St. Lawrence, and undoubtedly one of the most remarkable rivers in the world. Its head-water is Lake St. John, 40 miles long and nearly as wide, which, although 11 large rivers fall into it, has no other outlet than the Saguenay.

The original name of this river was Chicoutimi, an Indian word, signifying deep water; and its present name is said to be a corruption of St. Jean Nez. The course of the Saguenay is about 140 miles from Lake St. John to the St. Lawrence, which it enters 120 miles below Quebec.

Per Grand Trunk R. R. via Coteau, and afterward per Canada Atlantic, and the Canadian Pacific Rail Roads, I continued my voyage to Ottawa.

The capital of the Dominion of Canada is situated one the S. bank of the Ottawa river, at the mouth of the Rideau. It is divided into the Upper and Lower Town by the Rideau Canal, which passes through it and connects it with Kingston, on Lake Ontario. Bridges also connect the city with the towns of Hull and New Edinburgh, on the opposite side of the Ottawa river. Ottawa was originally called Bytown, in honor of Colonel By, of the Royal Engineers, by whom it was laid out in 1827. It was incorporated as a city under its present name, 1854, and was selected by Queen Victoria as the seat of the Canadian Government in 1858.

It has 40,000 inhabitants, and is the entrepot of the lumber-trade of the Ottawa and its tributaries, and has a number of large saw-millls, several flour-mills, and manufactories of iron-castings, mill-machinery, agricultural implements, etc.

The Government Buildings are the chief feature of the city and cost $4,000,000. They contain the various Government bureaus, the Post-Office, the Model-Room of the Patent-Office, the Senate Hall, the Chamber of Commons, and the Library, containing 40,000 volumes.

The official residence of the Governor-General, is in New Edinburgh, across the Rideau river.

After the Government Buildings the most imposing edifice in the city is the Roman Catholic Cathedral of Notre Dame. In the interior of the Cathedral is a painting by Murillo, representing the "Flight into Egypt." The Ottawa University, the Ladies College, and the Normal School, and Model College, the great geological Institute, are eminent schools.

There are in the city two convents, two hospitals, three orphan asylums, a Magdalen asylum and the Grey and Black Nunneries.

The scenery in the vicinity of Ottawa is really

grand, at the W. extremity are the Chaudière Falls. The Rideau Falls, two in number, are very attractive.

Returned to Montreal for the purpose of obtaining official statistics, and than to explore the Adirondacks, Lake George, and Lake Champlain before starting for New York; I consider it my duty to publicly express my sincerest thanks to the numerous friends, left behind in the hospitable Dominion of Canada, for the many favors conferred upon me; especially to the German Consul Mr. Munderloh and his Secretary, the amiable families of Messrs. Boas and Moss, and the learned body of McGill University, in particular the Botanist Penhallou, and to several clergymen in Montreal; to the acting Prime Minister, Mr. Pierre Garneau, and the German Consul in Quebec; to the Scientists of the Geological Institution, and to Professor Fletcher of the Experimental Agricultural Station in Ottawa, by whose kindness I was enabled to send a rich collection to Europe.

The most populous Province of the Dominion of Canada is Ontario, established in 1867. Previous to 1791 it formed part of the Province of Quebec; from 1791 to 1840 known as Upper Canada; in 1840 reunited with Quebec, under the name of Canada.

Area, (census of 1881), 101,733 square miles. Total land occupied, 19,259,909 acres; improved, 11,294,-109 acres, of which 8,370,266 acres were under crops; 2,619,038 acres in pasture, and 304,805 acres in gardens and orchards.

Temperature at Toronto: winter, 4.8° to 62.5°;

summer, 38.7° to 92.7°; mean temperature, 44.16°. Rainfall at Toronto, 28.43 inches. The surface of the country is diversified by numerous lakes and rivers.

The agricultural resources are very great, and the mineral wealth varied and rich.

Public affairs are administered by a Lieutenant Governor, assisted by an Executive Council of 6, and a House of Assembly of 89 members. Ontario sends 24 members to the Dominion Senate.

Population of the Province, 1881, 1,923,228. Number of churches, 5,075; of which 2,375 are Methodists, 852 Presbyterian, 680 Church of England, 389 Baptist, and 367 Roman Catholic. There are 21 hospitals, and 22 orphanages. Number of colleges and universities, 17; boarding schools, 44.

There is an excellent system of free schools under the control of a Minister of Education and a Chief Superintendent. School population, 405,857. Number of high schools, public and private, 410; public elementary schools, 5,313.

The agricultural products are wheat, barley, oats, rye, beans, peas, buck-wheat, corn, potatoes, turnips, hay, grass and clover seed, flaxseed, tobacco, and hops.

Timber in abundance; and the 681 fisheries in the Province very important.

Quebec is one of the most important of the Canadian Provinces. Earliest settlements made by Europeans, in 1541; first permanent settlement made by the French on the present site of the city of Quebec,

1608. Country occupied by the French until 1759, when, through the victory of General Wolfe, it fell into the hands of the English.

Area, census of 1881, 188,688 square miles.

Total amount of land occupied, 12,625,877 acres; improved, 6,410,264 acres, of which 4,147,984 were under crop, 2,207,422 in pasture, and 54,858 in gardens and orchards. Population, 1,359,027. While the climate is similar to that of Ontario, it is colder in winter, and warmer in summer. At Montreal the winters are very severe, the temperature often ranging from zero to $10°$ and even $30°$ below it, and in summer it is frequently $90°$ in the shade.

Public affairs are administered by a Lieutenant Governor, assisted by an Executive Council, a Legislative Council of 24 members, and a Legislative Assembly of 65 members.

The Province sends 24 members to the Dominion Senate. The surface of the country is varied, consisting of extensive forests, large rivers, lakes and prairies, and bold rocky heights. The Province abounds in numerous minerals. Among the agricultural products are wheat, barley, oats, rye, peas, beans, buckwheat, corn, potatoes, turnips, grass and clover seed, hay, tobacco and hops. Public instruction is under a Superintendent of Education; school population, 209,623. Number of elementary public schools, 4,404; pupils, 170,858; colleges, 44; academies, 246; special schools, 18; normal, 3; model, 333.

The forests are extensive, and the lumbering and

shipbuilding interests are large. The products of the fisheries are very valuable.

The prevailing religion is Roman Catholic.

The number adhering to that faith is, 1,170,718, or about seven-eights of the entire population. Number of churches in the Province, 1,280, of which 712 are Roman Catholics.

Number of hospitals, 29; orphanages, 11.

Among the statistics, those of British Columbia were also kindly given to me, and, since I had extensively traveled in that distant Province, I am only too glad to reproduce the same.

The Colony of British Columbia was established 1858, and admitted into the Dominion, 1871. Area, including Vancouver's Island, 341,305 square miles. Population, 49,459. Climate milder than that of same latitude on the Atlantic coast. Country traversed by Rocky and Cascade Mountains. Loftiest peak, Mount Browne, 16,000 ft. high. Government consists of a Lieutenant Governor, an Executive Council, and a Legislative Assembly, elected by the people. Amount of land occupied, 441,255 acres; improved, 184,885 acres. The grain product, potatoes and hops, important, and timber in abundance. The mineral wealth of the Province is very great, the chief source being coal. On the mainland and Vancouver's Island large deposits of bituminous coal are found, and on Queen Charlotte's Island a fine grade of anthracite. Gold is found in various localities. In ten years the yield in the Province exceeded $22,000,000.

The Adirondacks, situated in the northern part of New York State, between Lakes George and Champlain on the E., and the St. Lawrence on the N. W., extend on the north to Canada and on the S. nearly to the Mohawk River. The mountains rise from an elevated plateau, which extends over this portion of the country for 150 miles in width and 100 in length, and is itself nearly 2,000 ft. above the level of the sea. Five ranges of mountains, running almost parallel, traverse this plateau from southwest to northeast, where they terminate on the shore of Lake Champlain. The most westerly, which bears the name of the Clinton Range, begins at Little Falls and terminates at Trembleau Point, on Lake Champlain. It contains the highest peaks of the entire region, the loftiest being Mount Marcy, or Tahawus, 5,337 ft. high, while Mounts Seward, McIntire, McMartin, Whiteface, Dix Peak, Colden, Santanoni, Snowy Mountain and Pharaoh are none far from 5,000 ft. high. The entire number of mountains in the Adirondack region is supposed to exceed 500, of which only a few have received separate names. They are all wild and savage, and covered with the "forest primeval," except the stony summits of the highest, which rise above all vegetation, but that of mosses, grasses, and dwarf Alpine plants.

There are many beautiful lakes and ponds in the mountain-valleys, numbering about 1,000. The general level of these lakes is about 1,500 ft. above the sea, but Lake Perkins, the highest of them, has an elevation of over 4,000 ft. Some are only a few acres in length, others cover 20 miles. Among the largest are Long Lake, the Saranacs, Tupper, the Fulton Lakes, and Lake Colden, Henderson, Sanford, Blue Mountain, Raquette, Forked, Newcomb, and Pleasant. This labyrinth of lakes is connected by a very intricate system of rivers, rivulets, and brooks. The Saranac and the Ausable run in nearly parallel lines toward the N. E., discharging their waters into Lake Champlain.

The largest and most beautiful river of the Adirondack region is the Raquette, rising in Raquette Lake, and after a devious course of 120 miles flowing into the St. Lawrence.

The mountains are covered with forests, whilst in the lower lands, along the rivers, a dense growth of evergreens is common. In these solitudes are found the black bear, the wolf, the lynx, the wild-cat, and the wolverine.

Deer is abundant, also numerous smaller animals, and birds, and the lakes and rivers swarm with fish.

Birmingham Falls, caused by the Ausable River flowing over the Alice Falls, and then descending a line of swirling rapids, where it plunges over a precipice 70 ft. high into a semicircular basin, is of great beauty. A few rods further down are the Horseshoe Falls, near which the gorge is entered from above by a stairway of 166 steps leading down a cleft in the rock. Below this the stream grows narrower and deeper, and rushes through Ausable Chasm, where at the narrowest point a wedged bowlder cramps the channel to the width of 6 or 8 ft. Still lower down the walls stand about 50 ft. apart and are more than 100 ft. high, descending to the water's edge in a sheer perpendicular line. The chasm is nearly 2 miles long and offers very striking and beautiful effects.

The Upper Saranac Lake, the largest and one of the most beautiful of the Adirondack lakes, is 8 miles long and from 1 to 3 miles wide, and its surface is studded with little islands.

To describe all the beautiful spots in the Adirondacks would fill volumes.

Lake George is a picturesque sheet of water in Warren and Washington Counties, in New York State. It is 33 miles long, and from $\frac{3}{4}$ of a mile to 4 miles wide. It is the most famous and most frequented of American lakes. The scenery of its banks is admirably pretty, and the lake is bordered on either side by high hills crowned with woods, etc. It empties into Lake Champlain, from which it is separated by a narrow ridge only 4 miles wide. The Indian name of Lake George was "Horicon," meaning "silvery waters;" when the French discovered it, early in the 17th century, they named it "Le Lac du St. Sacrament," but its English conquerors called it after King George II., then on the throne.

Lake George fills a conspicuous and romantic place in American history. In the French and Indian War it was repeatedly occupied by large armies, and was the scene of several battles. In an engagement near the S. end of the Lake, September 8, 1755, between the French and English, Colonel Williams of Massachusetts, the founder of Williams College, was killed, Baron Dieskau, the French commander, severely wounded, and the French totally defeated.

In 1757, Fort William Henry, at the same end of the lake, was besieged by the French General Montcalm, at the head of 8,000 men. The garrison capitulated after a gallant defense, and were barbarously massacred by the Indian allies of the French. In July, 1758, the army of General Abercrombie, about 15,000 strong, passed up the lake in 1,000 boats, and made an unsuccessful attack on Ticonderoga. A year latter, July, 1759, General Amherst, with an almost equal force, also traversed the lake, and took Ticonderoga and Crown Point. The head of Lake George was the depot for the stores of the army of General Burgoyne before he began his march to Saratoga.

The most interesting points on the route to Lake George are Glens Falls, on the Hudson river, at a fine cataract 50 ft. high, and Caldwell, near the ruins of old Fort George.

The nearest island to Caldwell is Tea Island, bordered with picturesque rocks, and a mile and a half beyond is Diamond Island, so named on account of the beautiful quartz-crystals found on it in abundance. Dome Island, richly wooded, is near the center of the widest part of the lake, and there are hundreds of other strikingly beautiful places in and around Lake George, which to describe is almost an impossibility.

Lake Champlain, extending from Whitehall, in the

State of New York, to St. John's, in Canada, is 126 miles long, and varies in breadth from 40 rods to 12½ miles; containing upward of 50 islands and islets. It depth varies from 54 to 399 ft., and vessels of 800 or 1,000 tons navigate its whole extent. The principal rivers entering the lake are Wood Creek at its head; the outlet of Lake George, the Ausable, Saranac, and Chazy, from New York; and Otter, Winooski, Lamoille, and Missisquoi, from Vermont. The outlet of the lake is the Sorel or Richelieu River, sometimes called the St. John's, which empties into the St. Lawrence, and with the Chambly Canal, affords a passage for vessels to the ocean. On the south it communicates, by means of the Champlain Canal, with the Hudson River at Troy. The waters of the lake abound with fish, and, filling a valley inclosed by high mountains, the lake is celebrated for its magnificent scenery, which embraces the Green Mountains of Vermont on the E. and the Adirondack Mountains of New York on the W.

Fort Ticonderoga is a station on the lake, at the foot of Mount Defiance. Ticonderoga village is 2 miles from the steamboat-landing, and about 1 mile to the N., on a high hill, are the ruins of the famous old Fort Ticonderoga, with fine views from the crumbling ramparts, though the views from the top of Mount Defiance are still finer. Mount Independence lies in Vermont, and Mount Hope, an elevation about a mile W. of Ticonderoga, was occupied by Burgoyne previous to the recapture of the fort in 1777. Leaving the landing at

Fort Ticonderoga the steamer runs to Shoreham, on the Vermont shore, and thence crosses the lake to the village of Crown Point, with fine mountain-views all the way. Six miles below, is the rugged promontory of Crown Point, which was the site of Fort St. Frederic, erected by the French in 1731, and of a much stronger work subsequently erected by the English, the massive ruins of which are still plainly visible. Fine views are obtained from the bastions of the old fort. Opposite Crown Point, on the Vermont shore, is Chimney Point. Between them the lake is very narrow, but opens out above into the broad Bulwagga Bay, on the W. shore of which is the pretty village of Port Henry, with extensive iron-works and ore-beds. Just beyond Port Henry the scenery is exceedingly fine. To the E. the Green Mountains with their lofty peaks, Mount Mansfield and Camel's Hump, rise against the distant horizon; and on the W. the Adirondack Hills mingle their blue tops with the clouds.

Here also as on the Lake George, the scenery is wild romantic and the eye gets dazzled at the many charmingly attractive spots.

Returned to Glens Falls, thence to Fort Edward, I reached Saratoga Springs, in the State of New York. This is one of the most famous places of summer resort in America and is frequented by Americans from all parts of the country, and by foreign travelers from all parts of Europe.

The Mineral Springs, which have given the place its celebrity, and the majestic trees, shading several of its streets, are almost the only natural attractions. As a mere spectacle, the brilliancy of this place during the summer-months, is nowhere excelled in the United States.

There are in all 28 springs at Saratoga, the most popular of which is the Congress Spring. The Geyser Spring, on Ballston road, 1½ mile from Saratoga, whose waters are so highly charged with carbonic-acid gas that it foams and exhilarates like Champagne, is very frequented.

Among buildings of interest at Saratoga, are the magnificent hotels, the High-School Building, the Temple Grove Seminary for Young Ladies, Yates Institute for Young Men, and the Central Fire Department Building. There are numerous fine private residences and suburban drives in and near Saratoga.

The Congress Park and the Boulevard are beautiful places. The population of Saratoga is 11,000, but during the season there are often 30,000 people in the place. The name Saratoga, Indian, Saraghoga signifies "the place of herrings," which formerly passed up the Hudson into Saratoga Lake.

In the vicinity of the Springs is Saratoga Lake, a beautiful lake, 8 miles long and 2½ wide, a favorite resort.

Another pleasant resort is Mount McGregor, 11 miles from Saratoga, lying 1,000 ft. higher than the Springs, and 1,200 ft. above the sea, now famous as the death-place of General Grant.

The cottage where he died has been ceded to the State of New York.

By way of Whitehall, an excursion was made to Vermont, via Rensselaer and Saratoga R. R., and in 9 miles the train runs to Fairhaven, where there are extensive slate-quarries, and one mile beyond is the beautiful village of Hydeville, at the foot of Lake Bomoseen. Four miles farther is Castleton, a pretty village, situated on a plain and surrounded by pleasing scenery. In the township are extensive slate-quarries, from which is made an imitation of marble of wonderful perfection. A State Normal School is located in the village.

About seven miles from Castleton is West Rutland, noted for its vast marble-works, and in 4 miles the prosperous town of Rutland is reached.

The town is picturesquely situated, and has 12,149 inhabitants. It contains some fine public and commercial buildings, the State Workhouse, and the extensive Howe Scale Works. In the vicinity are numerous quarries and marble-works. Seven miles E., is Killington Peak, 3,924 ft. high, and the view from its summit is very fine.

Brandon, a manufacturing village of 3,500 inhabitants, with marble-quarries, large deposits of excellent bog iron-ore, and several factories where mineral paint is made from kaolin-mines in the vicinity, is 17 miles from Rutland. The beautiful mountain-lake, Lake Dunmore, nestles at the foot of the loftiest range of the Green mountains.

Middlebury, situated on Otter Creek, at some fine falls in that stream, has a population of about 3,000, and is distinguished as the seat of Middlebury College, founded in 1800. There is a library in that handsome-built village, containing 14,000 volumes and a small natural history collection. Fourteen miles beyond Middlebury is Vergennes, the oldest city in Vermont, and one of the smallest in the Union, with a population of little more than 1,500. It is situated on Otter Creek, 8 miles from Lake Champlain, and near the Falls, which have a descent of 37 feet. Commodore McDonough's fleet, which won the naval battle of Lake Champlain, September 11, 1814, was fitted out at Vergennes.

The last place visited in the State of Vermont was Burlington, the largest city in the State, finely situated upon the eastern shore of Lake Champlain, on a ground gradually rising from the water to a height of 367 ft. It was first permanently settled in 1783. In 1885 the population amounted to 13,500, and it has some of the largest mills in the country for planing and dressing lumber, and extensive factories of articles of wood, such as doors, packing-boxes, spools, etc., and of cotton and marble. The city is beautifully built, and several of the churches are superb architectures, as are also most of its public buildings. The Fletcher Library contains 18,000 volumes. The University of Vermont, incorporated in 1791, organized in 1800, is open to both sexes; its corner-stone was laid by Lafayette in 1825. The State Agricultural College was united with it in 1825. It has a library of 27,000 volumes, and a museum containing upward of 50,000 specimens in natural history. The Billlings Library given to the College at a cost of $100,000, contains the collection belonging to the late Geo. P. Marsh, and is the best collection of books in the nothern languages in the world. The Mary Fletcher Hospital, from the top of which the finest lake-view in America is obtained, is an admirably beautiful building. Lake View Cemetery, on the shore of the lake, is one of the finest in the State, and in Green Mount Cemetery lie the remains of Ethan Allen, under a granite shaft 42 ft. high, surmounted by a marble statue of the old hero.

The Depot of the Vermont Central R. R. is an extensive building, and the Court House, Custom House and Post-Office, and the City Hall and Opera House are very handsome. Other buildings of interest are the Lake View Retreat (a private insane asylum), and the Providence Orphan Asylum (Roman Catholic).

The "Green Mountain State," State of Vermont, was first settled by Massachusetts emigrants near Battleboro, 1724; admitted, 1791. Vermont was the first State to join the original 13 States.

Area, 9,565 square miles; length, 150 miles; breadth, 35 to 50 miles. Lake Champlain frontage, over 100 miles; Burlington the chief harbor.

Temperature at Burlington: winter, 18° to 33°; summer, 66° to 71°. Rainfall, 34 inches.

Death rate, only 1.07 per cent. per annum.

Montpellier, capital, is beautifully situated on the Winooski river, in a narrow valley surrounded by hills. Its population is 4,000, and in the portico of its beautiful Capitol is a marble statue of Ethan Allen. In the building is the State Library, containing 15,000 volumes, and the historical and geological cabinets, and the flags carried by the Vermont volunteers during the civil war.

Population of Bennington, 6,333, and of St. Albans, 7,193.

Number of farms, 35,522. Average value per acre, cleared land, $17.73; woodland, $15.28. Mineral wealth of great value, manganese, copper pyrites, iron ore, and gold deposits have been found. Black, white, red, and variegated marbles are abundant; annual value of marble, over $3,000,000, and of slate, about $1,000,000.

Number of different industries, 2,874, giving employment to 17,540 persons. Number of butter and cheese establishments, 85; flour and grist, 227; furniture, 56; leather tanning, 53; lumber sawing, 688; marble and stone work, 69; wares of tin, sheet-iron and copper, 95.

Population: 332,286, incl. 1,057 Colored and 11 Indians.

Number of Colleges, 2; school population, 99,463; school age, 5-20.

Devoting my time to a repeated exploration of the State of New York, the city of Schenectady, 17 miles from the capital of New York State, was begun with.

Schenectady is a city of 13,675 inhabitants, situated on the right bank of the Mohawk River, on a spot which once formed the council-grounds of the Mohawks. It is one of the oldest towns in the State, a trading-post having been established here by the Dutch in 1620, and is distinguished as the seat of Union College, founded in 1795 and now a famous institution.

Leaving Schenectady, the train crosses the Mohawk River and the Erie Canal on a bridge nearly 1,000 ft. long, and traverses a rich farming country to Amsterdam, and in 11 miles to Fonda.

Sharon Springs is reached from the latter place by stage. Situated in a narrow valley surrounded by high hills, the village of Sharon Springs in Schoharie County, New York, is chiefly noted for its mineral springs, of which there are 4; chalybeate, magnesia, white sulphur, and blue sulphur. The Magnesia and White Sulphur Springs resemble the White Sulphur Springs of Virginia. Though the waters are drunk to a considerable extent, the specialty of the place is its baths. Besides the water-baths, mud-baths are administered. The drives and rambles are very pleasant and from the summit of the hill over the village, a beautiful view is obtained, including the Mohawk Valley, the Adirondacks, and the Green Mountains of Vermont.

Little Falls, which is remarkable for a bold passage of the river and canal through a wild and most picturesque defile; and the already described beautiful city of Utica, the great railroad and canal center and where there is located the State Insane Asylum; and Trenton Falls, on the W. Canada Creek, a tributary of the Mohawk, whose descent is 312 ft. in a distance of 2 miles by a series of beautiful cataracts, have to be passed before Oneida Lake is reached. Chittenango and Syracuse are on the line on which, in 17 miles, the charming Lake Skaneateles is reached. The lake is 16 miles long, from 1 to 1½ miles wide; 860 ft. above the sea, and is surrounded by hills rising 1,200 ft. above the surface. Eight miles farther on is the handsome city of Auburn, with 21,924 inhabitants, situated near Owasco Lake, which finds its outlet through the town.

Auburn State Prison covers 18 acres of ground. The city was long the home of the late Wm. H. Seward, and his grave is in the pleasant cemetery on Fort Hill. The County Court House, the Theological Seminary, and the Churches of St. Peter (Epicopal), St. Mary's (Rom. Cath.), and the First Presbyterian are exceedingly fine edifices. Owasco Lake, 3 miles from Auburn, is a summer resort, and Cayuga Lake, 8 miles from the former lake, is 38 miles long, and from 1 to 3½ wide. At the S. end lies Ithaka, one of the loveliest cities in the State, noted as the seat of Cornell University, and surrounded by the most charming and romantic scenery. Founded in 1865, this institution has already become one of the leading educational establishments of the country. There are a series of cascades and waterfalls in its vicinity, varying from 30 to 160 ft. in height. The beautiful Ithaka Fall, 150 ft. broad and 160 ft. high, is about a mile distant in Ithaka Gorge, said to contain more waterfalls within the space of a mile than any other place in America.

The celebrated Taghkanic Falls are 10 miles from Ithaka. The Taghkanic Creek flows through a comparatively level country until it encounters a rocky ledge lying directly across its course, and then the waters fall perpendicularly through a chasm, which the stream has succeeded in excavating 215 ft. into the rocky basin, forming a cataract more than 50 ft. higher than the Niagara. Five miles beyond Cayuga is the manufacturing village of Seneca Falls, and 10 miles farther is the Academic City of Geneva, beautifully situated at the foot of Seneca Lake, noted for its educational institutions, of which Hobart College (Episcopal), is the most important. Seneca Lake, one of the largest and most enchanting in the State, is 35 miles long and 1 to 4 miles wide, is very deep and never freezes over.

Fatigued from my last, rather long lasting journeys, I proceeded to New York city, only to start anew after a short rest and thus terminate my explorations in the State of New York, and in the United States in general.

West Point is one of the most attractive places on the Hudson River. It is the seat of the National Military Academy. The most noteworthy of the buildings are the Barracks of the Cadets, the Academic

Building, the library, containing 26,000 volumes, and in which is the Observatory and the Mess Hall.

The Museum of Ordnance and Trophies, and the Chapel are interesting. The Parade-Ground is very spacious, beautifully laid out and contains several fine monuments.

Fort Putnam, on Mount Independence, 600 ft. above the river, is not far from here, and from the crumbling walls of the Fort excellent views are obtained.

New York City, the commercial metropolis of the United States, and largest city of the Western Hemisphere, is situated on New York Bay, in latitude 41° N. and longitude 71° W. from Greenwich, at the junction of the Hudson or North River, and of the East River. It occupies the entire surface of Manhattan Island; Randall's, Ward's, and Blackwell's Islands in the East River; Bedloe's, Ellis's, and Governor's Islands in the Bay, used by the U. S. Government; and a portion of the mainland, annexed from Westchester County, north of Manhattan Island and separated from it by Harlem River and Spuyten Duyvel Creek. The harbor of New York is one of the finest and most picturesque in the world. The outer bar is at Sandy Hook, and is crossed by 2 ship-channels. The villa-crowned shores of Staten and Long Islands, the massive battlements of Fort Wadsworth and Fort Tompkins, and on the Long Island shore, Fort Hamilton and old Fort Lafayette, famous as a political prison; Bedloes Island with the colossal statue of Liberty which France has presented to the City of New York, and Governor's Island with Castle William and old Fort Columbus, lie majestically on both sides of the bay and harbor, a panorama of phenomenal beauty and grandeur.

The site of New York is said to have been discovered by Verazzani, a Florentine mariner, in 1524; but authentic history begins with the visit of Henry Hudson, an Englishman in the service of the Dutch East India Company, who arrived there September 3, 1609. Hudson afterward ascended the river as far as the site of Albany, and claimed the land by right of discovery as an appanage of Holland. In 1614 a Dutch colony came over and began a settlement. At the close of the year the future metropolis consisted of a small fort and four houses and was known as New Amsterdam. As late as 1648 it contained but 1,000 inhabitants. In 1684 it was surrendered to the British, and passing into the hands of the Duke of York, was thenceforward called New York. In 1667 the city contained 384 houses. In 1670 the population had increased to about 6,000. In 1696 Trinity Church was founded. In 1711 a slave-market was established in Wall Street; and in 1725 the New York Gazette was started. The American army under Washington occupied the city in 1776; but after the battles of Long Island and Harlem Heights, it was captured by the British forces, and remained their headquarters for 7 years. The British troops evacuated the city November 25, 1783. Within ten years after the War of Independence, New York has doubled its population. In 1807 the first steamboat was put on the Hudson; the completion of the Erie Canal followed in 1825, and since that time the growth of the city has been rapid. Its population in 1800 was 60,489, it was 812,869 in 1860 and in 1880, 1,206,590. Commerce and industry have kept pace with the population. More than half the foreign commerce of the United States is carried on through the customs district of which this is the port, and about two-thirds of the duties are here collected. In 1883 the exports from this port were of the value of $361,425,361, and the imports $496,005,276. The manufactures of New York, though secondary in importance to its commercial and mercantile interests, are varied and extensive. In the value of products, according to the census of 1880, it was the first city in the Union, though surpassed by Philadelphia in the value of materials used, amount of capital invested, and number of establishments. The whole number of manufacturing establishments in 1880 was 11,162, employing 200,000 hands, and producing goods valued at $448,209,248.

The principal churches in the city are Trinity Church with the Astor Memorial Reredos in the chancel, one of the richest and costliest in the world (the Trinity Parish is the oldest in the city); St. Paul's Church; Grace Church; St. Paul's Methodist; St. George's Episcopal; the Jewish Temple Emanuel; and the Roman Cathedral of St. Patrick.

Of the numerous public buildings the following deserve special mention: the U. S. Sub-Treasury, the site of old Federal Hall where Washington delivered his first address as President, (the bronze statue of Washington on the entrance was erected here in November 1883); the U. S. Custom House, the new Post-Office, the new Court House, the City Hall, etc.

Among the numerous educational institutions of New York the most prominent are the University of the City of New York, Bellevue Medical College, College of Physicians and Surgeons, Columbia College, the oldest in the State, having been chartered in 1754; the Normal College, the College of Pharmacy, Homœopathic College, Cooper Institute, founded and endowed by the late Peter Cooper, a wealthy and philanthropic merchant, containing a free library, free schools of art and telegraphy for women, a free night-school of art for men, a free night-school of science for both sexes, and free lectures; the Bible House, headquarters of the American Bible Society, next to the British the largest in the world; the Mining Academy; the Astor Library, containing 250,000 volumes; the City Library; Mercantile Library; New York Free Circulating Library; the Library of the Historical Society; the Geographical Society's valuable series of maps, specimens, etc.; the Harlem Library; and several Colleges of Dentistry.

The National Academy of Design; the Metropolitan Museum of Art, containing the famous Cesnola Collection of Cypriote Antiquities; the Abbott Collection of Egyptian Antiquities and the Lenox Collection of Nineveh Sculptures both in the Historical Society's Building; the American Art Gallery and numerous private Galleries and Collections rank among the first in the country.

The Battery, a pretty little park at the southern extremity of the city, looking out upon the Bay, was the site of a fort in the early years of the city, being then the fashionable quarter. At the S. W. end is Castle Garden, a depot for immigrants, and at the S. end stands the handsome granite U. S. Barge-Office. Just north of the Battery, at the foot of Broadway, is Bowling Green, the cradle of New York, it was the court end of the town in the times of the Dutch.

The Business Buildings of New York have nowhere in the world their equal; some of them are palatial structures. I mention only a few: The Produce Exchange, Standard Oil, Stock Exchange, the Equitable Life Insurance Company's, Western Union Telegraph Company's, the Boreel Building, Wells, Stewart Buildings, Union Bank Building, Manhattan Company's, the United Bank Building, the Drexel and Mills Buildings and thousands of others are to be found in the business quarters of the city.

The Buildings of the leading Newspapers are also of colossal dimensions and the following are the most prominent:

Tribune, World, Herald, Staats-Zeitung, Sun, Times, Puck, and Post.

The Broadway is one of the finest, if not the finest thoroughfare in the world, and the elegant Avenues in New York have no rivals, and are intersected by lovely parks. Of monuments and statues, which are numerous in New York, those at the Union Square, of Washington's bronze equestrian statue, the bronze statue of Lafayette, and the bronze statue of Lincoln are of extraordinary beauty. On Madison Square, another pretty little park, is the bronze statue of Admiral Farragut, the monument to General Worth, and the bronze statue of Seward.

The Masonic Temple is a spacious and pretty building, and there is an abundance of Opera-Houses, Theatres and other places of amusement in the city. The principal Clubs in New York are the Century, Knickerbocker, Manhattan, Union, Union League, the Lotos, Army and Navy, St. Nicholas, the University Club, and the Athletic.

Of the many musical and singing societies of New York City, the "Liederkranz" is the most celebrated in the country, its President (since many years) is the well-known Mr. Steinway, the manufacturer of the world-famed Steinway-pianos.

There are comparatively more charitable institutions in New York than in any other place in the world; suffice to mention a few of the most important, viz.: the Deaf and Dumb Institution, the buildings which are the largest and finest of the kind in the world; the Bloomingdale Asylum for the Insane; several Orphan Asylums, among which the Hebrew Orphan Asylum is the finest in the Union; the Bellevue Hospital, the largest in the city; the Foundling Asylum; and the Five Points House of Industry and Mission; the Howard Mission; and on Blackwell's Island, 120 acres in extent: the Alms-house, Female Lunatic Asylum, Blind Asylum, Charity, Small-pox and Typhus-Fever Hospitals; also the Hospital for Incurables, and Convalescent Hospital; on Ward's Island: the Lunatic Asylum for Males, the Emigrant Hospital, and the Inebriate Asylum; and on Randall's Island: the Idiot Asylum, the House of Refuge, the Infant Hospital, Nurseries and other charities provided by the city for destitute children. Besides these, there are numerous Homes and other Institutions for Indigents of both sexes in the city.

The pride of New York is the Central Park. It is one of the finest parks in the world, embracing 843 acres and in it are the two large Croton Reservoirs. The Mall in the Park is the principal promenade; it is a magnificent esplanade and at various points are fine life-size bronze statues of Shakespeare, Scott, Morse, Goethe, Halleck, Daniel Webster, and among the bronze busts, the bust of Humboldt. The Zoölogical Gardens, or Menagerie, in the Park contains interesting collections of animals, birds, and reptiles, etc., and opposite the Metropolitan Museum of Art is the Egyptian Obelisk (the Needle of Cleopatra), one of the most ancient of the world's monuments. Originally hewn and inscribed by Thothmes III., one of the sides is also inscribed with the victory of Rameses or Ramses II. (a contemporary of Moses), who lived three centuries afterward. It was presented to the City of New York by the late Khedive, and brought to this country at the expense of the late W. H. Vanderbilt. Adjoining the

Park is the American Museum of Natural History, containing Indian antiquities, minerals, shells, and stuffed and mounted specimens of birds, fishes, quadrupeds, insects, etc.

Riverside Park, within the city limits, is the burying-place of General Grant.

The great East River or Brooklyn Bridge, is the largest suspension-bridge in the world and is 5,989 ft. long. Its width is 85 ft., which includes a promenade for foot-passengers, 2 railroad-tracks on which run steam passenger-cars, and two roadways for vehicles. This stupendous triumph of engineering was planned by Colonel John A. Roebling and completed under the charge of his son, Washington Roebling. It was thirteen years constructing, and cost about $15,000,-000.

The elevated Rail Roads in New York, four distinct lines, running almost parallel and traversing the city, are among the wonders of the city.

The new Aqueduct in course of erection is one of the most gigantic structures of its kind. In High Bridge, the Croton Aqueduct is carried across Harlem River in a length of 1,450 ft. This noble structure is well worth seeing.

Of the City Prisons, the Tombs, a massive, granite, sombre looking building in the Egyptian style, and of a shape resembling ancient Egyptian tombs, is undoubtedly a unique.

The Penitentiary and Workhouse are on Blackwell's Island.

New York is one of the greatest Rail Road Centers in the world and the Grand Central Depot one of the finest and largest in the United States.

Staten Island, the largest island in the harbor, has an area of 58½ square miles; it is separated from New Jersey by Staten Island Sound and the Kill Van Kull, and from Long Island by the Narrows. From the heights there are broad views over harbor and ocean. New Brighton is the largest village on the island.

The most popular of all the resorts near New York is Coney Island, just outside the entrance of New York Bay, and consists of a very narrow island, 4½ miles long, with a gently sloping beach, affording unsurpassed facilities for sea-bathing. It is a part of the town of Gravesend and is separated from the mainland by Gravesend Bay and Coney Island Creeks on the north, and has the broad Atlantic for its southern boundary. The island is divided into 4 parts known as Coney Island Point, or Norton's at the west end, West Brighton Beach, and Manhattan Beach at the east end. From the Observatory in Coney Island an extensive view is obtained. The drives are superb, especially on the Ocean Parkway.

Rockaway Beach and Long Beach are likewise excellent sea-bathing resorts, and the colossal tubular Iron Pier in Rockaway Beach is well worth seeing.

The other great summer resort in the vicinity of New York is Long Branch, on the Jersey shore of the Atlantic, where an extensive beach affords excellent facilities for bathing.

The Beach Drive on which the superb villas of the Wealthy are situated is an elegant road. The place is very attractive and is the Rendez-vous of the better situated class.

Opposite New York, just across the river, at the W. end of Long Island, lies the third largest city in the United States, Brooklyn. On the heights back of the city the battle of Long Island was fought, on August 26, 1776, and the Americans defeated with a loss of 2,000 out of 5,000 men.

In 1800, the population of Brooklyn was 3,298, and in 1880, 566,689.

Brooklyn was settled in 1625, near Wallabout Bay, by a band of Walloons.

The city is exceedingly pretty, most of the streets aborned with shade-trees.

Its public buildings and private residences are of great beauty and the commerce large. The City Hall, County Court House, Municipal Building, and Post Office are spacious and elegant structures. The Long Island Historical Society contains a valuable library and many curious relics. The Academy of Design, and the Academy of Music are highly ornated buildings. The Long Island College Hospital, the Mercantile Library, with 60,000 volumes; and several of the theatres are noteworthy. Of the many churches, the following deserve special mention: the beautiful Church of the Holy Trinity (Episcopal), Plymouth Church (formerly the church of the late Henry Ward Beecher); the Tabernacle (of the famous orator Rev.

Talmadge), the largest Protestant church in America; the Congregational Church of the Pilgrims (R. S. Storrs, Pastor); and the Presbyterian Church (Dr. Cuyler).

The County Jail and the Penitentiary are castellated, immense stone piles.

The Atlantic Dock has a basin which covers an area of 42½ acres and is surrounded by piers of solid granite, on which are spacious ware-houses. Prospect Park is one of the most beautiful in America. It contains 550 acres, lies on an elevated ridge, and commands magnificent views of the two cities, of the inner and outer harbor, Long Island, the Jersey shore, and the Atlantic. In the center is a fine fountain and a bronze statue of President Lincoln. It is beautifully shaded, has splendid drives, and was the site of extensive fortifications during the Revolutionary War.

The U. S. Navy Yard is the chief naval station of the Republic and contains 45 acres.

The trophies and relics preserved here are of great interest.

Greenwood Cemetery is the most beautiful in the world. It contains upward of 500 acres tastefully laid out. The grounds are traversed by 19 miles of carriage-roads and 17 miles of footpaths and there are many beautiful monuments.

The "Empire or Excelsior State," the State of New York is one of the 13 original States; named in honor of the Duke of York to whom the patent was granted; first settled by the Dutch, on Manhattan Island, 1614.

Area, 49,170 square miles; extreme length, east and west, 412 miles; extreme breadth, 311 miles; two-thirds of boundaries formed by navigable rivers; total water frontage, 880 miles.

Temperature at Albany: winter, 22° to 36°; summer, 67° to 73°. Rainfall at Buffalo, 34 inches, and at Penn Yan, 28 inches.

First railroad, from Albany to Schenectady, 1831; present railroad mileage, 7,349; artificial water-ways, 907 miles.

Number of farms, 241,058; average value per acre, cleared land, $58.48; woodland, $40.88. Ranks first in value of manufactures, soap, printing and publishing, hops, hay, potatoes, buckwheat and milk cows; second in salt, silk goods, malt and distilled liquors, miles railway and barley.

Population, 5,082,871, incl. 65,104 Colored, 909 Chinese and 819 Indians.

Number of colleges, 28; school population 1,681,101; school age, 5–21.

. . . . . . . . .

The United States, a Republic occupying the central portion of North America, together with Alaska, in the extreme northwest, contain 38 States and 10 Territories.

Area land surface, 3,547,000 square miles; greatest length, east and west, about 2,800 miles; average breadth, about 1,200 miles; British American boundary, 3,540 miles; Mexican, 1,550; coast line, exclusive of land indentations, 5,715 miles; lake shore line, 3,450.

New York ranks first in population; Pennsylvania, second; Ohio, third; Illinois, fourth.

New York City, metropolis of the Republic; Philadelphia ranks second; Brooklyn, third; Chicago, fourth. Washington, capital.

Railway mileage: 1830, 23, having increased to 126,718, January 1886. Increase, 1885, 3,214.

According to Statistics for year ending June 30, 1884, the total value of dutiable merchandise imported, was $457,813,509, and of imported merchandise free from duty, $209,884,184. The exports of merchandise for the same year amounted to $740,513,609.

The total value of products of industry, according to census, 1883-4, $10,000,000,000; average annual coal production, 77,908,874 tons; average annual exports, domestic merchandise, $794,060,103; average annual value imports, domestic merchandise, $635,227,511; average annual value exports of cotton, $12,322,428; and average annual value imports, cotton manufactures, $32,285,660.

Leaving this beautiful country in which I have stayed longer than in any other during my eight years travels, and thanking all my friends in the City of New York for the many favors bestowed upon me during my repeated long sojourns, I beg leave to bid Good-bye! Au revoir!

www.ingramcontent.com/pod-product-compliance
Lightning Source LLC
Chambersburg PA
CBHW020242240426
43672CB00006B/612